SPLIT
SECONDS

Balanchine

Q. My greatest desire is to dance with George Balanchine's New York City Ballet. How does he select the dancers?

A. In so many words, the 75-year-old ballet master says it all boils down to horse sense. "First, their proportion must be right. Small head, long neck, long legs, long feet and turned out. They must have a technique that I want," says Balanchine. "In the end, it's ability to move that counts. They're all thoroughbreds, all look beautiful, all trained the same, but this one or that one breaks away from the pack and wins. I have my own. taste. I am dictator."

SPLIT SECONDS

A remembrance by

TAMARA GEVA

Harper & Row, Publishers

New York, Evanston, San Francisco, London

FIRST EDITION

STANDARD BOOK NUMBER: 06-011512-2

LIBRARY OF CONGRESS CATALOG CARD NUMBER: 72-79666

Designed by Patricia Dunbar

SPLIT
SECONDS

1

I AM WALKING DOWN A DIMLY LIT CORRIDOR
. . . then . . . to my right, there are heavy draperies fringed
and slightly parted in the center. I go through the opening
and walk in.

Now there is light . . . bright light all around me . . . plum-
colored walls . . . mirrors . . . mirrors, and across the room,
near the window—Mother.

She is sitting in front of her dressing table. Her full bosom
rises above her corset, and her profile is chiseled against the
darkness of the window behind her. The lace curtains framing the window are framing her too and she looks like a pretty
Valentine.

Then the shutter clicks and there is nothing.

That is the first moment of consciousness registered in my
memory—a lightning bolt that opened the world to me. Till

then, it's a dark, deep void. I must have been about three years old.

Soon after its initial flash, the picture of entering Mother's boudoir was to repeat itself often, each time growing in dimension, gathering sound, smell, touch, detail, until it became a complete experience that launched the chain of events, some important, some frail, that were to be my life.

It was my mother's habit to call me in when she was getting ready to go out in the evening. The boudoir encased in its mauve walls was lush and soft, with a lot of gilt and wood carving. Everything was ornate—the tall Victorian mirror, the marble-topped washstand, the rounded love seat littered with silk cushions with a low table in front of it where a frosted vase in the shape of a squatting cupid sprouted a bouquet of artificial lilacs. Feet sank into the luxurious carpet that was generously patterned with roses, and the lights of the crystal chandelier played hide and seek on the bric-a-brac. The draperies at the entrance made this room seem protected from the disturbance of the outside world.

I would pull up a stool and sit by Mother's side, watching her in rapt fascination as she applied her makeup. This was gilding the lily, for she was young and fresh-looking. Her table was laden with imported beauty preparations that were the envy of her women friends. I distinctly recall the label "Institut de Beauté." Later, when I lived in France, I saw that label in many a Paris window, and it never failed to pinch my heart.

Stretching her neck forward, Mother applied eye shadow and outlined her eyebrows. She also used some black paste, a forerunner of mascara, which she brushed on her lashes with a toothbrush. In those days, ladies didn't wear much makeup, but being a kept woman, Mother defied all rules. She even smoked in public, languorously drawing on long, thin cigarettes with gold tips.

On her dressing table, next to the jars and bottles, stood a tin casket the size of a shoebox, and that crude object was to me, as indeed it was to her, the high point of the dressing ritual. When her face was powdered and her lips lightly rouged, and she seemed satisfied with the result, she would flip open the lid of the casket, and out came layers and layers of cotton, each layer displaying a dazzling array of jewelry—brooches, earrings, necklaces, with large precious stones staring up from them. Having laid them out on the table, Mother would sit there, pondering the most effective combination for that night. With total concentration, she would move the pieces like chessmen in a game, arranging them in sets or complementary colors. There was also an endless trying on of rings —she wore them on all her fingers except her thumbs.

We both gazed at the jewels, and I remember that it gave me an eerie feeling. If I squinted my eyes, I felt myself transported to some magic world, flickering and blinking, a shining field of burning flowers, and I saw myself running through it, picking those flowers and whirling and tossing them in the air. Perhaps that was when the vague idea of dancing first flitted through my brain.

Sometimes, in jest, Mother would ask me to suggest what jewels she should wear, and I invariably pointed to my favorite—a June bug made of multicolored stones. And she would pick up another, more important piece of jewelry and say, "Wouldn't you rather I wore this?" and as I would always stick to my first choice, she would throw her head back and laugh. She had a low, sensuous laugh.

"You'll learn in time," she always said.

But she was mistaken. I never did.

3

Bedecked with glitter, Mother would ring for the maid, and a few minutes later Daria, a chubby spinster, was pouring rose-scented water over Mother's bejeweled hands. Then she helped her into the dress.

Somehow, I remember Mother best in a lavender sequin gown that clung to her hourglass figure like shimmering fish scales, an amethyst and diamond necklace hanging low over her décolletage. (She was partial to violet hues.)

The final step in the procedure was to move to the mirror.

Many people claim that their mothers were beautiful, but mine really was. Her beauty was her meal ticket. Standing in front of the tall mirror, scrutinizing her appearance, she made a handsome picture. Chestnut hair piled up high in an intricate coiffure; large gray eyes that had the mysterious ability to change from cold detachment to a disarmingly warm glow; a short chiseled nose; a figure voluptuous yet arrogant in its stance; and, when she smiled, teeth the like of which I've never again encountered—even and round like meticulously chosen pearls.

To my asking where she was going, the most frequent answer was that she was going to see operette. For some reason I was ashamed to ask her who or what operette was, and in my imagination that word took on the form of a fat jolly lady.

We remained in the boudoir until the doorbell rang and her gentleman caller came to fetch her. Then she would either kiss me good night and dismiss me right there, or take me into the living room to be introduced to her beau of the evening.

"This is my little dove," she would say casually, and he would pat me on the head just as casually and tell me how much he liked me, but with the infallible instinct of children I knew that he didn't care for me one way or the other.

4

Once or twice a week, Father took her out. On those occasions I would forgo my visit to the boudoir and sit with him in my room until the very last minute. I would listen to the stories he told me, and try to envisage what the beautiful-sounding words described. I was heartsick when it had to end.

Mother had many admirers, young, old, handsome and ugly, but one man came more often than the others. His name was Michael. He had some kind of title, and he wore a magnificent uniform with a gold-braided jacket that hung miraculously on the tip of his left shoulder. I think he was the only one who genuinely liked me; he even brought me presents.

After Mother and her beau departed, I had supper in my room. And then the governess would escort me into the living room to practice my piano lesson while she sat nearby reading or knitting. The house was quiet, disturbed only by occasional splashes of laughter coming from the servants' room. On the piano, the candelabrum rested in its hazy halo of light and outside the window snow fell lazily in big flakes. My fingers diligently pounded the keys with primitive beginner's exercises, but my mind was far away. I thought of Mother. And I saw her going up a marble staircase, where the jolly operette met her. Operette stretched out her hand and tickled Mother under the chin, and Mother laughed and laughed until tears were running down her cheeks. Then they floated up the stairs and were gone.

The governess was dozing. The snowflakes slowed down to a standstill in the air.

2

Mother was of Swedish blood. Her family came from way up north and settled in St. Petersburg before she was born. She had two sisters, Irra and Alexandra. Grandpa was a bookbinder, who had a small shop in the poor section of the city. Apparently he was also quite a man with the bottle, an affliction that left a permanent mark on his daughter, Alexandra, whom he hit on the head with his favorite container when she was a little girl. The blow injured her brain, rendering her a semi-idiot for the rest of her life. This devotion to spirits was, no doubt, the reason for his untimely death, which left the family destitute. Grandma, suffering from overweight and handicapped by a limited knowledge of Russian, was not equipped for any job. Thus Mother, being the oldest of the daughters, became the provider at the ripe age of twenty. What she did and where she worked at first were never made clear to me, but eventually her looks and a pleasant singing voice landed her a job in an elegant music hall on the outskirts of the city. It was a popular hangout for rich young dandies. That's where my father saw her.

The east and west met and exploded—my father being an Oriental, half Tatar and half Turk. Dark, moody, brilliant, way ahead of his time, he lived on a plane much higher than hers, which left a lot to be desired in the communication between them, but flesh called and she became a need. He would have married her at once if it hadn't been for two important factors: the respect of an Oriental for his parents—they would

not give their blessing to his marrying so disreputable a creature as a singer in a music hall—and their firm decision to
disinherit him should he disobey them. The latter threat
didn't bother Father—money was not paramount in his scheme
of things—but Mother was not one to acquire respectability at
such a price. Since Father was very rich, she preferred to be
kept. Then I came along.

We lived in a very large apartment. Grandma and Mother's
two sisters also lived with us. Mother had a deep affection for
her family, but she was temperamental and at times, when she
was angry or irritated, she treated them badly, accusing them
of being a burden, though in reality she didn't mean any of
it. Each of them responded in a different way. Grandma,
grateful for the security, forgave her everything; Alexandra,
in her demented placidity, had no reaction whatsoever; but
Irra, the youngest sister, secretly hated Mother with the sharp
hatred that comes from dependency and envy. Not being able
to take it out on Mother, she took it out on me in devious
ways.

Our staff consisted of a cook, Masha, and two maids, all
crowded into one room near the kitchen. They were an ignorant lot, illiterate and very superstitious. Masha always
cried when we played the gramophone; she considered it an
invention of the devil and was fearful for the souls of those
who used it. There was also a governess to take care of me,
and that lady slept in my room.

With all the rooms, halls and ample space, there was only
one bathroom. A tub decorated with a plaster garland and elevated on what looked like six bronze chicken legs stood next
to the water heater, which was a combination of a barrel-like
stove, a variety of weird coils and a funnel that pierced the
ceiling. When in use, this contraption puffed and spat and

belched out clouds of smoke. The servants went to a public bath, but everyone else bathed twice a week, taking turns, except Mother, to whom no rules ever applied.

Right after breakfast, I was allowed one hour to myself. I liked that hour. The house was all whispers and tiptoeing, because Mother slept late, and any noise was an invitation to a wrath everyone tried his best to avoid. I wandered through the apartment, watching people at their early chores, but the best part of that hour I spent alone in the living room.

All children dream, but my capacity for it was truly limitless. I spent more time dreaming than living in reality. Perhaps it was an instinctive protection from the confusing atmosphere around me, an escape from something I felt was not the way it should be.

The living room, with its paintings, figurines and other decorative objects, presented a fertile stage for my imagination. Everything was a key to a dream world: for instance, the golden Buddhas in the glass cabinet whisked me to a place where bells rang with human voices and maidens washed their hair in perfumed streams; the pictures came to life and I could walk right into them taking on any form I chose, and the tall French windows . . . oh, those windows, opening on a snowy world with white fluffy stars eddying in the air, and a little snow queen, spinning on the window ledge, inviting me out . . .

By squinting my eyes I could fly anywhere. Squinting makes one feel little and not there.

Sometimes Alexandra would join me. She, too, was a wanderer around the house, her restlessness coming from a different confusion; it was as if she were looking for a door to open up her brain.

We would stand together by the window, gazing out.

"See that castle up there, on top of that cloud?" I'd ask.

"Oh, yes, I do, I do!" she'd reply eagerly. "It's very pretty. But the roof leaks."

"Let's go there," I'd propose.

"Yes, let's," she'd agree and then add cautiously, "You go first, you're smaller, you can climb better. I'll follow."

I have no doubt that she could see the things I saw; it showed plainly in the happy smile that would come to her normally sad face.

She was quiet, with eyes that held a constant fear. Her speech was slow and deliberate and only occasionally unintelligible. Though twenty-five, she didn't look a day over sixteen, and her mentality was that of a girl of ten. She adored wearing aprons and insisted on helping with the housekeeping, but her poor coordination and memory made her break or misplace things, and then the apron was taken away from her and she cried pathetic, soundless tears. All in all, most of the time she behaved rather rationally, if not for one peculiar habit. Before retiring, she would secretly collect certain unlikely objects and hide them under her pillow—pots and pans, strainers, mixing bowls, even tea and coffee pots. Every now and then she would change to shoes or vases, but her preference ran to kitchen utensils. To this day, I cannot understand how she could sleep on those lumps, but sleep she did, and as there seemed to be no harm in it, she was permitted to indulge in this fancy. Then one day, a large kitchen knife was found tucked in her pillowcase, and that gave cause for some alarm. A family council was called, and a long conference ensued, but nothing much was done about it except to take the knife away.

At ten o'clock my tutor came in. She was a young lady, very plain, very proper and obviously very bored with teaching one

9

so young. However, she taught me well. I learned to read and write at an early age, and Father instilled in me a real love for the written word. The reading matter in our apartment was restricted to cheap romantic novels, and those were snatched away from me the minute I laid hands on them, but Father saw to my supply. He brought me stacks of books—fairy tales, children's classics, illustrated books on travel—and would sit with me explaining whatever was beyond my understanding so that I became convinced that Father knew more than anybody. If it came to something that was particularly difficult for me to grasp, he used to say, "Don't get discouraged. What you read must be one step ahead of you and you must reach for it. Then you'll grow forward instead of just up."

I was in awe of him. He was a serious man, withdrawn and pensive. He walked with a slight stoop, his longish black hair fell over one eye, and he had a habit of twisting that lock. There seemed to be an invisible shield around him that made people approach him with care and respect. No one would ever think of slapping Father on the shoulder and saying, "Hi, pal."

What puzzled and disturbed me most was that he didn't live with us. I thought fathers always lived with their children. But he stayed with us only over the weekends and on rare occasions would spend a night during the week. However, he came to see us every day, mostly at lunchtime. At that early age, I was no judge of marital relations, but this situation gave me a sense of inexplicable insecurity and preyed on my mind. Yet some inner warning prevented me from bringing it up. Then, one day, it finally slipped out.

We were sitting down to afternoon tea. Mother was out, which gave the rest of them an opportunity to gossip freely.

There was a short lull in the conversation.

"Why doesn't Father live with us all the time?" The question popped out of my mouth before I could catch it.

A hush fell around the table. Irra giggled. My governess looked down and coughed.

"No worry, little one," Grandma said, leaning toward me, "no worry. You too young to understand." With the rise of her blood pressure, her accent always grew thicker.

But Irra was not going to miss an opportunity to release her venom.

"It's because he has another house much better than this, and he has other loves," she said, giggling viciously.

"Shut yourself up!" Grandmother said.

Something caught in my throat. "What loves?"

"Books, books, and theaters and crazy things!" Irra was obviously enjoying herself. "Oh, he's a smart one! We're just trash! He's up there with the big people. And his parents are infidels . . . and they live in a big house . . . and do you know what you are? You are—"

"Shut yourself up, I say! Fool!" Grandmother's voice rose to its highest pitch, drowning out Irra's words.

The governess got up, took me by the hand, and without a word dragged me away to my room.

A fog descended on me—that dense grayness in which all thoughts and feelings are so mixed up that one is helpless and there is no way out. One can only sit in stillness. I remember my governess suddenly getting very busy with something inside a drawer. I don't know how much time elapsed, and then I ventured again.

"What is an infidel?"

She cleared her throat and continued to rummage in the drawer. "It is a man who isn't Christian."

"Is Father an infidel?"

"No, he isn't," she said, and after a pause added, "Not now."

With that she slammed the drawer shut and marched out. The fog in my head thickened. What did she mean? Had Father been an infidel or did he intend to become one? My idea of Christianity wasn't very clear either. Mother was very religious. Icons hung all over the apartment, each with its own votive lamp burning day and night, and Mother crossed herself often and automatically, especially after she had a row with someone in the family. But that gesture didn't shed any light on my nebulous understanding of religion.

Did Father believe in God? Did the infidels believe in God? And why did he have to have another house? Did he love his other loves better?

The necessity to know was urgent. Whom should I ask? Surely not Mother—her reactions were unpredictable and I was a little afraid of her. Maybe I should ask Father himself?

Next time he came to my room he brought with him a huge tome of Fenimore Cooper. It must have been some special edition for he was very proud of it. He planted himself at the table and at once began lecturing me on the lives and customs of the American Indians. I stood by his side, watching his finger travel over the illustrations, but I could barely hear what he was saying. Inside of me a whirlpool of conflicting emotions was churning at high speed. Shall I ask him now? What do I say? It's so difficult to find the words. How should I begin? Suppose it is something one shouldn't talk about. What if I hurt him? What if he gets angry and goes to the other house, never to come back? What then? No, no, I couldn't risk that.

So I stood next to him, aching, and never said a word.

3

Every afternoon, at three o'clock, I was taken to Catherine Square for my daily outing. Russian winters are severe, and to brave the subzero weather required a lot of clothing.

First, woolen tights pulled up to my armpits and held up by braces, then high felt boots and a quilted padding with sleeves—a coat in itself—and finally the real coat. A fur bonnet was pulled down over my head and a shawl wound around my neck so that it covered my mouth and nose, leaving only my eyes exposed. Finally my hands were stuck into heavy mittens and then into a muff that hung on an elastic band lassoed around my neck. Eskimos wear less.

Catherine Square was about ten blocks away from where we lived and the governess and I walked that distance slowly, because the air was very dry and still, and for the first half-hour or so one didn't feel the cold at all. The penetrating winds came only with the snowstorms.

St. Petersburg was—Leningrad is—a beautiful city: majestic, with wide streets, hundreds of cathedrals, churches and palaces, its many canals and parks and bridges adorned with statues. Whitened by winter, it acquires a special dignity.

It is amazing what snow does to sounds. Everything is muted. The beating of horses' hoofs sounds like padded castanets, the sleighs leave the faintest hiss in their wake, and the ringing of the church bells, though they may be near, seems to come from far away, the reverberation cut short at a certain point. Even voices, no matter how shrill, are velvet-coated.

The whole world seems shy and gentle and suspended in waiting.

We walked across the bridge over the Fontanka Canal, the water below us frozen, passed the sprawling palace of the Dowager Empress, and continued along the straight line of Nevsky Prospekt to our destination.

I always looked forward to one specific corner where a row of rissaks was lined up next to the curb, waiting for customers. The word "rissak" is derived from the verb "to pace" and is applied to a fast thoroughbred pacer harnessed to a small elegant sleigh. The horses were beautiful, their necks arched and their skins quivering in anticipation of the ride. Loosely knit blankets were stretched across their backs from shaft to shaft, the long edge weighed down with heavy pompons to protect the customers from the flying snow thrown up by the horses' long stride. The bearded drivers, padded into shapelessness, sat on their narrow, elevated seats like glued-on toys. To attract customers they shouted at the top of their lungs, trying to undercut each other. When one of them took off, it was a pleasure to watch the sleigh shoot forward like a bullet, overtaking every other vehicle on the street. The rides were expensive. One didn't hire a rissak just to get someplace. One hired it to show off.

A huge statue of Catherine the Great stood in the center of the little park of Catherine Square. Time and weather had painted the bronze with a green patina, and strips of snow hid between the metal folds of the Empress's dress. Around the statue the snow paths were scraped to an even surface, but the lawns were left virginal, rising like waves of whipped cream. The governesses formed little groups and walked along the paths (it was too cold to stand still), and we, the children, played in the shallower reaches of the lawns, screaming and laughing, invigorated by the frost and the temporary freedom.

We amused ourselves as children do all over the world— threw snowballs, made snowmen—and pretty soon my mittens were wet and a crust of icicles formed on the shawl around my mouth. Evenings came early in the winter, and by the time we started for home it would already be dark. We walked back along the same route, only now the street lamps were lit, glowing like yellow moons, and everything was blue, and little diamond sparks sprang up from the ground.

One afternoon, on my governess's day off, Irra took me to the Square. On the way back she veered away from Nevsky Prospekt, taking a roundabout route and leading me through streets I had never walked before. Surprised, I asked her where we were going, and she replied that there was more than one way to get home. I didn't mind. Anything new always pleased me.

We came to an intersection and there she stopped. I looked up and saw her staring at an imposing house on the opposite corner. Built of gray stone, with a turret protruding into the sky, it stood taller than the houses surrounding it. The exceptionally large windows of the two top floors were lit with a glaring light, and from where we stood we could see the silhouettes of people darting about. On the lower floors, some of the windows were also lit, but here the glow was amber and warm. The massive entrance door was carved into squares, and next to it a double iron gate shut off the courtyard.

Irra's eyes were fastened on the house and she showed no intention of moving on.

"Come on," I urged her, pulling at her sleeve. "Why are you staring at that house?"

"No, wait," she said and looked down at me. There was a strange curve of a smile on her face as if she were deliberating about something.

"Do you know who lives there?" she asked.

"No," I said, "I've never seen that house before."

"Of course not. They are trying to keep it from you. But I will tell you. Your father's parents live there—your grandfather and grandmother."

"The infidels?"

She laughed. "Who cares what they are? They are very rich. See those top windows? That's the factory. They make gold cloth there—it's called lamé. You know, the stuff they use for priests' vestments. And those lower floors are where they live."

I became very excited. "Let's go and visit them," I said.

Her lips curled up higher.

"We can't," she said.

"Why not? Please, Irra," I pleaded, "please."

As long as I live I'll remember the malice on her face. Through all the years nothing could ever erase it. When she spoke again, it was slowly, to give me a chance to absorb the meaning of each word.

"No, no, we can't. They don't want to see you. They won't even let us in. You're not their kind. You're illegitimate."

"What's that?"

"One day you'll know. I can't explain it to you now. You're too little to understand."

There it was again. Grandma had used the same excuse when I had asked her about Father.

Suddenly, I didn't want to see the house any more. I hated it. I turned and ran. She caught up with me and grabbed my hand, but I kept pulling forward, my face averted and my breath coming short because of my rising tears. Home! I wanted to get home quickly. . . .

In the vestibule, I yanked myself out of her grip, and still in my street clothes ran through the apartment into my room. Grandma was sitting there, snoozing, the bulk of her body overflowing the armchair. I fell on my knees before her, buried my face in her lap and gave way to sobs. She woke up instantly.

"What is it? Who hurt you, little one?" she asked tenderly, her fingers fighting to remove my shawl and bonnet. "Tell Granny."

At first, I couldn't speak, but then the words burst out in spasms.

"Grandfather . . . and . . . the other Grandmother . . . she showed me a big house . . . they don't want to see me . . . she said I'm . . . something . . . I'm . . . I'm . . ."

Grandma didn't let me finish. She pushed me aside gently, lifted herself up and went by me, letting my head fall back on the seat of the chair. A second later I heard a slap, followed by Irra's screams. I turned. Irra was pinned against the door frame, her face distorted with fear and hate. With one hand Grandma was holding her by the neck and with the other slapping her across the face over and over again.

"Bitch! Bitch!" Grandma shouted, "You told . . . Why? . . . She clothe you . . . she feed you . . . but you hate her. . . . Why? Why?"

Irra was wriggling and screaming like a creature possessed. Attracted by the commotion, Mother came flying to the scene. Her entrance produced a magical effect: they both quieted down instantly.

"What's all this? What are you two fighting about? Oh, Lord, what have I done to deserve this?" Immediately, Mother became the injured party. "I do everything for you, and what do I get in return? Nothing but trouble! Ingrates, parasites!"

It never occurred to her to stop and find out the cause of the fracas. She was winding up on her favorite theme—her charity, her patience and the advantage others took of her. She berated them harshly, insultingly, and they listened with

17

heads bowed in subservient silence. When she stormed out, they followed her like two whipped dogs.

Left alone, I jumped on my bed and buried my head under the pillow. I didn't want to see any of them ever again. . . . I wanted to hide, to run away. . . . I wanted to do something, but I was not sure what it was.

Somebody touched my shoulder. Cautiously, like a turtle, I pulled out my head. Alexandra was leaning over me, her eyes full of compassion, and her apron bulging with something hidden under it.

"Don't cry," she whispered. "You know something? I'll tell you a secret. They are crazy. Oh, yes, they are. I know. One day, I'll fix them. Look, I brought you a present."

And she stuck a skillet under my pillow.

4

Up until Irra's unsolicited disclosure of my unwelcome state, I never gave my father's parents a thought. Now another taunting riddle had come into my life. I realized from Grandma's reaction that this, too, was a forbidden subject, and that questioning the elders would get me nowhere. But bottled-up frustrations must find an outlet, and one by one I began to test my playmates in the park. With an air of indifference, I would ask them all the same question—"How many grandparents have you?"—and the answer, as a rule, indicated two sets. If one or more were missing, there was always a logical explanation; they were either dead or gone away someplace. Then I'd go after my main target.

"Do you see them?"

"Of course, I do. Aren't you silly!"

"I mean, do you see them often?"

"Of course. They come to see me and I go to see them. They're nice. What are yours like?"

Refusing to appear different, I would invent stories about my grandparents. They lived in a big house, they loved me dearly, in fact I was going on a trip with them in the near future. Where? Oh, I don't know. They didn't tell me.

Then I'd fall silent, my thoughts spinning. Everybody saw their grandparents. Why was I not like the others? What was wrong with me? Irra had said I was . . . I was . . . The actual word eluded me, but the darkness it carried lingered.

Everything Irra had said about the house was true; it was my grandparents' house, and the top windows belonged to the factory, but she underestimated the establishment. She also neglected to point out the most interesting feature. Next to the main house stood a modern two-story building, slender columns holding up its portico. The sign above it spelled out in orange letters "THEATRE MINIATURE."

That was Father's theatre. He built it to promote new ideas and encourage new talent. In those days—and, in Russia, still —tradition had its claws out for every new development in art, and anything avant-garde was deliberately squelched. Father was that rare phenomenon in his time and environment—a private angel who was for the daring, the new and the experimental. Many a talent that eventually gained recognition would have perished had it not been for Father's moral and financial support. His interest in art took in a wide territory; among other things, he was one of the first backers of the famous Russian director, Meyerhold, and I was told that long before the Revolution he imported from abroad the first exhibition of the Cubists, which earned him the nickname of "Father of the Futurists."

Ironically, the money for all this activity came from the most traditional of all institutions—the church. For the church was Father's real business. The factory did make lamé for priests' vestments as Irra had said, but that was only part of its business. Father's company built and decorated churches, made miters, chalices and other religious articles, using mostly gold, gold leaf and precious stones, and since Russia was littered with churches and monasteries, the business, to put it mildly, was extensive. There was one special cloth of pure gold thread, woven by hand, a yard of which took six workers a year to complete. That gold monstrosity, weighing a ton and prohibitive in price, was made solely for the Imperial family and kept at the factory to await the proper occasion—that being a royal death, when the coffin would be covered with it. I remember Father coming in one day and gaily announcing: "Another Grand Duke gone. Now I can buy a Renoir."

Every Saturday, he changed all the paintings on our living room walls. I used to sit and watch him take down the old paintings and replace them with a new crop. As far as I recall, he never repeated them. Balancing on the ladder, he whistled cheerfully, obviously enjoying this pastime.

"Where do you get all these pictures, Papa?" I would ask him, and he would bend down and whisper confidentially, "Oh, I've got thousands and thousands of them."

Most of the paintings were way beyond the comprehension of anyone in our family, and a great deal of scathing comment was voiced behind Father's back. "He's crazy. Look at that woman with a green face" or, "Have you ever seen sky like that?" Grandma said that given a brush she could do a lot better, and Irra nearly died laughing when she saw a Modigliani. Mother tried to silence them, but from the expression on her face as she glared at the pictures it was evident that she, too, wasn't quite sure whether Father might not be playing a joke on her.

One day, Father hung six pictures everybody understood. They were large engravings of Maria Taglioni, caught in quite improbable dancing attitudes—floating on a cloud, balancing on one toe on the tip of a flower, or leaping high over a brook. In her diaphanous tutu, with her swanlike neck and spiraling curls, she transcended anything that my imagination had concocted thus far, and she promptly entered my private world of dreams as a reigning fairy queen. Now everything centered on her. Father explained to me that she had gained fame by being the first dancer to get up on her toes, and that information was nearly fatal. I almost broke my ankles trying to imitate her. She became a diamond pinpoint on the horizon—a goal.

Next Saturday Taglioni was gone, and paintings of clouds took her place, but her ghost was to remain with me for years and years to come.

5

Mother's social activities were not limited to going out; she also gave many parties at home, and on those occasions I was sent away to spend the night with my friend, Nina. Nina was the daughter of mother's closest friend, whom I respectfully called Aunt Pauline. In fact, all the adults, unless they were employees, were called aunts and uncles. It was considered impolite for a child to address anyone as Mr. or Mrs., and the size of my family of aunts, and especially uncles, was impressive.

My governess would deposit me at Nina's late in the afternoon and return to our apartment to help with the festivities.

I liked staying at Nina's. The apartment was small—only three rooms—but it had an aura of peace and warmth, and the security of simple love. They, too, had a part-time father, but the reason for it was understandable: he was a naval officer, at sea most of the time. Nina's relationship with her mother was wonderful; they were like loving sisters, discussing everything and sharing each other's experiences. Naturally, Aunt Pauline would be going to Mother's party, and shortly after my arrival she would begin preening herself for that event. Nina took an active part in it. Excitedly she would jump around, bringing out dresses, shoes and trinkets, and making suggestions: "Oh, Mama, you must put on this dress! Oh, Mama, you'll look so pretty!" she'd exclaim, only to change her mind a minute later, and drag another dress out of the closet.

One feature of Aunt Pauline's countenance stands out in my memory; she had no eyebrows, but, unlike Mona Lisa, she substituted for this deficiency two half-moons thickly painted with a black pencil high above her eyes, which gave her a look of perpetual surprise. Aunt Pauline was no beauty, but she was a darling; she was kind and sweet, and easy to be with.

Later, when she had left, Nina and I were served supper in the tiny dining room by an old Nanny, and it made me feel very important, though I would never dare show this in front of Nina. Being a few years older than I, she treated me with the condescension appropriate to her seniority, and I accepted it as something normal and inevitable.

In our beds, we talked for hours, even after Nanny turned out the lights. We speculated about the party, and invariably the conversation would turn to my Mother.

"Well, your mother is rich," Nina would say. "She can give these big parties."

"Doesn't Aunt Pauline ever give parties?"

"Not that kind. We can't afford it. Your mother is different from other mothers."

"How is she different?"

"I don't know. I just heard that she was."

And she would dismiss the subject. "I don't want to talk about the party any more. Tomorrow Mama will tell me everything about it."

There lay the difference. Tomorrow she would be told, and together she and Aunt Pauline would relive the party in detail. Not so with me.

In the morning, I returned to a silent, sleepy house. The servants moved about like ghosts, noiselessly clearing up the debris of the previous night. Nobody spoke to me. Only Irra would throw an occasional dart.

"My. That sure was a brawl we had!"

Came Christmas, the enchanted time for all children, when their supremacy is unchallenged—but it was not my holiday. I was left somewhere in the background. For instance, I was not allowed to participate in wrapping packages or trimming the Christmas tree. It was the elders who did it on Christmas

Eve after I had been sent off to bed. Presumably, this was done so that I would get the full impact of the decorated tree in the morning, but the sense of desolation it brought as I lay in the dark, listening to distant voices and laughter, was a very high price to pay. Sleep wouldn't come. Even when the house became quiet again, it took hours before sheer weariness closed my eyes.

Anxiety woke me up early, which only meant that again I had to lie in bed for an interminable time, waiting for the governess to show signs of life. At long last I was sitting at breakfast, and finally the governess gave me the sign: "You can go in now."

Together we opened the heavy double doors of the living room, and there it stood, the glistening marvel, so tall it seemed to go straight through the ceiling, and so laden with ornaments that one could hardly see the green. The governess connected the plugs, and it burst into life with a million tiny lights—red, blue, gold, like wondrous eyes peeking through the branches. Most people used candles on their trees, but we, at Father's insistence, used electric bulbs. The ornaments were porcelain angels with real hair, flying in the air and playing all sorts of instruments; little baskets of fruit made out of candy; miniature villages, complete with people and cattle; and strings and strings of beads interwoven with icicles and dripping snow. Under the tree, a mass of packages was spread out invitingly, but the governess instructed me not to touch anything, presents or ornaments alike. Then she'd leave me alone.

And so I sat there, cross-legged in front of the tree—waiting. It seems that most of life is made of waiting. Waiting for that next moment which will be better than the one we live, waiting for the groceries to be delivered or the telephone to ring, waiting for our hopes to materialize. Even as we are engaged in some activity, we are already waiting for the result it will bring, and when misery engulfs us, we wait for it to end. Only in those rarest of moments when we are truly happy do we forget about waiting—for a while.

I waited for three o'clock. At that hour the family and friends assembled around the tree for the celebration. There were tea and cakes, champagne and caviar, and oranges—the most expensive delicacy in Russia. Mother, wearing some fabulous creation by a great designer and bejeweled as ever, presided over the gathering like a gay, benevolent queen. Aunt Pauline and Nina were there, of course, and a dark handsome woman whom they called Marianne and who was a close match to Mother in jewelry—a friend of old days, a demimondaine who had done pretty well for herself too. And many gentlemen, including Michael. Best of all, Father was there in one of his rare gay moods. As a rule he was not given to small talk, but that afternoon he politely joined in the general chitchat. Only one person didn't share in the festive mood; she was Mother's half-sister, Aunt Eugenia. Plain, sweet and thoroughly respectable in her middle-class marriage to a German merchant, she obviously didn't approve of Mother, her life, morals and behavior. Wearing a pained expression on her face, she observed everything with an air of saintly tolerance as if to say, "Father forgive them, for they know not what they do." Whenever I happened to be near her, she would grab and hug me, and whisper tragically, "You poor, poor little girl."

In due time, we opened the presents, and there was something for everybody. For me there were toys which I didn't care for, games, lots of books and, for some reason—a violin. Who thought it up I don't recall, but I remember being rather surprised since I had never mentioned that I wanted one.

25

Gifts for Mother excelled all others. Exhibit A was Father's offering—a large stole and muff of blue-dyed fox, a new fur that he had ordered from Paris. Mother was jubilant; she threw it around her shoulders, and paraded up and down like a fashion model, and Marianne nearly fainted with envy, which gave Mother no end of pleasure. Then she went back to her other presents. Here something strange happened. She picked up a box, opened it and quickly slipped it under a discarded piece of tissue paper, while her other hand was already on the next present. A few minutes later, Father got up and slowly walked to where the box was concealed. As he pulled it out from under the tissue paper, opened it and looked inside, the room sank into silence. Marianne alone was still bravely carrying on a *sotto voce* conversation with one of the gentlemen. But even that was cut off abruptly when Father quietly put the box down and walked out into the entrance hall.

Mother ran out after him. Everyone in the living room was silent, listening to Mother's voice rising higher and higher in the hall. Then we heard the entrance door slam.

When she came back, she looked wild. Tearing the stole off her shoulders, she threw it on the floor and kicked it.

"He can't do that to me!" she screamed. "I am a free woman!"

"I wouldn't say that," Marianne said icily. She disengaged herself from her gentleman and came to Mother. "Don't press your luck. You have a pretty good setup here. He knows that no man would give you a present like that unless he had a right to."

Mother flung herself into a chair, dissolved in tearless moans and dramatically announced that a heart attack was coming on. Immediately everyone rushed to her side, and Aunt Eugenia threw up her hands and then clutched me. Before I knew it, Nina and I were pushed into my room. I didn't care, for nothing mattered any more: Father was gone, and Christmas had walked out with him.

"What do you suppose was in that box?" Nina asked. "I thought I saw something sparkle."

I had no answer, and she sat down at the table and proceeded to amuse herself by making patterns with dominoes. I picked up the violin. A sound resembling a Bronx cheer came from beneath the bow.

7

Father didn't come back until way after New Year's Day. In the interim, it seemed that tension would burst the walls of the house. Mother was irritable, finding fault with everything and everyone, and her mood made the members of the family scatter into their corners like mice. Father's reappearance dispersed the gloom, and everything went back to normal, if we may call it that.

Right after the holidays two things happened: the governess quit without notice—she couldn't stand it any longer, she said—and two weeks later, I became very ill. A new governess was summoned, and this good woman looked like an egg. Everything about her was oval—blank face, hair rolled up into an egg-shaped coiffure, oval body, plump hands with fingers like short sausages. She was German and spoke Russian poorly, which forced me to learn German quickly—an acquisition that eventually was to be of great help to me.

As for my illness, it was first diagnosed as a chest cold. The treatment for it, however, was so extraordinary that I wonder why it didn't kill me.

I was to be kept in compresses, and the idea of what constituted a compress was unique. A sleeveless linen jacket soaked in hot water was put on over my bare skin, followed by a similar jacket of oilcloth, topped by another made of flannel. Then I was wrapped in cotton wool and swathed in bandages so tightly that I could hardly breathe. Still, with the slightest movement, the air would filter under this armor, making me cold and clammy. I would begin to shake and immediately everything would be ripped off and the whole procedure repeated from the beginning. It was a constant change from heat to chill, with a lot of standing naked in between.

Three weeks of this cure and I developed a spot on my lung. It created a great deal of frantic excitement, and I heard a lot of talk about the dangers of traveling in wartime. Still, in the end, it was decided to ship me off to the Crimea. The Crimean climate and a special type of grape that grew there were supposed to do wonders for all lung ailments. Grandmother and the new governess were to accompany me.

I remember the last moments at the station, when everybody rushed around, and dozens of packages were brought into the compartment, including baskets of food—there was no restaurant on the train. And I remember Mother kissing me madly. She always either smothered me with demonstrations of affection or ignored me completely for days. My reaction to her tended to be negative: she was there—she was in charge of my life—she was someone to reckon with, but the connection, the core, was absent. It was not her deeds—for at the time I didn't understand them—but the apprehension she evoked in me that stood between us.

The train moved and began to crawl. Through the window I looked at Father, who, keeping pace with the train, walked along the platform. There were apology and sadness in his face. Then the train gained speed and I lost him.

Three days later, at dusk, we arrived at Sevastopol, a beautiful white city overhanging the Black Sea. From there we had to travel by surrey since our destination, the estate of Countess Panini, was nowhere near a railroad.

The horse trotted merrily, and with each mile the beauty of the land unfolded more and more, dazzling and soothing all at once. There is nothing like the Crimea—it is one of the most picturesque places on earth. From the snow-tipped mountains to the deep-green sea, here and there splashed with pink stripes, it's like a garden of Eden, the air so clear and faintly scented that every breath is a pleasure. We traveled along winding roads between cypresses, oleanders and acacia trees bursting with white, pink and yellow bloom; wild roses hung over the rocks; fig and olive trees grew in profusion; and vineyards spread their terraces in jagged design. We passed great villas, sugar-white amidst the green magnificence, and Tatar villages where on the flat roofs of the huts fruit was spread out to dry in the sun. The journey was long—we had to change horses many times—and I fell finally asleep, so I don't remember how we arrived.

The little house assigned to us was once occupied by the head gardener, who had moved closer to the vineyards. It stood in a clearing beside the acacia alley which started at the entrance gate and ran all the way to the palace at the center of the immense property.

In the mornings, I was handed a basket of grapes and sent out to do as I pleased, and except for a brief return for lunch when my basket was refilled, I wandered around all day long.

Nibbling at my grapes, I explored a world of never-ending surprises. The estate was a mixture of formal landscaping and jungle-like wilderness, and the scenery changed quickly as in a magic garden. Overgrown with roses of every shape, color and scent, it was laid out formally around the palace; then a web of paths and trails led to different nooks where statues were mirrored in ponds that sprouted green lilies, or to fields of wild flowers, or to dense forests of blooming trees that would suddenly open on terraced steps descending to the sea. And below, pines, black and sweet-smelling, guarded the archaic rock formations of the pebbled beach.

At one time, it had been Tatar territory, and the Countess was able to buy it only with the proviso that the Tatars would retain the right to use one particular fountain, inside the estate, a few yards from the boundary. There, a narrow path cut through an opening in a fence and crept up the hill, where, at the very top, a mosque stood alone and proud against the sky, marking the beginning of a Tatar village.

At sundown, the muezzin came out on the minaret of the mosque and chanted his evening prayers to the sinking sun. Shortly after, the Tatars would start coming down the hill single file, the men leading their horses and the women balancing jugs on their heads and carrying baskets of laundry. Dressed in their native costume, with their pale yellow skins and slanted eyes, they were a beautiful sight—a procession from ancient days. I was always at the fountain at that hour, waiting for them.

Jabbering and laughing, the women would throw the laundry into a trough and wash it by shuffling their bare feet in the water. Their hair, partially dipped in henna, was braided into what seemed like dozens and dozens of tiny snakes, and these wiggled and danced around their faces to the jingle of the coins hung on chains around their necks and wrists. More coins were sewn on the tiny round hats they wore over a short veiling. The men sat around watching and exchanging comments, and their faces reflected humor and a dash of viciousness. They were handsome people. Most of them were guides who made their living by taking lady tourists for rides in the mountains.

A blond little girl is a tasty dish to an Oriental. Their concept of age differs from ours; besides, those guides were no pillars of morality. In time, the Tatars got used to me, and we became friends: I even learned a few words of their language. The better the understanding, the shorter grew the distance between me and a young guide named Hirey, until he edged his way right next to me. I liked him. He was like a prince in his gold-embroidered black jacket, his cap set far back on his curly black hair. And he had beautiful hands, like Father, whose hands were forever being noticed by artists. Hirey spoke broken Russian that made me laugh, and often brought me figs in exchange for a few nibbles from my grape basket. He called me strange names, and once put his cap on my head, which delighted the Tatars.

Then one day he asked me if I wanted to ride his horse. He lifted me onto his dappled stallion, and led it through the acacia alley to the entrance gate. Once we were outside the gate, he jumped into the saddle behind me. His body was pressed against mine, and his arm was hooked tight around my waist as he gave the horse a kick and sent it into a gallop. It was thrilling to fly like that. Then he slowed down, and his hand went up my neck and buried itself in my hair, holding it tight while his other hand began slowly exploring my body. Terrified, I looked up to find a grinning, slit-eyed face leaning over mine. I squirmed to release myself from his hands, but the grip on my hair was like an iron claw, and the traveling hand sank itself in my thighs. He was saying something in his native tongue, the sounds coming out harsh and guttural through his quickened breath. I pulled and pushed and tore, and finally fell off the horse, leaving a strand of my hair in his hand. Scrambling to my feet, I started running. He let me run for a distance, and then I heard the horse's hoofs behind me. As he galloped by, he leaned down and picked me up on the run, and I found myself on the horse again, now lying across its back, face down. Hirey, his mood totally changed, was slapping me on the backside, laughing and repeating, "Bad girl, bad girl, bad girl." In this fashion we galloped back to the fountain. The Tatars found it riotous: they shrieked with laughter and pointed their fingers at me, and, as I slid off the horse and began running toward the cottage, it only increased their merriment.

Near the cottage, I slowed down and stealthily walked up the steps of the porch. My face was flushed; my scalp hurt where the hair had been torn out; and along with the emotional shock, I felt a bewildering sense of shame as if I myself had been an accessory to what had been done to me. I wanted to hide, to bury my experience, and I was scared to face Grandma and the governess since I had a notion that they already knew about it and were ready to question me.

Luck was with me. Hiding behind the porch door, I heard a violent argument inside. The governess was leaving: she was fed up with this place, with nothing to do and no one to talk to, with this boring life. This bustle provided me with the opportunity to slip unnoticed through the parlor into my room. I sat on my bed waiting for my face to pale and the thumping of my heart to lessen while the angry voices continued the fight.

Supper was late that night, and all three of us sat dejected for different reasons. Very few words were spoken, and little attention was paid to me, for which I was grateful. But during supper, and all through the night, I saw a grinning face and felt hands crawling over my body.

8

The egg-shaped governess departed next morning, bag and baggage, leaving us with the memory of a sickly smile and a wave of the hand.

Now there were just the two of us left—Grandma and myself. Grandma was a loving woman, but she was clumsy in her love. Her outbursts of affection, like Mother's, were spasmodic, and usually ill-timed. Uneducated, and not too bright to begin with, she never learned that children are delicate mechanisms, with thoughts and longings and doubts. She treated me more like a puppy than a human being; as long as I was fed, kept comfortable and petted, all was well. There was no communication between our senses, and whenever I tried to tell her about something that disturbed me, she would subdue me with her favorite phrase, "No worry, baby," followed by a strong dose of kisses. Still, I loved her, on her own terms, as a cub loves mama bear.

Grandmother was a short, stout woman, suffering from high blood pressure, and the hot climate was beginning to tell on her. Every day, after lunch, she had to lie down to rest, her heart pumping, and her forehead glistening with perspiration.

My routine had not changed; I still wandered around all day with my basket on my arm like Red Ridinghood. Though I tried to keep away from the fountain, I was strangely drawn to it, with an urge so strong that I usually found myself hiding behind a tree, watching the Tatars from a distance. And I was always waiting for Hirey to come down. When I caught sight of him, I was lost between revulsion and fascination, wanting to run away but compelled to stay. I remained behind the tree, watching his every move, until the Tatars shut up shop and the last of them disappeared over the hilltop.

Time went by. Days rolled into weeks, and I was growing very lonely. Before I left home, I had been told that my parents would come to see me, but in the letters we received there was no mention of their visit. One day, Grandma informed me that a new governess was being sent to us, but since no specific date was mentioned, it did not register in my mind.

There were a few other children on the property—sons and daughters of the workmen—but they were rough, and I didn't like to play with them. Besides, they always questioned me about my family—and it made me feel even lonelier. So, I slowly drifted away from their company.

The Easter holidays were nearing. A blanket of new violets covered the ground and the soft winds got softer.

We dyed some eggs, and Grandma, puffing and sighing, managed to bake the Easter cake, and we two ate it, sitting alone in the kitchen. It was a far cry from Easter at home, but neither of us mentioned it.

By the third day of Easter, I gave up hope of seeing my parents. I felt forgotten, forlorn, and though my face was dry, my heart was full of tears. Grandma didn't seem to notice my sadness. She was getting more and more tired, moving very slowly and letting me fend for myself.

And so I wandered listlessly about the estate, always ending up behind the tree at the chant of the muezzin. Out of loneliness, one day I emerged from my retreat and joined the Tatars. They greeted me with shouts and cheers, and Hirey came up to me right away and sat by my side. I didn't care. I didn't care what he might do. Any attention was welcome. But he acted very sweetly; with great tenderness, he stroked my hair, and then he took off an amulet hanging on a chain around his neck and pressed it into my hand. I sat with the Tatars until they left, and then, with the amulet clutched in my hand, walked down the acacia valley to the entrance gate. I climbed on the stone fence surrounding the property and settled on top of it with my feet dangling over the roadside. My head was empty—there wasn't a thought in it, no wish, no intent. I just sat there in the deep lavender of the evening and watched the white whiffs of the road dust move ever so slightly in the breeze. It was quiet, except for the birds gossiping in the treetops.

In a while, I heard in the distance the sound of an approaching carriage, and presently it drove past me. All I could make out was a stack of suitcases and the outline of a figure partly hidden behind them. The carriage drove by and was about to turn into the gate when it suddenly stopped. A woman, graceful and willowy, stepped out of it, walked back to where I sat and asked my name. Then she returned to the carriage, and I saw her speak to the driver, her hand drawing an invisible map in the air. A minute later, the carriage with the suitcases, but minus its passenger, drove through the gate. She stood there for a few seconds, looking after it as if to make sure that the driver had followed her instructions, and then slowly walked back to me again. Picking up the skirt of her white linen suit, she climbed the stones of the fence and sat down on my left. She didn't speak for quite some time. Then she said, not to me, but as if into the air, "How beautiful. I never dreamed it would be like this. It is my first trip south."

I glanced at her sideways and saw the clean-cut line of her profile, tranquil and serene, and softened by an upward curve of the mouth, and the slim column of her throat rising above the ruffled collar of her blouse. Her skin was very white, and she looked like marble, but live marble because of the warmth about her.

Again we sat in silence until she turned to me and put out her hand.

"We might as well get acquainted," she said. "I'm your new governess. Fräulein Rosalia is my name."

We shook hands as grown-up people do, and when I looked into her eyes, clear as spring water, I knew right there and then that she was unlike anyone I'd ever known.

Talk came easily. She told me how much my parents missed me and how sorry they were not to be able to come and visit me, and how lucky she considered herself to be chosen to take their place.

We sat and talked until darkness fell, and then, hand in hand, we walked back through the acacia alley to the cottage, where her suitcases were already piled up on the porch.

Thus began a relationship which would never be duplicated in my life.

If angels walk among us, Fräulein Rosalia was one of them. She had a kindness and wisdom not easily to be found in a mortal. And she had strength—quiet strength, entrenched so deeply that nothing could shatter it.

I often wondered what kind of a human being I would have become had Providence not guided her my way. From the first day, she seemed to have looked into my soul and, seeing the lack, supplied what was needed. She gave me her undivided attention and concern, her gentleness, but, more than anything, she gave me love—not the erratic outbursts of it that had been bestowed upon me from time to time, but a steady, ever-present stream of tenderness and understanding.

There was a bond between me and my father, but that bond was sealed in silence, as if we both were afraid to bring certain things into the open. Nothing was ever hidden between Fräulein Rosalia and me. She invited trust, and I gave it to her in the comforting belief that she would never fail me. There wasn't a thought or deed I didn't share with her, no doubt or question I didn't run to her with, and she always listened with interest, and eventually led me to the straight road. Even a question that was unanswerable was discussed, and she always managed to deflate its importance, so that I would dismiss it from my mind.

She straightened me out on the subject of the "infidels." No, she said, my father was not an infidel. He had been brought up in a different faith—Mohammedan, she called it—but he had turned Christian when he became a man. Besides, she said, only those who were very stupid used the word "infidel," because there was one God, and everyone was free to worship Him the way that suited that person best.

She impressed upon me her hope that I would remember this for the rest of my life. When I asked why my grandparents refused to see me, she simply said that she would find out about it later, when we returned home, and let me know. But in my happy life with her I soon forgot about them.

She took over the running of the household, giving Grandma the leisure she badly needed. And for the next two months the old woman seemed much better, all her wants attended to, relaxing on the porch, knitting or just admiring the scenery. With Fräulein Rosalia around, I stuck closer to the cottage. The search had ended—there was no reason to lose myself in other worlds, because for the first time in my life I felt good in the one in which I lived. And when the wanderlust came over me, Fräulein Rosalia would come along, sharing and enjoying my adventures and exploits.

Summer was reaching its zenith and it was getting very hot. To cool off, Fräulein Rosalia and I would go down to the sea and dip into the water. Swimming was risky along that stretch of shore. Rocks, some of them submerged, created currents and small pools, and all I could do was splash or float, held up by Fräulein Rosalia's hands. But it was fun and refreshing, and everything around was beautiful: the intense blue of the sky, the fantastical designs of the stones, the aroma of the pines steaming in the sun above the beach.

One afternoon after swimming, Fräulein and I stretched out on the rocks to dry off in the sun. All of a sudden everything around us began to change rapidly. Clouds rushed toward each other, and in no time the sun was shut off by a puffed gray ceiling. The sea turned from emerald to black, exploding into angry waves. Thunder was rolling toward us.

Quickly, we pulled our dresses over our bathing suits and, scrambling up the rocks, dashed up the hill, hoping to make it before the cloudburst. Big drops were already falling, and we raced each other laughing and ran up the porch steps just in time to avoid the downpour.

There we stopped dead, stunned by the sight confronting us. Grandma was lying on the floor, caught in the swinging door between the porch and the living room. Her face was ashen, and her breath was coming in gasps and gurgles, as if something had stuck in her throat and she couldn't get it out. One of her hands was flopping against the floor planks like a fish out of water; the other lay limp against her stomach, pressed in by the edge of the door.

I screamed. Fräulein Rosalia quickly knelt and put her fingers on Grandma's pulse.

"Prepare yourself to get really wet this time," she said to me calmly. "Because you'll have to run to the head gardener to tell him to call the doctor." There was no phone in our cottage.

The gardener's house was quite a distance from us. I ran all the way without ever slowing down. My heart was pounding and I was getting a stitch in my side, but still I ran, slipping and falling on the wet grass, picking myself up and running again. The thunder was roaring, and the rain was lashing me mercilessly, and when I got there, I could hardly speak, but as soon as I had delivered the message, I turned and ran all the way back at the same speed. I was soaked to the bone, my dripping hair clinging to my scalp and face, and I didn't feel it.

Fräulein Rosalia was waiting for me on the porch, a big towel in her hands. Right there, she stripped me, dried my hair and wrapped me in the towel. Only then did I notice that Grandma was not in the doorway any more.

Fräulein Rosalia sat me down on the porch swing. "I want to talk to you," she said, "and I don't want you to be afraid." The calmness of her tone was reassuring. "Grandma has left us for a while. She is sleeping and will sleep for a long time. That's what people call dying, for they've found no other name for it. We all come out of a sleep, see, feel and do things which we call living, and go back into sleep again. Now you, for instance—one day you woke up, and suddenly saw things for the first time . . . didn't you?"

As she spoke, the picture of walking down the dim hall toward Mother's boudoir flashed somewhere within my vision, and though the connection was vague, I felt that there was truth in what she was saying.

Fräulein Rosalia went on: "She was very tired—you know that—she had lived a long, long time and needed rest. So God sent her rest, and he will look after her now. It isn't up to us any more. Now—are you ready to see her?"

She led me inside. With a superhuman effort, she had dragged Grandma's bulky form into the living room, and now Grandma was lying in the middle of the floor, a pillow under her head and a coverlet pulled over her up to her chin. She looked very peaceful. Fräulein Rosalia had already attended to the closing of her eyes and mouth, wiping away the ugliness of death.

"People will come and take her to a place where she won't be disturbed." Fräulein spoke quietly. "Do you want to wait here, with me, until they come, or would you rather I took you to the neighbors on the hill?"

I preferred to stay with her. We sat on the sofa, and I cuddled up to her, while she talked softly about this and that, as if what had just happened was the most natural, the simplest thing in the world.

And so we waited. The rain had stopped. A pale sun was coming out.

It was my first encounter with death, and Fräulein Rosalia carried me safely past that milestone. She took fear out of death and gave it dignity.

10

Shortly after, I was pronounced cured and we went back home. A few days before our departure, a letter had arrived that Fräulein Rosalia read very carefully. She put the letter down, thought for a minute and smiled. She had a nice smile, slow in coming but so warm it was contagious.

"There's a surprise for you at home," she said. "You have a little brother."

I took it in my stride. I remember having no definite reaction.

"Aren't you glad?" she asked.

I said I didn't know. I had never had a brother, so I couldn't predict how I would feel.

On the train, as we were getting closer to the station, a feeling of apprehension began to rise in me. The few months with Fräulein Rosalia had been so happy that I was not sure I wanted to go back to the old surroundings. She must have read my thoughts. With no provocation she said, "It will be different now." She had an uncanny ability to know what bothered me before I could put it into words.

And different it was; she could not change the conditions, but she made them easier to bear.

The house was in a turmoil. The little brother, only two weeks old, was installed in my room, and I was transferred to what had previously been a den. There was also the presence of another new person—the wet nurse. In Russia, ladies of means didn't nurse their babies—it was believed to spoil the shape of the bust. A healthy peasant, herself recently a mother, was brought into the house to attend to the feeding, and during her stay this creature literally ruled the household. An old superstition that any aggravation would spoil the milk played in her favor, and the wet nurses took full advantage of it. Our wet nurse was a monster. She bullied everybody—even Mother didn't dare to contradict her. Only Fräulein Rosalia stood her ground, mostly by ignoring her, which caused a slight friction between her and Mother.

Another person the wet nurse found hard to bully was Alexandra. During our absence, she had taken a turn for the worse. A haunted, dangerous look was now in Alexandra's eyes, and her actions were unpredictable and ominous. After a couple of collisions, the wet nurse was afraid to tangle with her.

According to custom, the nurse wore a traditional national costume, and the richer the family, the more magnificent it was. Our nurse wore wide skirts of bright colors over starched petticoats, a peasant blouse made of the best linen and lace, and rows and rows of beads, tied together with ribbons that fell down her back in a cascade of color. Around her waist a string of real amber was held by a gold clasp—amber was supposed to prevent illness—and her hair was kept in place by a small, jeweled cap called a "house kokoshnik." In this splendid raiment, the wet nurse swaggered around the house as if she owned the place.

Mother now paid even less attention to me than she had before. She had another child, this time a male, and knowing full well what a male child meant to Orientals, she concentrated on him, hoping that Father's parents would accept her, and approve her marriage to Father.

But there was talk of old Grandfather ailing. Behind Mother's back, Irra wondered aloud if the old man had found out there was another little bastard, and Fräulein Rosalia had to cut her off sharply. Being basically a coward, Irra cringed and, with an air of abused innocence, disappeared from view.

Two other events of importance occurred after our return. My friend Nina passed the examination and was accepted by the famous Imperial Ballet School, and Father took me to the theatre for the first time.

Father's decision to take me to the Maryinsky Theatre met with resistance from Mother; she said I was too young to be dragged out at night, and that I wouldn't understand a thing. Standing by, Fräulein Rosalia listened intently, and by the eagerness in her face I knew she hoped Father would win.

He did, and the following Wednesday, dressed in my prettiest clothes, a big bow in my hair, I walked by his side down the aisle to his subscription seats in the third row. Even before the rise of the curtain it was an unforgettable experience; the magnificent theatre, all powder-blue and gilt, the elegant audience, the soft growl of the orchestra tuning up in the pit, the immensity of scale—it all seemed like a fairy tale come true. And when the curtain went up, I was bewitched for the rest of my life. The stage of the Maryinsky Theatre is enormous, and it seemed to be filled with thousands of people dressed in beautiful clothes, and singing like angels, and even the rather fat Juliet couldn't spoil the illusion. After the second act, despite my protestations, Father took me home. He said that it was quite enough for the first evening, and that I would see this opera and many others more than once, and that little by little he would let me stay longer.

He kept his promise; from then on, he took me to the opera every week, and finally he took me to the ballet. That night my life was shaped. As I breathlessly watched those lovely creatures leap and spin to the sound of beautiful music, my mind went back to the pictures of Taglioni, linking a dream with reality, and suddenly I saw a way to the fulfillment of my dream. My friend Nina was now a pupil in the school where those dancers were trained, and I couldn't wait to see her and find out all about it. But she wasn't very receptive. If her attitude toward me had been condescending before, it was now imperious. It didn't disturb me in the least: she was a real somebody, a girl chosen to become a fairy queen, and I felt it quite proper for her to behave in conformity with her high status.

In the meantime, home continued in a dither, all the attention focused on the baby and the wet nurse. Six weeks went by, and the household was torn asunder.

The baby died. Mother's grief was on the order of Greek tragedy. Screaming hysterically, she tore out her hair, rolled on the floor, invoked curses on the world. Father, in his civilized way, suggested that the body be taken away to a church or chapel, but she would have none of it. As a consequence, the living room was transformed into a chamber of mystic horror. The tightly drawn curtains plunged it into darkness, and the little coffin was placed on a table draped with black velvet that fell to the floor in heavy folds. Four huge candles in tall church candlesticks, one at each corner of the table, provided the only illumination, making the room, filled with flowers and permeated with burning incense, look and feel like a tomb. Two nuns took turns in the vigil at the foot of the coffin, and there was always a black figure, prayer book in hand, mumbling something unintelligible in Slavonic.

Mother wailed, and the wet nurse, having lost her income and position, wailed too. Even Irra obliged with a goodly flow of crocodile tears. The rest of the house was deathly still, and the effect was terrifying. The incense fumes were slowly oozing through the whole apartment, spreading the ghastly mood.

I dreaded even to walk by the living room, but Mother dragged me inside.

"Look," she moaned, lifting me and bending me over the coffin, "look at your little dead brother . . . you'll never see him again. . . ."

I looked at the little face, waxen by candlelight—a little face alien to me, a dead doll lying amid flowers in the shadow of the black nun—and terror seized me.

"Kiss him!" she cried hysterically, pressing my head down. "Say good-bye to him!"

I stiffened, and tried to push myself away from the coffin, but I was paralyzed. Just then, I felt other hands on me. Fräulein Rosalia freed me from Mother's hold, pulled me back and protectively encircled me with her arms.

"Madame," she said respectfully but firmly, "I fully appreciate your sorrow, but this is barbaric. Remember, she is your own child too. You're frightening her. May I have your permission to take her away until all this is over?"

Mother's answer was lost in her sobs. Taking advantage of the moment, Fräulein Rosalia quickly took me to my room. Big, bodyless ghosts were hovering about my head. In those few minutes, Mother almost succeeded in undoing all the good Fräulein Rosalia had accomplished at Grandma's death. But Fräulein Rosalia was determined not to have my spirit destroyed.

"Listen to me," she said urgently. "Sit here, and don't move. I'll be back as soon as I can."

She grabbed a shawl and ran out.

I had no idea where she was headed, but later I found out

that she went straight to the big house, forced her way in and asked Father to help her take me away.

Father came with her when she returned. Together they dressed me in a hurry, and Fräulein and I drove to Aunt Eugenia's, where we remained until after the burial.

This episode, I think, describes Mother's level of intelligence better than a long analysis. Superstitious, emotional, she was a true manic-depressive, swinging from elation to complete despair in a matter of minutes. Her greatest fault was, probably, a total lack of self-criticism. I never saw her cry sincerely except in rage, when she could not have something her own way. Yet, with all these traits, she had extraordinary horse sense in dealing with everyday problems, and a miraculous ability to recuperate from her moods. So when we returned from Aunt Eugenia's, she was her old self again, bearing no visible signs of her ordeal.

Except that, when she looked at Fräulein Rosalia, there was something new and hard in her eyes.

The war between her and Fräulein had begun.

II

The week following the funeral, Father, as usual, took me to the theatre. This time Mother objected violently; she said it was unchristian to indulge in such frivolities instead of mourning the dead. Father stood his ground; it was no frivolity, he said, it was education, and he intended to continue it without interference. Opposition collapsed, and we went to hear Tchaikovsky's *La Pique Dame*.

Father's method of educating me in music was well thought out. After each opera I attended, he would bring me a simplified piano score of it, and being still under the visual spell, I would take great delight in trying to play it with one or two fingers. It was impossible to get me away from the piano, and without effort, I soon learned many operas by heart.

Whether it was opera or ballet, with each visit to the theatre my determination to be part of it grew stronger. I wanted to be sent to the school where Nina was, and become a ballerina. But at the same time, I didn't exclude the possibility of becoming an opera star. I incessantly talked about it to Fräulein Rosalia, who calmed me down by saying that I still had a few years before coming to a decision, and that it was not the proper time to bring up the subject.

She must have possessed a sixth sense, because a few days later another death struck the family.

The ailing grandfather suddenly gave up the ghost. Though nobody on our side had ever seen him, the effect was powerful. There was something ominous in having two males in the family, the youngest and the most ancient, depart almost simultaneously into another world without ever having met in this one. Despondency hung over the house. I suppose everyone was wondering how the two deaths would affect our welfare. Whatever Mother felt, this time she kept it to herself. But there was a lost look about her, and once or twice she mentioned that she thought she was being punished for her sins. Outwardly her despair took on the face of charity; the war was at its peak, and she was constantly sending donations to various war-relief organizations. And every evening the whole family, including the servants, assembled around the dining room table, where they made packages to be sent to the soldiers at the front. Individual pouches were filled with bandages, bottles of iodine, bars of chocolate, cigarettes and other useful articles. This job was done mostly in silence, and as the group sat under the shaft of light falling from overhead, the atmosphere was thick with voiceless woe. It was as if they suddenly realized that life was not going the way it had been planned, and that something sinister lay in store.

One evening this silence was broken by the ring of the doorbell. Daria, the maid, went to the door and returned to announce that Father had come in with some lady, and that he requested Mother to step into the vestibule.

Mother shrugged her shoulders and, getting up, remarked: "Now he doesn't even use his key any more."

The vestibule was next to the dining room, and, as she reached the door and looked out, she gasped and pressed her hands to her bosom. Blood left her face, and she ran out.

Everyone in the dining room tensed up. Obviously something of great importance was happening on the other side of the door. In a moment we heard voices in the entrance hall bursting into loud sighs, sobbing and laughter, with Father's sober voice trying to calm the hysteria.

We waited. Then they walked in—Father, Mother and a very fragile old lady with parchment-like skin and dark, narrow eyes. Dressed all in black, with a lace shawl over her silver hair, a single strand of pearls around her wrinkled neck, and her right hand on the knob of a cane, she was the perfect picture of a matriarch, the standard portrait of centuries.

She walked with dignity, slowly and deliberately, her head held high. Father was supporting her elbow, while Mother, still crying and laughing, was hanging on to her from the other side. The old lady, too, was in a state of high emotion, a tear rolling down her cheek.

48

Everybody rose. The old lady's eyes took in the table with its bandages and other paraphernalia, and her head nodded in approval.

There was a moment's pause, during which I felt Fräulein Rosalia gently pushing me forward until I stood face to face with the old woman.

She stared at me, and I stared at her, as Fräulein Rosalia behind me said, "Curtsy, darling. This is your Grandmother Sofia."

12

What persuaded this woman to make that dramatic entrance after years of refusing to acknowledge our existence? She was a converted Christian, and perhaps the two deaths made her realize the meaning of "Forgive us our trespasses as we forgive those who trespass against us." Perhaps she, too, felt that she was being punished for her sins. Or was it because Grandfather, a man of iron will and an unbending Mohammedan to his last breath, wasn't there any more to impose his will on her? Had she been against his closed mind all the time?

Only Grandmother Sofia could shed light on these speculations. Since she didn't choose to do so, it was to remain a secret forever.

Her appearance changed the atmosphere as if by magic. Gone were the long faces; gone was the table with bandages; gone was concern for the poor soldiers; gone was repentance. Salvation had walked in.

Mother seemed in excellent spirits, and the whole household seemed drenched in sunlight. The only sad note was Alexandra. She was getting progressively worse. She was morose and erratic, frequently exploding into violence. Fräulein Rosalia tried to make Mother realize that it was psychologically wrong and physically dangerous for me to be growing up in the company of someone so close to insanity, but Mother shouted her down and told her to mind her own business.

Fräulein Rosalia's concern was well founded; one morning, in a fit of fury, Alexandra ripped her bed to shreds with the knife she had again concealed in her pillowcase. When Mother apprehended her, Alexandra sprang at her and, with the strength of the mad, threw her down on the floor, and nearly choked her to death. It took three people to pull her away. Spittle dripped from her mouth and she was screeching like an animal. A doctor was summoned, and the next morning the poor soul was taken away to an asylum. I was never told what became of her. One just didn't talk about Alexandra any more. She simply vanished from our lives.

Except for this unhappy development, everything was going swimmingly. Mother's friend Marianne and Aunt Pauline were constant visitors, and there was a lot of whispering and chuckling going on among the three. A dressmaker came in often, almost every day, but the clothes were always tried on behind the closed doors of the boudoir. Then Mother decided to give one of her big parties, and, as usual, I was dispatched to Nina's.

That afternoon, Nina and I were watching Aunt Pauline get dressed for Mother's party, and I thought that she took extra-special care with her appearance. Her outfit was brand-new and elaborate. The dress was a mass of beige ruffles, and a little beige hat was set on top of her coiffure. Long white gloves were laid out on a chair next to a new handbag adorned with brilliant stones, and there was even a nosegay of flowers that she picked up before she left. At the door she turned to me, kissed me with especial tenderness and said that there was a box of chocolates for us in the kitchen cupboard.

After dinner, Nina surprised me with the news that she would live at Theatre School, starting the following week, to come back only for Christmas, Easter and a short summer vacation. How I envied her! In my eyes she was already a prima ballerina, standing on the stage in a white tutu, with fame at her feet.

She put on her new ballet shoes and showed me a few exercises, which I tried to imitate. To my surprise, I found that I could do them quite easily. That took a bit of wind out of her sails, but she regained her supremacy by telling me that they were the very simplest exercises and that she wouldn't think of showing me anything difficult.

We spent the evening dancing and playing games, unaware that at the same time, in our apartment, my mother and father were being married.

13

We moved into the big, gray house that once upon a winter afternoon had caused me such anguish. Before that important event, everyone in our family was elated—and rightly so. After all, at long last we had made it: another rung up the ladder, another, and final, step toward security, wealth and, this time, position. The unattainable attained. Expectations ran high, filled with visions of Oriental splendor, liveried lackeys and marble halls.

All these delusions crumbled into dust as soon as we entered the house. Not a lackey in view—not even an Oriental rug. In fact, there were no rugs at all.

In place of marble, plain stone steps led to the living quarters. These consisted of two separate apartments, one above the other. Grandmother Sofia moved to the upper one, letting us take the apartment below.

It was a large place, but simple—almost austere. In comparison, our former dwelling looked like a small Versailles. Even the layout was monastic. From the vestibule, a long straight corridor divided the apartment into two sections, with all the bedrooms of equal size and shape on one side, overlooking the courtyard, and Father's museum and the living and dining rooms on the other, facing the street. There was one extra bedroom right off the vestibule, before one reached the door to the corridor. Only the bedroom windows boasted simple white curtains—the rest, unadorned except for strips of wood carving, and polished to crystal-clearness, looked out on the world like cold, accusing eyes. Gleaming parquet floors made footsteps resound; heavy furniture seemed to have grown roots, and the subdued colors—greens, rust and deep gold—were still as earth against the white of the walls. There was no bric-a-brac of any kind—nothing that could have been considered superfluous. A few paintings, sparsely hung, and a cluster of real plants in the corner of the living room broke this chilling solidity, but only the icons spelled wealth; coated with gold and studded with precious stones, they were masterpieces of workmanship.

Whereas in our house books had been almost nonexistent, here they were everywhere. Not only the walls of Father's museum, but the vestibule and the whole length of the corridor were lined from floor to ceiling with glass-enclosed book-shelves, leaving not an inch of wall exposed.

One feature, however, was just the same as in our former home—the service entrance off the kitchen. That passageway, appropriately called the "black walk," was more like steps into a dungeon than anything that belonged above ground. Dark, dirty, with rough-hewn uneven steps and narrow horizontal windows that prohibited ventilation, it remained damp and cold even in the heat of summer.

More than its physical aspect, however, it was the feeling of the place that differed so powerfully from our old home, where everything attracted and challenged the world, like a peacock spreading its tail. Here the house seemed to turn in on itself, complete and quiet, as if it had reached its desired goal and there was nothing more to seek.

This atmospheric change had a restraining effect on the new inhabitants. Irra held her tongue, looking around in awe-some bewilderment mixed with distaste. "Looks naked," she would mutter under her breath. But the servants were ecstatic. At the end, the corridor made a fifty-degree turn and there began the servants' quarters—two good-sized rooms, a pantry, a laundry room and an enormous kitchen with a special din-ing table for them. Such consideration for the lowly was rare in Russia in those days.

Mother took to her new status and surroundings with the enthusiasm of an actress finally getting a chance to play a coveted role. The metamorphosis was spectacular. She became the picture of respectability, her manners controlled, her voice held down to softness.

To make the image perfect, her wardrobe underwent a drastic change. All the Paris creations stayed in the closet; she wore white blouses and dark silken skirts. The jewels, too, were missing—only a small cameo was cradled in the ruffles at her throat. Perhaps it was a precaution, in order to be always prepared for Grandmother Sofia, who, having kept her key, had a bad habit of dropping in on us whenever the fancy took her. Sometimes she was accompanied by Tatiana, a young girl of eighteen whom she had picked up nobody knew where. A more unlikely ward for that righteous woman would be hard to imagine. Shifty-eyed, wet-lipped, she immediately telegraphed some inner malignancy.

The gentlemen callers vanished, all except Michael, who turned out to be a friend of Father's and who in former days had apparently been around not to court Mother but to keep an eye on her. Of the other intimates, only Aunt Pauline and Marianne remained. Naturally the members of the family were always welcome.

A new custom—entertaining at tea—came into Mother's life, and the first time Marianne appeared for this social event, she nearly exploded. One look at Mother in her demure attire, her legs gently crossed at the ankles and her hand placed ever so delicately on the handle of the teapot, and Marianne threw up her hands and dissolved into convulsions of laughter.

"Girl," she said finally, getting hold of herself, "all you need is a cross and a few nails."

Mother was furious. "I don't see what's so funny," she said grandly.

"Everything!" answered Marianne, gulping down the remains of her laughter. "Whom do you think you're fooling? You can put a leopard in a cage, but you cannot change his diet."

I was promptly sent out of the room. From the distance I could hear them arguing and screaming, and then a piece of crockery was smashed, but later, when Marianne was leaving, they had their arms around each other.

Through all this, Fräulein Rosalia remained unchangingly serene. She and Grandmother Sofia got along very well—they appeared to respect one another; they conversed with ease and when they agreed on some point, Grandmother Sofia would always make some gesture of approval, like patting Fräulein's hand or giving her cheek a gentle pinch.

And I? What did this change do to me? It made me feel good because—glory of glories—Father was with us all the time. Nobody volunteered to tell me what had happened, why we had moved, or what the reasons were for Father's constant presence, and I was afraid to ask for fear of spoiling things. He was there, and that was good enough for me. Of course he was out part of the day, attending to his various interests, but he slept at home, he dined with us and, in his spare time, worked with his secretary in the museum.

Now that I was well again, my studies were resumed. Fräulein Rosalia, being a Lithuanian, attended to my German; the same young lady tutor reappeared for general subjects; and a French teacher was added to the roster. Her name was Madame Callot. Vivacious beyond her middle years, and full of oo-la-las and gestures, she was overflowing with spontaneity and Gallic charm. She was also the possessor of a most outrageous figure: it looked as if someone had sawed her in half at the waistline and put her back together carelessly so that the two parts didn't quite meet. This made her derriere stick out in a most ferocious fashion. Her lessons were fun and her method effective.

Since I had no other friends, I missed Nina very much. She was in school until Christmas, and that was still two months away. I asked after her so much and so often that Aunt Pauline decided to take me to Theatre School on what was called "Reception Day."

The Theatre School was—and still is—located on Theatre Street, right behind the Alexandrinsky Theatre, which in turn was right in back of Catherine Square, where I went for my afternoon airings. A long, pale-yellow building, it stretched the whole length of the street, housing the Ballet School, the Drama School and part of the Theatrical Archives. It had its own code, its own traditions, and nothing much has changed to this day.

We entered the building, walked up two flights of stairs to a landing that opened on a wide hall, and were ushered into a large ballet studio. One of its walls was covered entirely by a mirror, and the floor was raked down toward it. Through the open doors, I could see that there was another, similar studio next to it, back to back, and that the floor there was raked down toward the mirror on the other side, creating a rise between the two rooms.

For this occasion, benches were placed along the walls in the first studio, a few feet away from the barre, and some of the pupils were already sitting around talking to friends and relatives.

The girls wore powder-blue uniforms with flaring skirts that fell all the way to the floor and starched white bibs over tight bodices. White aprons were tied around their waists. Every girl's hair was arranged in the same way, pulled back in either a braid or a low knot, depending on their ages, which ranged from nine to eighteen. I searched their faces. To me, they were not human beings—they were goddesses possessing sublime qualities unknown to others.

A prim lady in a high-collared black dress was walking around surveying the proceedings with a sharp eye and an air of strict formality. A strange hush prevailed—as in church. Everyone spoke in undertones.

Aunt Pauline gave her name to the lady in black, and presently Nina emerged from somewhere—I was too busy gaping at the girls to notice. Nina looked different; she seemed more mature, her carriage was assured and her nose high in the air. She sat down, aloof and dignified.

At once, I began bombarding her with questions.

"Do you like it here? Where do you sleep? Who is your teacher?"

She smiled a queenly smile. "Of course I like it. And we sleep in the dormitory. It's very nice."

"Can I see it?"

"No."

"Why not?"

"No visitors are allowed anywhere but this studio."

"Never?"

"Never!"

I was overwhelmed. Truly this was a sacred place—a temple that no ordinary mortal could set foot in. I touched Nina's uniform. It was made out of soft wool, and I held on to it trying to absorb the magic of this symbol, and wishing, wishing, wishing. She pulled it out of my hand. "Don't crumple it. We must look neat at all times."

"Why is everybody's hair parted in the middle?"

"We're not allowed to wear it any other way. The maids fix it for us in the mornings."

It all sounded so glamorous. I marveled at her nonchalance and poise.

"Why have you two studios?"

"Because we need them," she answered brusquely. "And there is one more, in the back. And the boys upstairs have just as many."

"Boys? You have boys too?" Somehow, I never questioned

the background of the leaping cavaliers I had seen on the stage.

"Yes, we do. But we don't see them yet. We'll meet them later when we are ready for ballroom dancing."

"Isn't there something you could show me?" I begged.

"No, I told you that no outsider can see anything but this room you're in."

She was reluctant to give any information, but I persisted and found out that there were classrooms on the other side of the hall, and a library and even a small theatre where performances were given by the pupils in all categories, from beginners to graduates.

Time flew by, and soon a bell rang—not an electric bell, but a hand bell that gave out a silver tinkle—and the dark-clad lady clapped her hands to announce the end of reception time. Quietly the little gathering began to disperse. The young ladies in blue curtsied gracefully; the black lady rounded them up and piloted them away through the back door of the studio.

I felt desolate. I didn't want to leave. I yearned to remain there forever, to wear a pale-blue uniform—to belong.

But Aunt Pauline was already walking down the stairs, and I had to follow. The Theatre School doors closed behind us, and we were in the street, back in the world of the commonplace.

That night I must have tossed a lot, because suddenly the light was turned on and Fräulein Rosalia stood by my bedside.

"What is it, dear?"

I told her of my yearning, and I pleaded. I pleaded for us to go to Father and ask him to send me to Nina's school. Could we do it tomorrow?

She pondered a while, her finger at her chin.

"No, not yet," she said then. "This is the worst possible time we could choose. Have patience. First, we must settle here securely. There are still many obstacles to overcome. Besides, you are too young. You're not yet seven. Nine is the age to enroll. However, we will talk to your father—soon. I promise you."

She kissed me, turned out the light, and I fell asleep secure in her promise.

14

"To hell with it!" Mother said one day. Off came the blouse, skirt, cameo and all, and she put on a flimsy negligée. I guess the leopard was beginning to long for its natural diet.

The next sign of this hunger was the arrival of tall mirrors that were set between the windows in the living room, followed closely by a carpet that covered the floor from wall to wall, and then, a few days later, her bedroom furniture from the other house was brought in. That presented a problem since the new bedroom was smaller than the old one, and the pieces had to be fitted in haphazardly, crowding one another. Still, now she had her favorite lavender bedspreads covered with Belgian lace and her gilded cupboards.

And at that point she stopped—for a few weeks—shrewdly realizing that the transformation had to be accomplished slowly, and with caution.

I was delighted with the mirrors. They reminded me of the big mirror in the classroom of Theatre School. I would cavort in front of them, making up pantomimes and dances, and often Fräulein Rosalia would sit and watch my improvisations. One afternoon, when I was about to turn myself into a moth by jumping about with a towel in my hands, my fantasy was interrupted by a harsh voice.

"Stop that! Stop it immediately!"

Grandmother Sofia was standing in the doorway, her face distorted with indignation and her cane raised in the air. Despite her fragile frame, she made a formidable figure, like a general about to order a charge.

Fräulein Rosalia rose from her chair.

"Don't you know what day this is?" Grandmother Sofia demanded severely.

Both Fräulein and I were momentarily struck dumb by this surprise attack, which gave her a chance to proceed uninterrupted.

"It's Sunday! The Lord's day—the day for peace and prayer! Shame! Don't ever let me catch you at this blasphemy again! And you!"—she turned directly to Fräulein Rosalia, addressing her in a sharp tone she had never used before—"You! The governess! Sitting there, watching this sinful behavior! How shocking! Don't you know any better?" Her eyes went to the icon in the corner, and she crossed herself and mumbled a prayer. Like most converts, Grandmother Sofia took her religion professionally and blindly.

Not a muscle had moved in Fräulein Rosalia's face.

"Forgive me, Madame," she said, "but nowhere in the Scriptures do I find a suggestion that people should not try to be happy on Sunday—provided that what they do doesn't hurt anyone. Surely the Lord won't begrudge a child a little enjoyment—be it even on His special day. He liked children, as I'm sure you remember. However, if it offends you, for your sake, I'll see to it that she doesn't dance or play her games on Sunday."

The voice was respectful, but the words "you" and "your sake" were faintly stressed.

The cane came down and hit the floor. I fully expected smoke to come out of Grandmother Sofia's nose, so blazing was her fury. But she only opened her mouth, held it open for a second and for some reason closed it. She watched us sternly, giving herself a moment to cool off.

"What denomination are you, Fräulein?" she asked after a pause.

"Lutheran, Madame—but it's all the same. There is only one Lord for everybody."

Apparently Fräulein's answer nipped in the bud the intended debate on the concept and practice of different religions, because Grandmother Sofia pulled herself up to her full height of five feet, turned her back on us and walked out imperiously. We could hear her footsteps on the bare floor of the corridor fading in the direction of the entrance door.

Shortly after, Fräulein Rosalia was summoned upstairs to Grandmother's apartment, where she remained for an alarmingly long time, but when she returned, she was all smiles.

"All's well," she said, "you can dance all you want any time —even on Sunday. Nobody's going to stop you."

The first hurdle had been taken without too much injury.

About a month later, draperies appeared at all the windows, and bit by bit, but with unswerving regularity, other objects of luxury began to creep in. I'm sure that in time Mother would have changed the appearance of our new home beyond recognition, had not onrushing events prevented her from finishing the job.

15

Father didn't seem to mind this gradual transfiguration of his ancestral habitat—or, more likely, he didn't care. Small vanities didn't concern him. He pampered Mother and gave her what she wanted to make her happy, but none of it entered into his private scheme. Besides, no matter how much she changed the trimmings, she could not alter the soul of the house, for the soul was Father's museum, filling the whole place with an aura that no quantity of silk cushions could smother.

At the age of nineteen, he had bought his first collection of manuscripts and from then on the fever seized him. He never stopped collecting. To track down treasures, he employed innumerable agents all over Europe and he himself made frequent trips abroad. That pursuit and determination had lasted nearly twenty years, and by the time we moved in he was the owner of one of the rarest private museums in Russia.

He loved it—his heart and soul were in it. And it was a fascinating place, indeed. A door off the vestibule opened on two very large rooms lined with bookcases. The ceilings, like those in Egyptian temples, were supported by square, hollow columns that enclosed shelves where paintings, lithographs, posters and other works of art lay stacked in black boxes. Cabinets of various sizes jutted out into the rooms at different angles, creating a maze, and crates filled with materials still to be catalogued were usually in the corners. Most of the time, in preparation for an exhibition, paintings and sketches stood leaning against the bookcases and models of stage sets rested on tripods. Amidst all this organized disorder, Father's own desk, long, heavily carved and always laden, squatted like some tired animal.

On Sundays, when his secretary was off duty and I knew he was alone, I would tiptoe in and watch him from the threshold, deep in his work, his head bent over some volume and his fingers twisting the lock of hair over his right temple.

"Come in, come in," he'd call as soon as he noticed me.

And I would be taken into his world. He'd sit me down across the desk, and bring out something for me to read or look at. Through the years, I learned a lot in those two rooms— the beauty of the written word, the flight of thought, respect for all that stood against conformity, and the importance of curiosity.

His words still ring in my ears: "Never be ashamed to ask questions. Never be satisfied with what you know, for you will never know enough."

We would sit there, he absorbed in his work and I lost in some new adventure—both quiet, both silently excited, beginning to know each other not through conversation, which was sporadic, but through our shared enjoyment.

"Books are friends," he always said. "They'll never fail you. Treat them with care."

He taught me to handle books—never to flip a page, but turn it gently by placing a finger between the pages slightly below the top right corner. To this day, my books are clean, bearing no fingermarks.

"How many books have you got, Papa?" I asked him once. He looked around, his gaze measuring the book-filled walls, and smiled. He had a smile that touched only his lips—the eyes remained serious.

"What you see here is not all of it," he said. "There is more upstairs, in your grandmother's apartment."

Suddenly I realized I had never been taken upstairs, but that thought didn't bother me; only the revelation of more books was staggering.

"You have more?" I gasped. "How many altogether?"

"You haven't learned to count that far. But I'll tell you anyway. As of today, exactly seventeen thousand, six hundred and thirty-two. Many of them are first editions."

"Oh!" I said wisely, pretending to understand this seemingly colossal figure.

He waited for a second and then said, "Haven't you forgotten something?" It took me by surprise. "No. What have I forgotten?"

"Haven't you forgotten to ask me what first editions are? Remember—questions. Always ask if you don't know."

And he explained the meaning to me in simple words, baiting my curiosity.

"And pictures? How many pictures? You told me once that you had thousands."

"Well, maybe I was exaggerating a little. Still, I have a great many. But now I have to work. Here, look at these. They are the costumes for a famous ballet."

He opened one of the black boxes and placed before me a collection of sketches by Léon Bakst for the ballet *Scheherazade* and other ballets which Diaghilev had recently produced in Paris. The brilliant colors were splashed on the paper in rainbow bursts. Staring at those beautiful costumes, I certainly could not imagine that one day I would be wearing any of them on the very stage they were created for.

Gradually, new people began to drift into our life—Father's friends—so different from the crowd that had surrounded us

64

before. Writers, poets, artists—some famous, well groomed and aware of their importance, some still unknown and fighting for recognition, usually shy and shabbily dressed. These last prevailed, because, Father explained, they needed him more than those who were established.

As a rule, they visited him in the museum, but occasionally he brought them into the living room and then, invariably, the same procedure followed. At first there was a feeling of discomfort while Mother and the guests valiantly hunted for some point of contact, then gradually the air began to clear, and in the end she always won them over. Unless, of course, there happened to be some handsome young man among them, in which case a special look would come to Mother's face, and the rapport was instantaneous.

And then one day a new member of the family appeared. His entrance, though different in character, was every bit as arresting as Grandmother Sofia's.

Preceded by the jingling of spurs, he came in like a jet of wind, tall and trim in his officer's uniform, his handsome head cocked to one side, and a shadow of a smile on his mouth, his entire aspect bespeaking supreme confidence in the effect he was creating.

He swept across the room to Mother, brushed his lips across her hand and murmured his apologies. He was so sorry not to have been able to pay his respects sooner—maneuvers, you know, such a bore—but alas, what can one do? The voice was lazy, the words sloughed over, but the heavy-lidded eyes sparkled with humor.

He fell into a chair with easy elegance, flung one knee over the other, casually adjusted his belt and looked us over with amusement, as though we were freaks in a side show. Having taken his time, he lit a cigarette and began chatting.

65

This high-powered dandy was Father's younger brother, Konstantin.

Irra's eyes nearly popped out.

"Just look at him. Isn't he gorgeous?" she whispered to me, choosing me as a confidante only because I was the nearest to her.

Mother, too, was obviously impressed. Her female luster was turned up to its most seductive, but it did her no good whatsoever.

He showed no preference for anyone, doling out his charm in equal packages to all present, and conversing briskly and wittily without revealing much beyond the fact that he lived upstairs with Grandmother Sofia when he was in town, that at the moment his regiment was stationed outside the city, and that he preferred certain restaurants because they had the best wine cellars.

Then he was gone—as swiftly as he had come—leaving behind him a fragrance of toilet water, a row of startled faces and a promise of intrigue.

16

Again the city was painted with snow, again the rivers were frozen and the powdery veil of winter muted sound. Christmas was rolling toward us, and with it a sadness began to nibble at my heart. Soon there would come that lonely night when I would be sent to bed while the others trimmed the Christmas tree. I dreaded it. I wished there were no Christmas Eve—only Christmas morning.

Nothing that concerned me ever passed unnoticed by Fräulein Rosalia.

"What makes you so sad?" she asked.

I found it hard to reply—even to her with whom I shared almost everything. Children, in their misery, are afraid to reveal the source of their torment in case they look foolish. The misery is there, all right, but it's formless, and the words to express it haven't yet been learned. I hesitated.

"I'm sorry you won't tell me," she said after a pause. "I thought you trusted me." The hurt in her voice broke the barrier.

"It's Christmas. . . ." I blurted out.

Her eyes grew big with astonishment: "But why? It is a lovely time. . . . We'll have a tree—"

I didn't let her finish: "Yes, we'll have a tree . . . and you will trim it . . . you and the others." Since she was an adult, I immediately accused her of collaboration. "You'll have fun . . . all of you . . . and I . . . I'll be in bed, alone . . . but I won't sleep . . . I'll be listening . . . alone . . . listening to you. . . ."

Her hands gripped my shoulders, restraining this barrage of words.

"Are you trying to tell me that you have never been allowed to trim the Christmas tree?" she asked.

"No . . . never."

"But that's incredible! And you would like to do it?" She checked herself. "How foolish of me to ask that! Of course you would!"

For the rest of the evening I could feel her eyes on me, and when she tucked me in, thoughts were playing on her face.

I don't know how long I slept before I was awakened by

some disturbance. As consciousness returned, I realized voices were battling in Mother's bedroom. One voice, Mother's, was rapidly rising to a pitch of no control. The other, an undercurrent to this broken dam, kept its low, tense level. The words were not distinguishable.

I listened to the sounds, a premonition of impending calamity creeping over me. Then, not being able to contain myself, I slipped out of bed and stealthily, step by step, began feeling my way in the darkness of the corridor toward Mother's bedroom. The door was closed, but I could hear every word.

"I'm fed up with your interference!" Mother shouted. "What do you know of our customs! A stupid German, trying to get the upper hand in this family. You are nothing and you don't know anything. I didn't choose you—he did!"

Fräulein Rosalia's voice was fighting back quietly: "Please, Madame, I only meant to bring it to your attention. . . . What harm is there in letting her trim the tree? She's very unhappy about it—it makes her feel rejected."

"And you! You're fostering it, so you can turn her against me!" Mother was getting out of bounds. "You're a menace! I will not stand it any longer. I'm sick of you. Tomorrow morning you'll get your month's wages, and then you're out! You're fired! Out! I want you out by tomorrow noon!"

Panic is a magician; it opens up roofs, caves in walls, swallows time, transports you from one place to another without your knowing how you got there. All I remember is that the air around me was spinning like a tornado, that a fierce crackling made unbearable sounds in my ears, that a big faceless mouth gaped open, black and immense, and I saw myself running around the apartment, looking for Fräulein Rosalia, who was nowhere . . . nowhere. . . .

Everything toppled down. I heard somebody's bare feet slapping the floor—and suddenly I was standing in the museum, facing Father.

As usual, he was at his desk, the light of the student's lamp falling on the manuscript before him, leaving his face in the shadows. It was like a dream. The room was swimming and his face was wavering because something was obscuring my view—a curtain of tears. He looked up, his head snapping back in surprise at the small apparition in nightgown and barefoot, confronting him way after hours. He appeared momentarily stunned, then:

"What are you doing here? It's very late," he said in a dispassionate voice.

Tears were rolling down my cheeks, trickling into the corners of my mouth, filling my throat. Finally, I managed to speak.

Mother was firing Fräulein, I said. She can't do that. . . . Fräulein is my friend. . . . I'll go away with her. . . .

He didn't get up or comfort me. He remained seated, silently observing me, his face a mask. A grimace of embarrassment crossed it for an instant and quickly disappeared, leaving it again devoid of emotion. Tears, anybody's tears, apparently even mine, disabled him. I learned my lesson early; to my best recollection, that was the only time I cried in front of him.

He lowered his eyes. His fingers picked up a pencil and twisted it for a moment.

"Go back to your room," he said in the same flat voice. "I'll see what this is all about."

I ran back, this time fully conscious of my movements, and stricken with a new despair. Even he . . . even he doesn't care—nobody cares about me—only Fräulein Rosalia.

In my room, I curled up in the armchair by the window,

pressing myself against the cushions. The commotion in Mother's bedroom continued. In a while, I heard Father's steps passing my room—he had a long, heavy stride—and then, as he opened Mother's door, the voices swelled and instantly fell into a barely audible muttering.

A clock on Fräulein Rosalia's bedside table was endlessly ticking away the minutes. The glow of the votive lamp threw a pink shadow trembling on the walls, and the austere image of the Saint peered into the surrounding darkness.

Then I heard steps again, hurried steps, and the door of my room was flung open. Fräulein Rosalia flicked on the light, glanced around and, finding me in the chair, ran to me.

"To bed, to bed!" she urged, lifting me from my crouched position. "You'll catch your death of cold. There's a big draft there."

I threw my arms around her. "You're leaving!" I sobbed out.

"No, no," came the soothing voice, "I'm not leaving. I'm staying with you."

"Are you sure?" I threw my head back to look her in the face.

"Quite sure," she replied. "How can I leave a wonderful girl like you?" A luminous smile lit up her countenance. There were love and pride in it, but her eyes for some reason were damp.

17

Not only did Fräulein Rosalia remain with us, but the Christmas curfew was lifted, and I was permitted to stay up and trim the Christmas tree. Mother's attitude toward Fräulein Rosalia was that of barely polite hostility, a simmering of impotent fury that throbbed in her every word and gesture, but since Fräulein bore up under it very well, showing no resentment, respectful and immaculate in the execution of her duties, there wasn't much that Mother could do. In the following years, Fräulein was to suffer a great deal of abuse on my account, but her devotion to me was stronger than all the insults, and nothing could make her leave her post. She knew I needed her, and that was enough to fortify her against all wrongs.

Fortunately, this friction was somewhat eased by the Christmas spirit, and by the time the actual holiday arrived, Mother's antagonism had subsided. It was a good Christmas, and certainly unlike the one before. The gathering of friends and family was moved ahead from Christmas Day to Christmas Eve. We had an early dinner, and just as we settled to the trimming of the tree, the guests began to arrive. All the old cronies reappeared, and spirits were unusually high, including the intake of liquid ones.

Champagne—buckets and buckets of it—boxes of Christmas trimmings all over the floor, cakes, fruit, everyone gay and lighthearted. I was ecstatic, running around the tree, decorating the lower branches, while the grownups took turns on the ladder to take care of the top. A lot of laughter and screaming and clinking of glasses—someone pounding the piano, someone singing a song. But no carols. I never heard any Christmas carols in Russia. My first introduction to them was years later, in England.

Grandmother Sofia, with Tatiana at her side, came to put her present under the tree. It was another icon, studded with enough rubies to make a necklace—a thought, I'm sure, that crossed Mother's mind as she looked at it.

Grandmother Sofia didn't stay long. The sight of Marianne in a crimson dress, stretched out seductively on the couch, with a champagne glass in one hand and a cigarette in the other, and the abandon with which one of the guests performed a kosatsky, stiffened her backbone and sent her into dignified retreat, dragging the unwilling Tatiana with her. A short while later, Konstantin swaggered in, resplendent in his parade uniform and carrying a bouquet of roses that he deposited in Mother's lap. Unlike Grandmother Sofia, he found the atmosphere well suited to his taste, approving of the wine, the wild gaiety, and clearly approving of Marianne, since in no time at all he was stretched out on the couch beside her.

When the tree was finished and shimmering, Mother announced that, instead of waiting until next morning as was customary, we were to open our presents then and there.

More scramble, more laughter interrupted by shrieks of delight, more champagne. The presents were especially elaborate that Christmas. A gremlin must have whispered into everyone's inmost ear that this was the end, the last gasp, the few remaining miles before the avalanche, and that they had better make the best of it.

Mother received a green evening coat lined with sable, and

then the "pièce de résistance" was wheeled in—a tall cupboard swaddled in a blanket. When the covering was peeled off, everyone was dazzled by the sight of a cut-crystal set—eighty-four pieces in all—each piece brimmed by a band of gold and bearing Mother's initials on its side. There were fruit bowls, pitchers and glasses of every size, from small sherry glasses to goblets. This little joke of a present had been imported from London—the only set of its kind.

Among my presents, I found a hatbox, and when I opened it, out came a ballet dress—a fluffy pink cloud dotted with sequins. It was a present from Fräulein Rosalia, who had made it in the laundry room late at night while the house slept.

I was beside myself. I threw off my clothes and slipped it on immediately, and gave the first performance of my life before my captive, intoxicated audience, which expressed unanimous approval by applauding and hooting. I whirled and jumped around until, exhausted, I had to be carried off to bed.

Next morning, I was awakened by Fräulein Rosalia, who brought my breakfast into the room on a tray. That, too, was a departure from the norm. Simultaneously, I became conscious of foreign noises—mumbling voices, the shuffling of many feet, and then a chant began.

"Try not to get in the way," said Fräulein Rosalia. "You can look, but keep your distance. Today the clergy is coming to wish your father a Merry Christmas."

Intrigued, I stepped out and cautiously moved forward, trailing the scent which brought me to the living room door. I peered in. Two priests, garbed in gold brocade vestments, their beards combed out into holiday magnificence, stood facing the icon in the left corner while, behind them, a deacon was vigorously swinging a censer that let out a ribbon of blue smoke. Monotonously, and with no emotion whatsoever, they were chanting a prayer, the deacon's zooming basso carrying the counterpoint. Mother stood nearby, looking on reverently, while at a safer distance, Father, with his head bent down, stood leaning against a wall. He seemed to have found something awfully interesting in the carpet, which he was inspecting with the toe of his shoe.

The prayer finished, one of the priests turned around and gave the blessing. He blessed everything—Father, Mother, the furniture, the carpet, the windows and every inch of air. His wrist was in perpetual motion. I think he made the sign of the cross at least twenty or thirty times. That accomplished, the trio were escorted into the adjacent dining room. I paralleled their moves by running down the corridor, and stuck my head through one of the dining room doorways.

A feast of delicacies and endless wine bottles was laid out on the table—a curious display for so early an hour—and the servants were standing by, waiting to serve what was pointed to. There was also something about the room itself that struck me as out of the ordinary—something that I could not at first detect. Then it came to me: all the chairs had been removed. The priests ate and drank standing—an unheard-of state of affairs in a Russian home, known for hospitality.

Irra joined me at my observation post.

"Why aren't there any chairs?" I whispered to her.

"Because if a priest sits down, he'll never get up. Can't risk that. Must keep them moving."

This bit of wisdom was substantiated almost immediately. I started back toward my room and was nearly trampled by a crowd of monks entering from the vestibule. Quickly, I sprang back and flattened myself against the bookcases to let them go by. They were ushered into the living room by Daria, the maid, while Father was gently leading the first three priests out of the dining room and toward the exit.

They came all day: priests, acolytes, monks, nuns. They came singly, in groups of two or more, and in veritable hordes. Every cathedral, church and monastery was represented. They went to the icon, chanted mechanically, blessed everything in sight, refreshed themselves with wine and food, and departed, accompanied by Father to the exit door. By midafternoon, traffic was so heavy it would have required a wizard to keep any semblance of order. While one group was eating, the other was already chanting, and several more teams were awaiting their turn in the vestibule. Everywhere you turned, you bumped into a saintly figure—it was impossible to control them and they roamed about freely.

I spent most of that day in corners or behind doors, unobserved, watching and listening. I saw and heard a lot of things. I heard monks swear obscenely in low voices, I saw priests yawn and pick their noses and scratch their buttocks, and I saw nuns sneak drinks with supreme dexterity. I also noticed that, every now and then, Father would turn away discreetly, pull out a wad of money from his pocket and peel off a note.

Peace came at eight o'clock, exactly twelve hours after the pilgrimage began. The door closed behind the last batch, and everyone collapsed. Weary as she was, Mother felt sanctified.

"The house is blessed," she sighed. "It's holy, holy!"

"Holy, my foot!" Father grunted sarcastically. "Holy hell! I'm out two thousand rubles!"

She looked at him, stunned. "What do you mean!"

To us, the day had been a new experience—to him, a yearly routine.

"What do you suppose has built up my business into one of the biggest in the country?" he said. "Quality alone won't do it. Those priests are a corrupt lot. I know them. I've been on the inside of it all my life. That's why my father remained Mohammedan. Do you think they came here to purify our souls? Let me assure you, they did not. They came here to collect another token of my appreciation—just another bribe masquerading as religious fervor. Believe me, that man died on the cross for nothing."

Mother pressed her hands to her bosom. "Man!" she exclaimed, horrified at this sacrilege.

"Yes, man!" Father repeated emphatically. "A man who hoped that by shedding his blood he could persuade his fellow creatures to take the right course. He was an optimist. Cain is still with us. Take a good look at our country. Barbaric, backward, with injustice and inequality for all except a chosen few. We need a parliament, we need a democracy."

"We don't need anything." Mother put up a heated defense. "God is looking after us!"

"Well, I don't know about that," Father mused. "What I do know, for sure, is that He is represented very poorly. High time we ourselves started looking after our fellow men. Lighting candles and singing hymns won't do it."

This difference of opinion persisted throughout the years, and nothing ever made them come to terms. Between the two opposing views, I grew up in spiritual confusion, searching, seeking, believing one moment and losing faith the next. Being a Lutheran, Fräulein Rosalia didn't dare enter this controversy. Thus I was left to find my own way.

18

Probably to compensate for the turmoil of that day, next afternoon Father took me for a ride in a rissak. Tucked up to my armpits under a fur blanket, I sat next to him, pulsating with excitement as we flew forward, leaving a wake of silver dust behind us. The pacer's even gait carried us onward in a swift unbroken glide, and his hoofs pounded a steady rhythm on the snow. Periodically, the driver encouraged the horse with mad outcries, which were quite unnecessary since the horse was only too eager to tear ahead. Around us the city was dozing in the approaching dusk, the crisp air bit into our faces, and the sky hung low with the impending snowfall.

We rode all the way down Nevsky Prospekt, swung to the right and passed under the arch that led onto the plaza before the Winter Palace. Guarded by sentries, the huge terra-cotta dwelling of the Czars (now restored to its original pale pistachio color) looked dead and uninhabited. We circled around the tall obelisk standing in the center of the plaza and came out on the Imperial Quay. On our left, the river Neva hibernated between its granite banks, dark silhouettes skating on its frozen waters, and on our right, the palaces of lesser royalty unfolded in an endless row.

Fast, fast, across the tiny bridges curving over the narrow canals, the outlets of the big river. On toward the lights of Vasily Island, where the globes of the street lamps hung frosted in the air. It was a lovely, breathtaking ride. At the mosque on Vasily Island Avenue, we turned back, taking the same course in reverse.

All went well until we were again at the arch of the Winter Palace plaza. And there, suddenly, we were faced by a roaring, disorderly crowd running toward us. Behind them mounted police were galloping in pursuit, and in a span of a few seconds the horses overtook the people, cut into the crowd, and the melee began. Whips and clubs swung in the air and fell on unprotected heads and bodies, people ran screaming in all directions, horses reared. A few feet away from us a man crumpled to the ground. Blood gushed out of his head, seeping into the snow in red rivulets. At that moment, Father's hand covered my eyes, and his other hand pressed me tightly to him.

I heard him yell at the driver to turn back and take the side street. I felt the sleigh swerve so violently that it stood on one blade, and then we were flying again, the roar of the crowd diminishing behind us and gradually fading out.

When Father took his hand from my eyes, we were on a dark, crooked street. I had no sense of fear, but rather of numbing shock. I looked at Father. His beaver hat pulled down low, his face looked grim. Deep furrows had knitted his eyebrows into a single line, and his muscles were tightened into stone. He stared ahead with concentrated intensity.

We took a circuitous way home at a much slower pace. A thin snow began to fall. The driver was silent, and so were we. Only the horse, being held back, snorted his objections and tossed his head.

19

In the days that followed the fatal ride, Father was especially nice to me. He took me to a gala performance of the ballet *Esmeralda*, danced by the great Mathilde Kchesinska, who was famous for her extraordinary technique and for her close relationship with Czar Nicholas. This lady, impersonating a poor gypsy girl, was bedecked with diamonds that looked somewhat odd against the rags she was wearing. The audience, however, didn't seem to mind in the least—they applauded and bravoed her every step, and went absolutely wild when she took her bows amid baskets of flowers carried on stage by liveried attendants.

A few days later, Father showed me the factory upstairs. I walked around, dwarfed by machinery, looms and all sorts of complicated contraptions. I looked at small furnaces where gold and silver were melted before being poured into molds. I watched the workers lean over the funeral cloth, working out minute designs with their flat needles, and I stood fascinated for a long time before the "studders" whose specialty was incrusting the objects with precious stones. Then we went up another flight of stairs to the turret, used as a storeroom, and I peeked out of the low corner window that gave a perfect view of both streets.

Mother, too, showed me unusual attention. She went as far as taking me for my afternoon walk to Catherine Square. But the outing was cut short, because she got bored walking up and down the paths while I played with the other children.

This rare harmony made Fräulein Rosalia believe that the moment was ripe for a confrontation with Father about my dancing ambitions.

Taut with anxiety, I sat in a straight chair in the museum listening to her repeat to him what I'd been telling her for months. She stressed that in her opinion it was not a whim or a childish fancy, like the desire of some boys to become firemen or streetcar conductors, but a real calling that should be given consideration. Indeed, she understood that I was too little yet to apply for the examination, but maybe if I were given a promise, I would find peace.

He heard her out. Then his eyes went around the room, as he collected his thoughts. A long, long silence, and then a carefully delivered response.

"I'm sorry, dear," he said. "How I wish I could give you that promise. But I cannot. In truth, I will do everything in my power to keep you out of Theatre School. It is not a place for my daughter. My daughter will have an education—a commodity sadly neglected in that establishment. The children there are trained like seals—for one purpose only—and the development of their minds is of secondary importance, if that. I want you to be a person, not a puppet. I want to give you tools to fight life with, for life is a turbulent sea, and its tides are hard to navigate. Perhaps, later, if you're still interested, I'll let you take dancing lessons privately. But no Theatre School—let us be clear about that. Go on with your piano lessons—I'm very pleased with your progress—and let me think about some other form of expression that might catch your interest."

The tone was kindly, but finality rang in every word. The dream fell apart. Hope ended. We missed the hurdle at the most unexpected place.

20

Let me explain what Father's refusal to send me to Theatre School meant to my future. It meant that no matter how good a dancer I might become I could never gain any standing because only the graduates of Theatre School were admitted into the ranks of the Maryinsky Theatre, the citadel of that art. The same condition prevailed at the Bolshoi in Moscow, where only the pupils of its own school became members of the company. There were a few small theatres operating in the provinces, but they were decidedly second-rate, without any permanent companies, and no one ever achieved any prominence by dancing in Kiev or Baku. Such companies as we now have in America and Europe did not exist. By being cut off from Theatre School, I was forever chained to mediocrity, for only the Maryinsky and the Bolshoi theatres provided the exposure and the chance for glamour and glory every dancer hoped for. It was held as a verity that only their own schools could discover and correctly train the talent suitable for those glorious establishments. That was a fallacy. Many good dancers were to be found in private schools, but, despite their talent, they were condemned to obscurity. The rule established for almost two centuries stood inviolate.

I brooded. Yet something inside me kept warning me not to give up. The cold facts were all against me, but that something was not to be stilled. Wait, wait . . . it said.

Father followed through on his attempt to interest me in other arts. A box of paints and brushes arrived, brought by a young artist who was to instruct me in drawing and painting. The experiment proved to be a disaster. Perhaps it was my unconscious resentment of this substitution for the one thing I really wanted, but all the efforts of the young artist failed dismally. I stared blankly at the still lives he set up in front of me, and then deliberately put down big blobs on paper or canvas, until, finally, in a fit of temper I broke all the crayons and paint tubes, and ground them into the carpet. For this outburst of temper I was to pay heavily. Mother, knowing full well how deathly afraid I was of the dark, chose to use it as punishment and locked me in a pitch-black bathroom for several hours, despite Fräulein's protests. The string to the electric bulb was too high for me to reach, and I sat there devoured by black visions that tore at my flesh. By some maneuvering, Fräulein managed to extricate me from my prison, but by then I was a bundle of exposed nerves.

Time went on. The holidays were over. New Year's Eve produced an extravagant all-night party that kept me awake most of the night—then all fell into routine.

Mother was getting noticeably fat—and dewy. She was pregnant again, and it gave her a glow, that singular radiance reserved for happy pregnant women. In her case, it was intensified by the hope that this time, legitimately and with pride, she might give birth to a male child, an heir to the fortune that now was hers. A contented look came into her eyes, and her disposition mellowed considerably.

I have often wondered how she looked when she carried me. There must have been some hope too—hope that the weapon growing in her womb would force the issue. I never fulfilled her expectations. The weapon didn't work. It was a boy—a little dead boy—who had done the trick.

Mother's condition being what it was, Grandmother Sofia

was visiting us every day. Her concern for Mother's well-being was overwhelming. It even made her more tolerant of our household, although she made it clear that this was by no means an acceptance of our way of living, only a temporary truce born of happy anticipation. Tatiana, too, was on hand. She and Irra struck up a friendship, which was a natural development between two minds that thrived on mischief and held dark, secret chambers. They cuddled in corners, their heads close together, giggling and contriving little evils.

Ever since I was legitimatized, Irra had lost a powerful tool to taunt me with. However, her ingenuity soon conjured up another.

Among Mother's friends there was a naval officer, a handsome blond man named Kaporin. During the Russo-Japanese War, he had been taken prisoner and he had remained in Japan until about a year before my birth. He used to amuse and bewitch me with tales of the cherry-blossom land, of the ladies in kimonos who lived in bamboo houses, and of the warriors who brandished flat swords and who shaved their heads except for a braid on top. We had a good time together; he was gentle and affectionate, and I liked him. One day, after one of his visits, I saw Irra and Tatiana eying me intently.

"See what I mean?" Irra said knowingly.

Tatiana chuckled her understanding.

"Blood will tell," Irra continued, "same blue eyes, same blond hair. There's none of it in our family. And he was around just then, exactly at the right time. I'll bet the old man knew it. That's why he wouldn't see her." And she pointed at me.

The meaning was obscure to me, but I felt that there was something wicked in her words, another buried secret concerning me, and my heart began to shrink.

"Did any of you suspect it?" Tatiana asked, playing along.

"Sure." Irra shrugged off the question. Then she came to me. "You like him, don't you?" she asked in a tone suspiciously too kind for her.

"Yes, I do," I said.

"How would you like him for a father?"

"I have a father."

"That's what you think!" They both broke into vicious snickers and left me to decipher the insinuation by myself.

From that day on, I never went near Kaporin, never asked him to tell me more stories; in my mind he became a villain, a partner to some wrong. And whenever he came to look for me, I would hide in a corner so that he could not find me. This change of heart puzzled Fräulein Rosalia, and, gradually, she got the truth out of me.

This time Irra didn't get away with it. Fräulein Rosalia found her and brought her into my room.

"Sit down!" she ordered in the tone used to a dog being trained.

Taken by surprise, Irra flopped into a chair.

"What was it you said to her the other day? What did you mean by it?" Fräulein Rosalia stood before her, rigid and determined. This normally gentle woman had turned to steel.

There was no answer. Irra sat contemplating her fingernails.

"What goes on in that polluted mind of yours? What pleasure do you derive from concocting lies and breeding misery?" Fräulein went on sternly. "Tell her—this very minute—tell her it was a joke, a mean and silly joke!"

Irra remained silent, pouting.

"Say it right now!" Fräulein Rosalia insisted, "or I will take you to the master of the house, and I'll expose you. I'm serious! You'll see where that will get you!"

84

Irra squirmed. She glanced up at Fräulein with naked hatred. "It was a joke," she mumbled reluctantly.

"That's better. Now you can go." Fräulein Rosalia dismissed her with a flip of the hand. Then she smiled at me. "You see, there's nothing to it. She doesn't know what to do with herself, so she invents all sorts of things."

That was the end of Irra's power over me. She had encountered a mighty opponent, someone who could crush her should she be caught tormenting me again. Fräulein's new face was a revelation, a warning sign, and being a shrewd girl, Irra wisely chose to let me be. Also, a short time later, she became so entangled in her own emotions that she forgot everyone except Konstantin. Her crush on him intensified, and she was beginning to pine away. To him it was a game, something to break the monotony. It amused him to lead her on, giving her a ray of hope one minute and taking it away the next. Irra was getting a taste of unrequited passion, and the uncertainty was sending her into a positively Chekhovian despair.

Meanwhile, the disturbances in the streets continued. There were clashes between the people and the police, though they were milder than the one by the arch. On our way to Catherine Square, Fräulein Rosalia and I always passed groups of people listening to a speaker shouting things I couldn't understand. Then the police would appear and the crowd would disperse. This lingering unrest caused some apprehension and, as a precaution, it was decided to move Mother's tin box with its jewels to a safe-deposit box in the "Bank de Lion," on Nevsky.

There was a lot of talk about a monk named Rasputin, who had apparently met with a spectacular end, and about the Empress, whom everybody seemed to hate, and about the war going badly, because the Empress was German and was on the side of the enemy. People were also saying that the ammunition sent to the front was deliberately defective.

Otherwise, life was following its usual pattern. One Sunday Father took me to his Theatre Miniature, and I listened to some play that made no sense to me, and watched two dancers perform a new dance called the tango, which was the newest Paris import. The theatre was lovely—small, cozy—and during intermission coffee and hot chocolate were served in the lobby.

On the surface the New Year started with only a few minor disorders, but February 1917 was not far away.

21

Revolution! I don't remember who was the first to utter that cry, but it was like the rending of the sky. The word flew from mouth to mouth until it became one solid, frightened wail, cracking the very air with its impact. Everybody was running around the house, aimlessly, hysterically, peering out the windows and quickly retreating, thrown back by the crackling of shots. The servants, being the most ignorant, took it for the end of the world. Daria fell on her knees, howling like a hyena, praying and begging the Lord not to take her yet. But Masha, the cook, probably remembering the saying that God helps those who help themselves, took a more realistic course. She wrapped herself—head and all—in a blanket, and crawled under the brick baking stove. Nobody bothered to lure her out.

The telephone rang incessantly. It was one of those crank-ing phones that hung on the wall. People were seeking com-fort in the sound of a friend's voice, and in confirming the fact that what was happening involved everybody. The at-mosphere was charged with fear, disbelief and hope that the eruption was not a lasting one, but a horrible incident, a nightmare that would subside, and tomorrow would vanish into the past.

The shooting was spasmodic. At times all was quiet, and then a new wave would come, with crowds running and roaring and bullets blasting. The noise swelled to thunder, losing any connection with human sounds.

"Away from the windows!" Father shouted, but nobody listened. They swayed back and forth, scared and glassy-eyed, like lost souls at the crossroads to eternity.

Grandmother and Tatiana came down to be with us. Kon-stantin was away, and, afraid to be alone, they came to find solace in the presence of others. Grandmother Sofia kept her outward composure. Her head high and her back arched, she sat proudly in a chair, immobile and silent, with both her hands on the knob of her cane. Only the chattering of her teeth belied her stoic stance.

A wild shot and a flying stone came through the dining room window, sending a cascade of splintered glass to the floor. Everyone screamed and ducked. A gust of freezing air followed through the hole. Quickly the doors were shut, iso-lating the room from the rest of the house, but the icy air kept seeping in through the slit under the door.

Mother was beside herself, her state of mind verging on insanity. Oblivious to the danger, and disregarding her own condition, she periodically threw on a coat, or a shawl, or whatever was handy, and ran out into the street. There was no stopping her. It was as if singlehanded she expected to hold back the tide that was threatening her welfare. After one of these excursions, she returned crazed and disheveled, and hurled herself, face down, across the table in the vestibule.

"They can't do this to me!" she shrieked, her fists pounding the table top. "They can't do this to me!"

Father and Fräulein Rosalia attempted to lift her up, but she pushed them away. "After all these years of waiting," she screamed, "I don't believe it! I won't have it! It's not fair!"

To her this great upheaval was a personal affront—a conspiracy designed for her ruination.

That night I slept on a double mattress placed on the floor below the window level. Fräulein Rosalia slept next to me, on the outer side, protecting me with her body.

The same disorder prevailed next day, only now everyone's face wore an expression of hopeless despair, for they were beginning to recognize this turmoil as no transient rebellion but an event of monumental force that was to wreck forever the lives they were used to living.

By three o'clock it built up to a climax. I remember the hour, because Fräulein Rosalia mentioned it while she was trying to force a cup of cocoa down my throat.

Crowds were converging and a real battle was raging beneath our windows. Then, very nearby, came the staccato of a machine gun, and people in the street began to drop. I was not allowed to see any of it, but I understood that the crowd was gathering closer and closer, surrounding our house as if it were a target. They shook their fists, and shouted something that was drowned out by the machine-gun rattle and the other shots.

"Somebody's shooting from upstairs," Irra screamed, peering through the corner of the window. "Somebody is mowing the people down!"

Father rushed to her side, and looked down at the crowd, straining to understand the meaning of the shouts. Below, people kept falling and the madness was rising. Then, out of nowhere, there appeared an armored car. It stopped near the corner in a strategic position, guns pointed at our building. A man climbed up on top of it, and yelled something over and over. For a moment, his voice carried above the general bedlam.

"Throw him down, or we'll level you!"

The crowd picked up that cry and now it could be clearly heard: "Throw him down! Or we'll level you!"

Father looked around in bewilderment. His hand went to his forehead and wiped off the glistening sweat. Everyone stopped, petrified, looking to him for leadership. Just then, a volley of gunfire hit the wall of the house and chaos set in.

Outward chaos creates chaos in one's mind, and for me the rest of this episode is chopped into several flashes. There was the thud of a fallen body, which nobody paid any attention to except Fräulein Rosalia, who ran and knelt over Grandmother Sofia, prostrate on the floor in a dead faint. Then there was a pounding at the entrance door, and a wild-looking man (I think he was one of the factory workers) rushed in yelling that a policeman was hiding in the turret. I remember Father riveted to one spot, his face pale with indecision. From then on the picture gets clearer again. I can see Father tearing to the entrance door, all the rest following him like a herd. Struck by some thought, he halted and ran into the museum, and we could hear the desk drawer open and close. When he came out, there was something in his hand.

He started up the stairs, the rest stampeding behind him. Carried by this momentum, and caught in the surge of hysteria, I ran with them, not knowing where we were running or why. From the bottom of the stairs came the rasp of the main entrance door being forced.

One flight up—two flights—gathering more participants on the run—through the factory—up the steps to the turret.

Father pushed the door open with his foot.

By the low window of the turret, we saw the hunched back of a policeman squatting over a machine gun that stuck out through the broken window pane, pouring death on the crowd below.

Father yelled at him to stop. The man didn't seem to hear, his shoulders shaking in rhythm with the barrage. Father stepped inside, again shouting a warning.

The man and his weapon swung around. A mad face glared at us from under a policeman's cap. For a split second, the black muzzle of the machine gun was aimed at us.

Father shot from the hip. The man toppled forward in a heap and remained still. There was no blood.

I don't recall how we got back downstairs.

22

Thus began a new era. One-sixth of the globe shattered into smithereens, and started shaping itself all over again into a new form.

A great deal has been written about the Russian Revolution, and I don't intend to recount it. I bring it into the story only as I saw it and lived it, as it related to my growth and influenced events and people around me, as it molded and dented me. Growing up is, even under the best of circumstances, a painful process—a voyage that begins in a labyrinth that gradually widens, straightens itself out and, if you are fortunate, opens on a meadow where you can see comparatively clearly. But when those years are lived in confusion, when the values you are supposed to learn are reduced to rubble and the adults who are your guides have lost the way, then growing up is a bleak dream at best.

One can never lose one's childhood. It stays with you throughout your lifetime, a second you—a vigilante that stands beside your shoulder and has a hand in everything you do.

For the first couple of months after the great upheaval, we personally were not much affected by the changes. Masha crawled out from under the stove and started cooking again, food was still plentiful and the welfare of the family was undisturbed.

But the general transformation had begun. The city was renamed Petrograd, and one day Father came in and announced that a new reform was about to take place. A parliament was being formed.

"Now we'll have some action," he said, gleefully rubbing his hands. "We may become a civilized country yet."

Mother reacted differently to the changes; she didn't like or trust anything that was going on, her primitive instinct sensing something more frightening looming in the future. And she was tearfully bemoaning the obsolete glamour of the era she knew was never to return.

In March two gentlemen wearing bowler hats and carrying umbrellas came to see Father. The three of them remained locked in the museum for a long time and at dinner Father divulged the purpose of their visit.

"Those were two agents from Great Britain," he said. "They offered to buy the museum. They tried to persuade me to sell it now, before it is too late. They said they'd pay in pounds."

"And I presume you have refused," Mother said sarcastically. She never had much respect for what she called "that silly hobby costing so many thousands," but up till then she had never dared voice her feelings quite so openly.

He looked at her with sadness. The chasm separating those two personalities was never more in evidence.

"I let you have your diamonds," he said edgily. "It's only fair that you should let me have what gives me pleasure."

She deliberately ignored the remark. "God knows what will happen to us, and English pounds might come in handy." Her voice was contemptuous.

He thought for a moment, then put his fork down and got up.

"I will not sell," he said and walked out in the middle of dinner.

It did not faze her. "Stupid idealist! Where will it get us?" she called after him.

She was getting progressively heavier and it added to her nervousness. I often caught sight of her standing before a mirror, inspecting her bulging figure with disgust. The impending arrival of a new child seemed to have lost its potency; the radiance had left her face, replaced by a haunted look.

Fräulein Rosalia, too, was saddened. She was a monarchist, and the overthrow of the monarchy was a real blow to her. Every day something reminded her of the loss. The sign "By appointment to His Majesty Czar Nicolas" was removed from the factory door, and similar signs and double-headed eagles, torn by angry crowds, were littering the gutters. Production at the factory was close to a standstill. With the overthrow of the system and the royal family, the status of the churches became doubtful and orders and purchases were reduced to a minimum. Everything seemed to be balancing on a seesaw—waiting.

When it was considered safe to go out in the streets, my walks to Catherine Square were resumed.

The city was rapidly losing its gloss. Tension vibrated in the air. Streets were filled with soldiers and sailors who mingled with the crowds, and the demonstrations on street corners took on a more violent aspect.

"Why are there so many soldiers?" I asked Fräulein Rosalia. She sighed. "I don't know, dear, I don't know. Stay by me. Hold on to my hand."

Political events were over my head. My only concern on those outings was to lure Fräulein Rosalia into taking a detour through Theatre Street, and, knowing how I felt, she often made that concession. The Theatre School building attracted me like a magnet, and even passing by it gave me a thrill.

That spring I was told it would soon be time for me to take the exams at a school called the Gymnasia for Young Girls—not to enroll, but to get a certificate for having completed the work of the first grade.

And so, one morning, weighed down by books, pens and pads, and crushed by kisses (Mother behaved as if I were going to the gallows), Fräulein and I embarked on this adventure.

At the Gymnasia, a scholarly-looking lady with a forbidding manner and pince-nez sitting on the tip of her nose received us at the office. She scrutinized me by throwing her head back and peering down the bridge of her nose toward the lenses of her pince-nez.

"We are ready for you," she said then. "Come with me."

Fräulein Rosalia took a step forward, but the lady raised her hand. "Not you," she said sharply, "you remain here and wait."

I was terrified of her, of her brusque manner. In silence she walked me down a long corridor. On either side of us there were closed doors, and we met a few pupils of the Gymnasia, who wore brown smocks and who also maintained complete silence. In this funereal atmosphere, we reached a door that apparently was our destination, and entered an empty classroom.

"Sit there," the lady ordered, pointing at a bench in the second row. Then she looked down at me. "Now stop trembling and behave," she said sternly. "The teacher will be here presently."

She departed, leaving me alone in the vast chilly classroom among empty benches, the naked walls closing on me like a trap, and silence singing in my ears. On a dais in front of me, the teacher's desk stood ominously superior.

My brain seemed to be melting. Trying to remember what I had learned, I discovered to my horror that I had forgotten everything and a humming emptiness filled my head. I broke out in a cold sweat.

"I bet they don't do this in Theatre School," I said to myself, finding comfort in that thought.

Then I began to exercise my memory. "Three and three make—what?" I questioned myself desperately, but the two threes remained stubbornly separate. After a while, I gave up, and resolved to tell the teacher when she came in that I had forgotten everything, and that I wanted to go home.

At least a half-hour passed before the door opened. The teacher turned out to be a he—a short dumpy man with a bald pate and a tooth missing.

"Well, well, what have we got here?" he said, looking at

me as if he had never seen a little girl before. That was the extent of our conversation. He took out a list of questions I had to answer, placed it before me and retired to the desk, where he opened a book and began reading peacefully.

I struggled, my memory returning slowly. When I had finished—doubtful of my efforts—he got up, picked up the paper without comment and instructed me to follow him. I was led again through the same hall, to another classroom, which was an exact replica of the first. He told me to sit down.

"The next teacher will be here soon," he said and made a quick exit.

Once again I sat and sat, waiting for the next inquisitor, who also took a long time to appear. This was a white-haired lady, whose questioning was a staccato onslaught. She was short-tempered, and must have been in a big hurry, because whenever I hesitated with my answer, she urged me on.

"Come on now, come on! Think, think! It's very simple!" she kept saying, her fingers continuously twisting her handkerchief. She left me completely flustered.

There were two more trips to other classrooms, with periods of waiting in between, and two more teachers to torment me—and then it was all over. By the time we got home, my mental state was not at its high point. A week later my parents were notified that I had passed the exams by the skin of my teeth.

23

That summer we went to the country, to a resort called Sestroretsk, about a hundred miles from Petrograd. Because of our dwindling finances, we couldn't afford a whole house, and so we rented the upper floor of a dacha, as Russian country houses are called. However, we had privacy because our stairs led directly down to the corner of the garden assigned to us, which was enclosed by a chicken-wire fence thickly overgrown with sweet peas. The garden was lavishly embellished with plaster statues of gnomes, dwarfs, storks and huge mushrooms, painted the most hideous colors. They could not be removed because the landlord, who occupied the lower floor of the dacha, was enamored of them, and peeked over the fence every day to make sure that his treasures were safely in place. The flowerbeds, such as they were, couldn't offset those horrors. Ugliness has power.

A month before we moved to the country, Daria and the scullery maid, afraid of conditions in the city, deserted us for the questionable safety of their respective villages. Masha, the cook, was still faithful to the family, but since the burden of the household was too much for one person, Fräulein Rosalia willingly took on a sizable part of the work. Irra was not much help in anything and Father remained in town, so the family was reduced to five people.

Our garden gate opened on a country road. Across the road stood a grove of splendid pines shielding a sandy stretch that sloped down to the railroad tracks. My favorite pastime was to sit on the warm sand and wait for the trains to go by. They were pulled by steam engines with clanging bells, and as they dragged slowly by, I could see the faces of the people in the windows and I would make up stories about them and where they were going. Actually, I knew that the train was heading for the next and final station—called Coursal—a community amusement center with a park, a mall with a bandstand, and a seaside building that contained a restaurant and a ballroom. But I disregarded those facts. Squinting my eyes, I sent the passengers on fantastic missions and made up their adventures any way it suited me. And I pondered over many things. I thought of the man who had fallen bleeding by the arch, and of the policeman Father had shot, and I thought how awful it was and wondered about the "revolution." It was during one of those "thinking" hours that I met the gypsy.

First there was a song—a plaintive melody unlike anything I'd ever heard before. It floated on the air, swelling and diminishing, carried by the soft breeze. Then I saw her. She was walking toward me through the pine grove, slowly and gracefully, her hips and her voluminous skirts swaying and her bare feet stepping noiselessly over the carpet of pine needles. In the shaft of sunlight piercing the pine branches, her baubles and bracelets sparkled, and her black eyes took on a red glow. She was still singing, softly now, which made the sound even sadder.

I jumped up and ran, but a flat voice glued me to a spot behind a pine tree.

"Little girl, where are you running?"

She was close, and now I could see that her clothes were dirty and that she was no longer young, but the animal vitality she exuded was hypnotic. She came to the far side of the pine, put her hands around the trunk, rested her face on her right upper arm and stared at me. A green kerchief was tied around her head, and a strand of her greasy, black hair was tangled in the loop of her earring. Her hands caressed the bark of the pine, loving it, and loving the spell she cast on me.

"Where's your mama, girl?" she said, baring teeth. They were very white against her dark skin. "Take me to your mama. I'll tell fortune, good fortune."

I couldn't move. I was weaned on the legend that gypsies stole children and that unless I was a good girl they would get me, and here I stood no more than a few feet away from one, with only a pine tree between us. She cackled, savoring her power over me.

"Don't be afraid . . . take me to mama. Where do you live? If you don't tell me, I put a curse on you. . . ."

I tore myself from the spot and ran through the grove toward our house, glancing over my shoulder. She was following me, lazily, her gait like a panther's. As I reached the front door she was already crossing the road. I ran upstairs to my bedroom, gave myself a few minutes to recover and then I looked out the window. She was standing by the gate, examining our windows. She stood there a long time. Then she started singing again and went away.

Other gypsies came by. "Don't talk to them," Fräulein warned me. "They are cheats and thieves. If you don't watch out, they'll steal the head off your shoulders."

The first gypsy came back one day, bringing with her a younger woman who carried a baby in her arms. Fräulein Rosalia made a valiant effort to shoo them away, but the older gypsy hissed and swore, and Mother, who was not the type to take a chance on a gypsy curse, invited them into the garden to tell her fortune. They sat on a bench under a tree, the older gypsy muttering over Mother's upturned palm, and occasion-

98

ally turning her hand over to admire her diamond ring. The younger gypsy stood by, watching. It didn't take long, however, before she started edging her way to the entrance door, and if it hadn't been for Fräulein Rosalia's eagle eye, she would have been inside the house.

To get rid of one gypsy is not easy. To get rid of two requires strength of character—and money. Before they left, they had to be paid over and over, and even then they swore at Mother, claiming they had been cheated.

A series of burglaries broke out. Times were getting rougher, police protection was nil, and since hordes of hungry and jobless deserters from the army roamed the countryside, the crimes could not be blamed on the gypsies alone. In fact, none of the burglars was ever caught, for the simple reason that there was no one to catch them.

Consequently Mother decided to get a dog. He was a big brute, part mastiff, part some indiscernible breed, and like most mongrels, extremely smart. Better still—he loved me, and a happy friendship blossomed. He was given the imaginative name of "Friend," which was only a half-truth, for he could also be ferocious, but with Friend at my side, I was not afraid of the gypsies any more. When Nina came to spend a couple of weeks with us, we took long walks in the woods, accompanied by Friend, gathering blueberries and flowers.

Once a month, at the Coursal, they held dances for children and teenagers, and one lovely Friday I was prettied up and taken there to attend my first real party. I remember in detail the dress I wore. It was of yellow organdy, embroidered with forget-me-nots, the full skirt billowing over two stiff petticoats. My hair was a very pale blond then, the color of champagne, people said, and it hung down to my waist. Mother didn't like to show herself in public in her blown-up condition, but in this case she made an exception, and wrapping herself in a ruffled cloak, she came with Fräulein Rosalia and me.

The ballroom was oval, the orchestra shell on one side and on the other an exit to a terrace where watery lemonade was served. Chairs stood along the walls, and mothers and their offspring sat around, waiting for the proceedings to begin. A slick-looking dancing master came in and made the rounds, greeting everybody and kissing some ladies' hands. There was no doubt that he fancied himself a Lothario, a summer conqueror. He called all the children to the floor, lined them up on opposite sides of the ballroom, and made a speech about how much fun we were going to have, and how absolutely delightful everybody was, and then told us to choose our partners. A big scramble ensued, and then the music struck up for the first dance. I found myself being partnered by a fat girl, who didn't inspire much confidence, but she surprised me by being very light on her feet and the first round went without a mishap.

There was a prescribed routine for dancing at these affairs: the couples moved counterclockwise, executing the simple steps of the pas de patineur, or czardas, and even the polka had to be danced inside the same circle, so that there was a degree of order on the dance floor. But this time it was short-lived. A certain girl in a yellow dress with forget-me-nots saw to that. A demon got into me, and suddenly I was whirling, doing strange, wild steps, and pulling the fat girl around with me. She tried to resist, not only because she was well mannered and sedate, but mainly because she couldn't keep up with me. In a paroxysm of exaltation, I twisted, turned and bent backward, kicking my feet up so high that my petticoats flew over my head. Exhibitionism, the inevitable ingredient in a performer, came to the fore, and I was possessed by the desire to be noticed, to be admired, to stand out from the crowd. The other dancers began to turn around and look, and, in the background, some of the mothers climbed up on chairs, craning their necks to see who that wild girl was. The fat girl fell, but it didn't stop me; I released her and continued on my own. Fräulein Rosalia ran out on the dance floor, weaving between the dancing couples and trying to catch up with me, but I was always a few steps ahead of her, a spinning, kicking dervish. Finally Fräulein Rosalia's grip was tight around my wrist, and she dragged me off the dance floor, through the crowd and onto the terrace.

"What is the matter with you?" she asked, pushing me into a chair. "Making such a spectacle of yourself! Shame on you!"

I was still under the spell, breathing heavily, my once neat hair now hanging loose and tangled around my face.

Mother stood by, laughing.

"Don't you know that a girl is a little lady?" Fräulein went on nervously, "that she should be modest, well behaved and—"

"Ah, leave her alone!" Mother's voice rose over Fräulein's words. "You get nowhere by being like other people. If she wants to show off—good—let her! Who ever got anywhere by being modest and sitting in corners? This is a mean, rotten world, and you have to fight it with everything God has given you!" She put her hand on my hair, smoothing it. "Come on. Let's have some lemonade and cookies. They may be our last."

I looked up and met a smile that was at once bitter and sweet. I think that when I was cavorting on the dance floor, she must, for the first time, have seen something of herself in me.

Whatever her motivation, I had found an unexpected ally— for the moment.

24

Mother sat doubled up in a chair, moaning. Her time had come, and Irra ran out to get a carriage that would take them to the station to catch the train for the city. Fräulein Rosalia was going too, for despite the friction between them, Mother knew who was indispensable in an emergency.

Irra drove up in the carriage. A lot of fuss was made about the baggage, making sure that nothing had been forgotten, and then a pyramid of suitcases was piled up on the seat next to the coachman.

It was early evening. A sweet fragrance rose from the warm earth, and the pine grove across the road stood still and straight—a black cathedral in the falling darkness. Masha, Friend and I waited by the gate while Fräulein Rosalia helped Mother into the carriage. Before they took off, Fräulein Rosalia repeated her instructions to Masha—the doors should be locked by ten, and I should not be allowed to roam too far from home while she was gone.

"I'll be back in two days," she said, throwing me a kiss with both hands.

We stood and watched them drive off, the placid clickety-clack of hoofs suggesting that the horse was unaware of the importance of his mission. The tops of three heads stuck out like bumps over the back of the carriage, and then the curve of the road swallowed them.

"I hope she doesn't die," Masha came up with a sudden, tearful pronouncement.

"Why should she die?" I asked, startled.

"Sometimes it happens," Masha said wiping her nose. "My sister died that way."

"Which way?"

I was already disturbed by Mother's pains, and though I had been told that she was about to have a child, the possibility of danger or death was never mentioned.

"Masha, tell me which way do you mean?" I persisted, pulling at her arm.

But Masha had already lost interest in the subject. Having tossed her morbid thought to the four winds, she turned to trivial matters.

"Come on," she said. "Supper is ready."

The thought of death lingered with me. Before following her inside, I looked back at the road, trying to read the to-morrow it held at its end, and I could swear that I saw the gypsy and a man standing immobile as statues in the shadows of the pine grove.

The doors were locked at ten, and all was well.

Adhering to Fräulein Rosalia's wishes, I stuck close to the house all next day. I didn't even go down to the sand slope, and amused myself as best I could. I read, counted flowers in the flowerbeds—a futile occupation—and stared at the hideous faces of the gnomes, wishing the earth would gobble them up.

And then, from somewhere, came the song. It was a man's voice this time, lengthening out the notes, vibrating in painful cadenzas, mournful, foreboding.

I listened, and I wanted to cry, and then, seized by sudden misery, ran into the house and up the stairs to the kitchen door. There I stopped, arrested by a strange sight. Masha, her face flushed, was sitting in the lap of a soldier. One of his hands was around her buttocks and the other was buried in her bosom. His face was twisted into a grimace, and he was muttering into her ear. In their involvement, they didn't notice me, and I backed out of the doorway without a word and ran into my room.

Where had I seen that expression on a man's face before? Oh, yes . . . of course . . . Hirey! But Hirey was beautiful . . . even then. This man was gross and ugly . . . and I hated him . . . and I hated her too, and I felt dizzy and ashamed of something I could not define.

So perturbed was I that it took me a minute to realize that the song that made me run into the house had changed into the sound of a hurdy-gurdy, and that it was close by. I looked out the window. A gypsy man stood by the gate, playing. A thick gold ring glistened in his left ear, and a monkey sat on his shoulder. The hurdy-gurdy whined and squeaked, and I stuck my fingers in my ears to shut out the sounds until the gypsy moved off.

At supper I couldn't bear to look at Masha. My head turned away in disdain, I barely nibbled at my food, feeding most of it to Friend, who was under the table. Masha, however, preoccupied with her own thoughts, didn't seem to notice anything.

Ten o'clock, and the doors were locked.

In the middle of the night—or what seemed like the middle of the night to me—I was awakened by the barking and scratching of a dog. Half-asleep, I sat up in bed. The flicker of the votive lamp filled the room with a faint reddish glow. Friend usually slept on a small rug near my bed, but I could see that he was not there. Yet the barking persisted, and now I could detect another sound, soft and secretive—a sort of rattle at the foot of the stairs. I yelled for Masha. There was no response. Was I alone? My heart began to beat faster, and, creeping out into the hall, I turned on the overhead light.

Below me, pressed against the glass pane of the entrance door, I saw a dark face, eyes black and steady looking up at me. The handle of the door was twisting and turning, the obvious source of the rattle I had heard. I screamed so loud that pain exploded in my head. Behind me in the kitchen Friend was barking furiously and tearing at the door. The man stopped his rattling while his eyes appraised the situation. Then, having correctly concluded that the dog was shut in and that I must be alone in the house, he pushed the door with all his might and was inside.

An earring—a gold ring in the left ear! He stopped at the foot of the stairs with his hands behind his back.

"Don't be afraid, girl, show me to your mama's room," he said and started slowly up the stairs like a cat, his eyes never leaving me. He was almost at the top when some saving instinct propelled me toward the kitchen door. I flung it open and Friend tore out, the impact of his forward leap knocking me back a few feet. The three of us collided somewhere in the middle of the landing, the gypsy crashing into us from behind. I saw Friend leap over me at the gypsy's throat. Something gleamed in the air, the gypsy fell and so did I, tripped by his fall, and then everything, including me, vanished in a blackout.

When I came to my senses, the gypsy and Friend were gone. Still dazed, I pulled myself into sitting position and stared blindly at the black gap of the open front door. The fingers of my right hand felt sticky. I looked down and discovered that it was blood trickling down my arm from my shoulder, where the nightshirt stuck to my skin in a red blotch. With this discovery came a gnawing pain. Still I sat, drained of all capacity to think or act. Friend came back, his hair still bristling but his tail wagging happily. He seemed unhurt. He lay down next to me and licked the blood off my fingers.

Masha came in when the doorway was pink with light and the rays of dawn were crawling up the stairs. She wept and groveled, and put wet towels on my shoulder, incessantly begging me to forgive her.

"Oh, little darling," she wailed, "I had to go and see my friend. I'm an old maid . . . I want to marry. . . . Never, never be an old maid . . . that's bad. . . . I locked the doors and locked in Friend so he wouldn't wake you when I came back. How was I to know? I'm a sinner, that's what I am. But I don't want to be an old maid. . . . Don't tell anybody . . . they'll throw me out . . . I'll never again leave your side. . . ." She stuck to her promise. She made me stay in bed all day, and sat by my side, changing wet towels and weeping. Her supply of tears was inexhaustible. I wished she'd go away— I didn't want to talk and I could not listen to her any more. Finally, I turned my face to the wall and pretended to go to sleep, and after a while this sent her back to the kitchen.

I lay there, and the thoughts in my head leapfrogged over one another. My shoulder was aching. What was this life? Why were people bent on hurting each other? She said, never be an old maid. . . . It must be awful to be an old maid if she could leave me all alone because of that. And the gypsy . . . She had seen Mother's diamond ring . . . and she had sent him. Did he mean to stab me? Or did he want to kill Friend?

Outside the sun was shining, but to me the world was ashen.

25

Despite Masha's gruesome thoughts, Mother didn't die. But the labor was hard and long, and it forced Fräulein Rosalia to remain in town for five days. By the time she returned and discovered my wound, a scab was already forming, and it was too late to take any stitches. As a result I wear the mark of that night until today—a scar, a perfect imprint of a dagger's point just under my right collarbone. For Fräulein's benefit, Masha threw another painful scene of repentance, but Fräulein comforted her by saying that it could have happened just as well if she had been in the house.

Mother didn't come back to the country. Irra arrived a few days later, but we didn't stay on long, and by the end of August we were all back in the city. Masha returned with us, her soldier friend having vanished without a forwarding address. Friend's size prevented his becoming a city dog, and he had to be left behind. Fräulein Rosalia found a good home for him, but it was a sad farewell for me.

In the apartment, a nursery had been made out of a servant's room for the new baby boy, whose name was Anatol, and a new wet nurse had been engaged. The other nurse's clothes had been exhumed from the bottom of a trunk and the new one was prettied up with laces, ribbons and beads. But somehow it wasn't quite the same. The clothes had a worn look about them, the nurse was frightened and docile, and the excitement that had been so apparent at the birth of the first baby boy was missing. History was washing everything pale.

Mother had lost some weight, but after this childbirth she was never able to thin down to her former figure, and she was to remain very plump for the rest of her life. Even the famine that was about to knock on our door didn't help.

October came, and overnight the change took place that was to tear our lives to shreds, and not only put its iron stamp on our country, but cast its shadow over the world.

"The Bolsheviks have taken over. The Communists are in." I heard the words repeated over and over. There was no screaming, no hysteria, only a lifeless calm. The words were spoken quietly, all hope relinquished, all energy vanquished by this new gigantic event.

The change began to bear fruit almost immediately. The two British dealers in bowler hats reappeared and had another long session with Father, and, when they left, I watched him walk up and down from the museum to the living room and back again, his shoulders stooped more than usual and his hands hanging limp. Next day, crates were brought in; some were placed on our landing, and others on the landing upstairs in front of Grandmother Sofia's apartment, and two men spent the whole afternoon packing. One-third of the museum kept at Grandmother's was packed in toto, and a considerable quantity of books and paintings were taken from our floor. Father stood looking on without a word. When the crates had been taken out and the main entrance door closed on them forever, he was still standing there, his hands clutching the railing, his eyes on the vacant stairs. Then he sat down on the top step; his head drooped forward, and he held it in his hands.

"I hope you'll never have to part with what you love," he said in a barely audible voice.

"If it makes you so unhappy, why did you let them take them away, Papa?" I asked.

He lifted his head, and his face was full of sorrow. "We have to live, daughter," he said. "We have to live and for that we will need money. Everything will be different now."

This prophecy was fulfilled with no delay. The calm was brewing a tornado, and not a day passed without something being torn out of our lives. The machines of the factory stopped, and the factory with all its riches was confiscated by the government. The same fate befell Father's theatre, where the first gesture of the new owners was to bar the doors and windows and tear down the marquee. Strangely enough, this loss didn't affect Father as strongly as the sale of the museum. He shrugged it off as inevitable.

Mother, too, suffered a severe blow; the Bank de Lion, where her jewels were presumably safe in a safe-deposit box, was taken over with the other banks by the new Communist regime. All access to it was prohibited.

"My jewels . . . my jewels! Is this the end?" she cried. And then she had a heart attack, this one real.

The whole city was in an uproar. Cries of "Long Live Lenin!" were shouted everywhere. Antireligious processions paraded down the streets, carrying banners showing Christ's face splashed with mud. The police were converted into militia, and were never to be found in the moment of need. The city was overflowing with soldiers; arrests and purges were in full swing, and it was impossible to distinguish friend from foe or from the bandits who took advantage of this anarchy.

The searches began about two weeks later. In order to catch people unaware, they were conducted during the night. I don't remember all of them, but because the first was a novelty and a shock, it stands out in my memory.

A terrific pounding at the entrance door woke up the whole family. Lights went up and everyone fell out of bed in a stupor. Through the open door of my room, I could see Father and the others, huddled in the corridor in their nightclothes, and looking at each other in bewilderment and fear. The pounding was getting brutal. Then Father walked into the vestibule and out of my sight. Next, the vestibule was filled with loud, coarse voices all yelling at once, with one word predominating in the cacophony: "Mandate!" "Mandate" in Russian means warrant. There was a stumping of heavy feet, and they walked into the corridor—two men carrying bayonets and three women wrapped in shawls—ghosts of Madame Defarge.

They went through the house looking for hidden money and jewelry and helping themselves to whatever pleased them. The men poked their bayonets through mattresses and upholstery, and the women concentrated on closets and chests of drawers and cupboards. Mother's diamond ring was taken off her finger and the silk kimono she wore torn off her shoulders. If they found three coats, they took one, and so it went with everything else. The bejeweled icons caught their eyes and one could see them being tempted, but they resisted, perhaps because possession of a religious article might have incriminated them. My room was the very last to be graced by this group.

"There's nothing in here." Fräulein Rosalia attempted to stand up to them. "This is a child's room." It had no effect. One of the men pushed her away, and, crooking his finger, motioned me to get out of bed. Fräulein Rosalia grabbed me, threw a blanket over me, and stood me behind her, her body a wall between me and the intruders. The man stuck his bayonet into my mattress, shook it and, finding no treasure sewn into it, walked out, followed by his comrades. Carrying their acquisitions in the women's shawls, they stumped out, leaving Father standing helplessly with the mandate in his hands.

A few more such visits, and our wardrobes were reduced to bare essentials, and if it hadn't been for a well-concealed storage room near the kitchen that the searchers never discovered, we wouldn't have had anything to sell later on.

Frightening as they were, the searches were minor compared with the day they came to arrest Father. His former wealth, his relation to the church, and the honorific, "By appointment to the Czar," made him a natural target, and I'm sure everyone had expected it to happen at any moment. Still, when it actually happened, it was a knockout blow. One late afternoon, two men in civilian clothes walked in, produced a summons—the officials were always loaded with papers—and ordered Father to come with them. They were polite and laconic—two robots with no feeling or compassion who wouldn't even let him pack a suitcase. They held him, and wouldn't let any of us come near him. Everyone stood in deadly silence, for this event was too big for tears, the chance of his return being one in a thousand. Hardly anyone taken away by the Cheka ever came back.

Father looked at his brood and forced a smile. "Don't worry," he said, but a specter of farewell in his eyes gave his words a false ring. Holding his elbows, the men took him out.

The house turned into a grave. Mother took to her bed, the wet nurse rarely came out of the nursery, Irra sat by the window most of the time, staring at the street in silence, and Masha, weeping again, now soundlessly, was seen only when serving food that nobody ate. Nobody spoke unless it was absolutely necessary, and hours and hours went by without a sound. It was so still that it was hard to believe that life was going on. Several times a day, Grandmother Sofia came down to inquire if Father was back, and having received the same answer walked away, her once proud body bent, her steps unsteady and her hands shaking.

Although I didn't realize the implications of Father's absence, I was very perturbed by it, and I repeatedly asked Fräulein Rosalia why he went away with those two men.

"He couldn't help it. He had to. . . . But God will bring him back. . . . God will bring him back. . . ." She said it over and over.

And he did come back, about two weeks later when all hope was fading. Shouts and tears of joy greeted his return, bringing life back into the house, and when the first excitement wore itself out, everyone gathered around him to find out what had caused this miraculous turn of the tide. It turned out that the news of Father's arrest had flown through the city's literary and theatrical circles with the speed of light, spreading beyond the city limits and arousing indignation and concern. At the beginning of the Revolution, the seat of the government was not at the Kremlin as it is now, but in Petrograd, at a college called Smolny, which had been converted to government use. Shortly after Father's imprisonment, an unusual petition was received there. It bore more than sixty signatures that included names famous in all the fields of art—directors, writers, painters, heads of museums and recently recognized revolutionary poets such as Mayakovsky and Yessenin, all united in a plea for Father's release. The document enumerated Father's past good deeds, testified to the help he'd given some of them during the lean years, and described him as an exceptional human being. The government investigated the claims and, finding them valid, resolved to act magnanimously. They not only released him, but gave him permission to keep what was left of the museum in our house, though he was forbidden to sell a single item from it.

Nevertheless, living continued to unhinge itself; food was getting scarcer; plumbing broke down and there was nobody to repair it; shops were closing all over town; and the atmosphere of hopelessness was suffocating.

In every situation, no matter how hard or complex, a certain element will find a way of profiting by it. And so one day a fat little woman and a man walked into our house. They produced proof that they were government employees in charge of the Bank de Lion and boldly laid their proposition on the line. They said the bank was to be confiscated within a week and Mother would lose everything she had in the deposit box. However, if they were given the keys and could open the safe-deposit box before confiscation, they would, in recognition of this courtesy, return to Mother two pieces of her own jewelry. They impressed upon her that she was already a loser but that in this transaction everyone would come out a little ahead. There was no choice and the keys were handed to them. The jewelry they returned was one pair of diamond earrings, each earring counting as a separate piece.

It was impossible to continue my education along the old lines; there wasn't enough money to pay the tutors. Madame Callot was the first to depart in a cloud of tempestuous goodbyes, a lot of hand-waving and a few teardrops. The young lady tutor was the second, her departure subdued and rather businesslike. Masha just waved and ran. Fräulein Rosalia didn't wait to be dismissed. She went to Father and begged to be allowed to stay with the family, offering her services without remuneration, and her request was granted.

Through the rest of the year, she helped me with my studies, and in the spring, following another torturous set of examinations, I was accepted as a pupil at the Gymnasia for Young Girls, to start the following fall.

Everything was changing relentlessly—habits, customs and way of life—and, in the process, people's characters were changing too. Irra was the most noticeable example: hate went out of her, and she began to show signs of affection and understanding, I suppose because there was no one to envy any more. We were all in the same boat and sharing the same load.

Konstantin alone took the change lightly. Without blinking an eye, he turned in his elegant officer's uniform for that of a sergeant in the Red Army, thereby delivering a mortal wound to Grandmother Sofia's pride.

"Oh, come on, Mother! Let's be sensible," he said when she reproached him for switching his allegiance so easily. "Life is a giant joke. I can't change history. A wise man goes along with it. I want to live and see what happens."

Not everyone was so lucky, even if they were willing to accept the change. Michael's title trailed behind him, a constant shadow of death, and one evening he walked in, wearing shabby civilian clothes, the collar of his coat turned up, his face gray and his fear showing in the way he jumped at every sound. It was hard to believe he was the same man. He stayed with us for several days, sleeping on the living room couch, and then one morning, when I woke up, he was gone. Father had arranged his escape, but there was never any confirmation that it had succeeded. Silence doesn't tell tales.

Mother's health was shaken. She was pale and listless, and continually complained about either her heart or a pain in her head, and it seemed wise to turn one of the earrings into cash and send us to the Crimea for the summer.

Before we left, I caught her sitting on the side of her bed, staring at the one remaining earring. She held it between her fingers, slowly turning it in the light of the bedside lamp, which made the diamond flare into sunbursts of sparks. Her mouth was curved down and her eyes were blind to everything but the glitter of that stone. She looked at it for a long time. Then she dropped the earring into a box and closed the lid, letting her hand lie limply on top of it.

I think it was then that she said good-bye to the past.

26

Along with other properties belonging to the nobility, the estate of Countess Panina was one of the first to be confiscated by the government, and so this time we went to a more plebeian part of the Crimea, nearer the town of Yalta.

There were no rocks here, no picturesque formations, no wonderland to inspect, just a curved stretch of sandy beach, soft as powder, slowly descending until it hid itself under flat, gently lapping waves. Wooden docks about a quarter of a mile apart ran out into the water for small craft and fishing boats; with the diminishing food supply, fish had become the mainstay of the diet in that part of the country.

In back of the beach, separated by a gravel path, stood a row of modest houses, each with its own rose-filled garden, or rather yard, and still farther inland the earth rose into hills, lush with greenery and punctuated by the darkness of cypresses tapering to the sky.

It was a quiet place, almost lethargic, in tune with the lazy rhythm of the sea and the stillness of the hills protecting it.

We had a small, two-story house. Mother's bedroom was on the ground floor next to the living room and the enclosed porch which also served as dining room. Our room was directly above hers, and the wet nurse and Anatol were installed across from us on the side facing the hills. Father didn't come with us; he remained in Petrograd to line up some work, for all his holdings were gone and he knew very well that the proceeds from the earring would not last very long. Irra also stayed behind, probably in the hope that on her own she would have a better chance to engulf Konstantin with her charms and perhaps subdue him.

Weeks went by and Mother showed no sign of improvement, sinking deeper into depression. The house was abominably furnished, with cheap curtains hanging limply at all the windows, paintings of hideous landscapes adorning the walls and antimacassars pinned to all the armchairs. Ordinarily Mother would have done her utmost to improve the place, but now all initiative seemed to have left her, and she was indifferent to everything except her personal despair. Ashamed of her plump figure, she refused to put on a bathing suit and go out on the beach, preferring to brood all day long in a hammock hung between two trees in the garden. At mealtimes, she would keep repeating that everything was finished, done with, that no one would ever look at her again, that there was no future or hope for any of us, and that it would be far better if the Good Lord in His mercy swept us all into the sea.

"Please, Madame," Fräulein Rosalia pleaded with her. "How can you say that? You have two children. They are your future. I'm sure there is a lot of happiness ahead of you."

But that would only touch off an eruption of abuse. What did she know about life? A servant, with no ambition, no accomplishment? How did she dare venture an opinion on something that had passed her by!

Fräulein Rosalia never answered, never retaliated in any manner, though she now bore all the weight of the household.

116

She sat silently, taking it, her eyes sadly appraising Mother's anguish, and only when Mother vehemently insisted that death was the only solution for us, would her body tense as she glanced at me.

Her anxiety was justified. Thanks to Mother's harangues, life was taking on the shape of a huge, inescapable enemy waiting for me around the corner with horrors dripping from its fingertips. I couldn't wait to go to sleep for, curiously enough, nighttime gave me a reprieve. Nights, I felt, were for sleeping, not living, and it was living I feared. Waking up in the morning was the beginning of uncertainty fraught with morose expectations.

Inevitably, it had to come out in the open.

"Will anything good ever happen to me?" I asked Fräulein Rosalia one day. The question visibly disturbed her, and for a while she was silent, biting her lip, and then she took my hand.

"Let's go out on the beach," she said, and fell silent again.

It was early dusk and the sea was splashed with golden licks of the departing sun. We reached the waterline in silence.

"I'll tell you what we'll do," she said suddenly. "We'll play a game."

"What kind of a game?" I asked, taken aback by this switch of subject.

"Let's guess the first thing we'll find on the beach."

"A dead fish," I said, unhesitating.

"All right," she said, "we'll see."

We walked along the waterline, our bare feet sinking into the wet sand, and then a soft wave rolled forward and deposited a garland of seaweed at our feet.

"You were wrong," said Fräulein. "It isn't a dead fish."

"Well, it isn't very pretty anyway," I said defiantly.

"Wrong again," she said, squatting beside the seaweed. "It is wet now, so it is difficult to see how delicately it is made. And, believe it or not, it contains iron and other minerals and ingredients that are put in medicines to help sick people get well. So, you see, it's a beautiful thing all around . . . and look . . ."

Her fingers untangled the wet fronds and disclosed a perfect little shell caught in the green web.

Looking for shells was my daily occupation, and a fairly successful one, but this shell seemed particularly lovely—iridescent, well rounded, with tiny sharp teeth closing its mouth.

"What does it mean?" inquired Fräulein Rosalia. Getting no response, she continued. "It means one never knows what the future will bring. You expected a dead fish and ended up with a beautiful shell. Doesn't that teach you a lesson? Life is full of surprises and adventures and you must be ready to accept them all. Don't look for a dead fish. Sometimes, indeed, you'll find it, but just a bit further there might be a treasure chest. Now, have I answered your question?"

I nodded, examining the wondrous shell.

"We'll take the shell home with us," she said, "just as a reminder."

For the rest of the summer, the shell was kept in a pretty box on my bedside table.

I was beginning to grow up. A slight curve appeared to indicate a waistline in the heretofore chunky body, a new hard tissue was raising the nipples, and my legs, thinning out at the knees and ankles, were beginning to suggest the shape they would eventually take. Boys began to notice me, but I hated them. Their way of showing affection was either to pull your hair or to pinch you when you least expected it, or, if there were more than one, surround you in a wolf pack and shout endearments and obscenities. One boy, however, was an exception. His name was Vadia, and he was undersized for his eleven years, with a long, dour face and a veil of freckles across his nose and cheekbones. Shyness kept him from speaking to me, but he followed me everywhere at a respectful distance and, when I sat down, he, too, sat down nearby, staring at me with an expression that was a blend of fascination and stupor. I didn't mind him. I fancied him to be my page in constant attendance.

One sunny afternoon, Fräulein washed my hair and sent me out to dry it in the sun. I crossed the beach and walked to the tip of the dock that jutted out at an angle across from our house. I liked that spot. Fishermen came in to unload once or twice a day, and I loved watching them spill their silvery catch into big buckets and carry them up the road toward the hills. And I dreamed that one day, for my personal benefit, they would fish out a mermaid and bring her ashore. The mermaid never materialized, but something else was sent by the sea—equally effective or maybe even more so.

I sat down on the edge of the dock, my hair covering me down to my hips like a tent. It was hot and still. The sea lay calm and glassy, stretched out to nowhere. No sound, no ripple. Even the seagulls forsook the sky and rested sleepily on the warm sand. At a self-prescribed distance, Vadia sat cross-legged, contemplating my presence.

Lulled into a pleasant limbo, I became aware of the sputtering of a motorboat only when it was quite close. The boat was heading toward the dock, and it carried two men—a sailor at the engine and a civilian, his white shirt open, who stood at the stern shading his face with his hand. The boat circled to the side of the dock behind me, the sailor threw the rope around the piling, pulled hard and brought the boat in. Over my shoulder I saw the man in the white shirt jump out with the agility of a cat, almost twisting in the air so that he landed with his back to me. I watched him lean forward and say something to the sailor, who was already releasing the rope, and in a moment the engine spurted with new vigor and the boat was off. The man on the dock stood with his hand up high, waving good-bye.

There was something disturbing about that back and the mold of the muscles under the white shirt, and it gave me a feeling of looking at something I should not be seeing. When he was about to start toward land, I quickly turned away.

I heard his footsteps on the water-beaten planks and then they stopped. When they resumed, they were coming toward me.

"Hey! Where did you get that wonderful hair?" a voice said right over my head.

I looked up and saw his face. He was smiling a broad, warm smile, his teeth white between full lips. It was a handsome face, strong and rugged, the raven-black hairline broken by a perfect widow's peak; a faint, irregular scar down the right cheekbone immediately conveyed to me some romantic deed, like a duel fought in defense of a lady's honor. But more than anything it was the eyes that hypnotized me—the deep blue of cornflowers in the bronzed skin—and as they met mine, my vision started narrowing down, shutting out everything around me like a camera focusing for a close-up. Suddenly there was nothing—no sea, no beach, no sky—but two blue centers absorbing me totally. A strange sensation rose from the pit of my stomach.

He waited, smiling.

"It must be a wig," he tried again. "Is it?"

The voice was kind and engaging, but I was unable to break the trance.

He made one more try. "Don't let your mother ever cut it off. Promise?"

I remained voiceless. Finally, he shook his head, and gave up, probably taking me for a half-wit.

I saw him walking away, down the dock toward the beach. The white shirt was shrinking with the distance. Now he stepped off the dock onto the sand. . . . He was going . . . and I would never see him again. . . .

Suddenly I was running in a blind response to some incoherent impulse. I ran, hair flying, feet fighting the delaying action of the sand, heart palpitating with excitement.

Halfway across the beach, I caught up with him, passed him and continued running ahead of him toward our house. There, I threw the gate open and leaped into the nearest flowerbed. My hands searched feverishly for the stems of the most beautiful roses. Insensible to the thorns that were tearing at my skin, I jumped from one bush to another.

Surprised by this behavior, Mother sat up in her hammock. "What are you doing?" she inquired sternly.

I paid no attention. My arms dipped into rosebushes up to my elbows, and my fingers brutally broke off the biggest and prettiest blooms. I heard the gravel of the path crunch under his feet and from the corner of my eye saw him walk past our house and out of sight. Not fully aware of what I was doing, I leaped out of the flowerbed and, clutching the roses in my fist, tore after him. I overtook him a few feet away from our house and barred his path.

He stopped. We were face to face again.

"For . . . for you . . ." I stammered, handing him the roses. There was a pause as he looked down at me, amused, and with that special, barely perceptible condescension of one accustomed to adulation.

"Well, well, so you can talk after all," he said, accepting my bouquet. The smile was back. "Thank you, they are beautiful."

"We have many more," I hastened to inform him, my legs set for a sprint back to the garden.

"No, no—" he put a restraining hand on my shoulder, his touch melting me—"these are quite enough. It was sweet of you to give them to me. You are a pretty girl, but you look like a little witch with your hair all tangled up this way. Where do you live?"

"She lives right here," a voice answered from behind us. Mother was leaning over the fence, observing us. "She's never behaved like this before. You must have made a great impression," she said, and, as he turned toward her and she caught a glimpse of his face, she added, "Oh, now I see."

Evidently he saw something too, for he promptly left me and walked to the fence to talk to her. At first I could hear the conversation clearly—it revolved around the heat, the place, how long we had lived here—but gradually the voices slid into a lower, more intimate key, with only a splash of laughter, or a word out of context, reaching me, and soon the gate was opened wide and he entered the garden. Neither of them looked back at me.

Discarded and forgotten, I was left alone in the middle of the gravel path. Gone was the elation that had given me wings, and I stood heavy on the ground as if I had suddenly put on extra weight. Suddenly the scratches on my hands were hurting, and I cringed under the pain of rejection and betrayal. I wanted to cry. Bewildered at myself, I looked around helplessly, and it was then that I noticed Vadia, who must have trailed me and, hiding behind a telegraph pole, must have witnessed the whole scene.

"Leave me alone! Go away!" I screamed and, swinging around violently, ran in the opposite direction.

Fräulein Rosalia and I had dinner alone that night. Mother said she was not hungry. The man in the white shirt was gone, but he came back later in the evening when I was already upstairs, preparing to go to bed. The window in our room offered a full view of the garden, and in my nightgown I watched him and Mother settle down cozily in two big chairs under a tree. The moon was pale, the night breeze low—a perfect setting—and shortly I saw him stretch out his hand and take hers, their fingers interlocking. I hated them both.

In the morning Mother was removing the hideous pictures from the living room walls. Her movements were languid and she was humming some bittersweet tune. Disregarding her cheerful greeting, I crossed the garden and walked out the gate. A small figure approached me. He came quite close, and I heard him speak for the first time.

"Give me a rose too," said Vadia. "Please give me just one."

I looked at him, and in his eyes saw my pain of the day before. So I went back into the garden, and brought him a fragrant yellow tea rose.

We didn't stay out the summer. Rumors of counterrevolution were circulating everywhere. People said that the White Armies were preparing to launch an attack and that civil war was inevitable. Fearful of being cut off from home, we hastily packed our bags and fled back to Petrograd.

I never saw the man in the white shirt again.

27

The dining room of the Gymnasia for Young Girls was quiet.
It was always quiet at the beginning of lunch when two el-
derly, lethargic maids shuffled between tables doling out the
food. Fifty-seven girls, ranging in age from eight to fifteen,
sat without making a sound. At other times, voices rose, and
the girls forgot themselves in play or study, but the sight of
the meager meal plunged them into reality. They sat, heads
down, staring at the contents of their plates, almost reluctant
to start eating in the knowledge that when they had finished,
the hunger sucking at their insides would be there still.

The food never varied: a smidgen of yellow, watery porridge barely covering the bottom of a china bowl, topped with
a couple of spoonfuls of frost-ruined berries cooked in glycerin. That was all, just enough to start the stomach juices
working and make the half-forgotten hunger assert itself and
whine for more. A piece of bread would help; it would provide
the necessary bulk to placate the gnawing worm. But there
was no bread. The bread ration was distributed daily only in
the district where one lived. It bore no resemblance to the
bread of the past—a small square piece made of dark flour,
full of husks and solid as a stone.

So we sat—each girl somewhere far away, alone with her
thoughts.

Then the worm won over, and the spoons hit the china. In
a few seconds the bowls were empty. Then we waited for the

tea. It was nothing more than tinted water without taste or aroma, but it was hot and therefore welcome.

The dining room was gloomy; everything was in shades of brown—the paneled walls, probably beautiful once upon a time, but now covered with grime; the narrow, wooden tables, scratched and stained; the rickety straight chairs; the bronze chandelier with one solitary bulb sticking out of it; even the girls, who wore brown smocks cut to the same pattern, but made of an extraordinary variety of fabrics. There were wools, cottons, velvet, burlap, anything brown one was lucky enough to get, and this conglomeration produced the effect of a desperate, one-tone masquerade. Look here, it screamed, all's well —we are adhering to tradition! The winter light fighting its way through the unwashed windows seemed brownish too, and if one watched closely, one could detect specks of dust shimmering in it and spiraling down on everything below, including the girls' heads. Not that it mattered—our hair was dirty and caked, and a bit of extra dust could do no harm.

The tea arrived, and was consumed as fast as the food. At the head of the table, the directress rose primly. Following her example, the girls rose too, and the room became alive with the sound of chairs being pushed back. The girls were streaming down the corridor toward their respective classrooms, and now a few words could be heard. Gradually the words linked into conversations, the voices growing louder and lighter in tone, and then a few giggles rippled through. Forgetfulness was back.

It had been almost two years since I had become a pupil in the Gymnasia for Young Girls, and in that time life had plummeted downhill. The civil war came and went, bypassing us. For a few days, when the White Army was only forty miles away from Petrograd, we had lived to the tune of booming cannons, but the army was thrown back and changed its course.

Meanwhile, not only the comforts, but the necessities of life were being wiped out. Famine raged, pipes froze, wood was nearly impossible to get, soap became a luxury to be used sparingly, and replacing it all, swarms of lice descended on the city bringing on an epidemic of typhoid.

Yet, somehow, we lived or, rather, went through the motions of living as if what was happening to us were normal. Strengthened by some distant hope, we made the best of it. We even laughed at times, as happy people do, self-preservation choosing its best medicine.

I hurried along the corridor, trying to catch up with a girl named Lisa whose carrot-red hair bobbed in and out of the crowd of other, less spectacular heads. Lisa was thin and lithe, her body was impatient, and she was addicted to skipping. It was this habit of hers that brought us together one day when, between skips, she executed a pirouette that landed her on the floor. I waited for her to scramble to her feet, and, breaking the rule of never addressing a senior until spoken to—she was two classes ahead of me—congratulated her on the brilliance of her technique. Our common interest in dancing surfaced right on the spot where she fell, and we became fast friends.

The redhead was getting away from me. I turned on more speed and caught up with her on the threshold of her classroom.

"Going today?" I asked, grabbing her elbow.

"Sure," she said. "But you can't come because I finish an hour earlier, and you have one more class."

"I'll tell them I have a toothache."

She laughed. "That's what you told them last week."

"No, that was a sore throat."

She looked at me gravely. "They'll catch you, mark my word."

"Why should they?"

"Well," she mused, "someone might come here to fetch you."

"Fiddlesticks! You know I always walk home alone. If I am late, I tell them I had an extra class. And here at the Gymnasia it's easy—a girl can get sick, can't she?"

"You're brave," she said admiringly. "I'd never dare do anything behind my papa's back. He'd skin me. All right then, see you later." And she skipped inside.

Walking back, I wondered if what she had said about her father was true. From what I had heard about him, he didn't seem to be a parent who would skin his daughter. A man of such foul habits would not provide his child with money to take private dancing lessons, and that was precisely what she was doing twice a week, right after school hours.

On those days I watched her pick up the satchel with her dancing clothes and joyously skip down the stairs, rushing toward that wonderful moment which was denied me. My heart would shrink with envy and I didn't want to go home. And many a day I was the very last to leave the school, trailing behind the other pupils. Finally it became too much to bear, and I asked Lisa if she would let me come with her and watch the lessons. Our last classes at the Gymnasia didn't always coincide, and this involved not only lying but missing quite a few school hours—both punishable sins. But although I was aware of the risk I was taking, I couldn't help myself. And so far, I had been lucky—my inventions had been taken at face value.

Using my acting ability to the fullest, I screwed up my face into a grimace of suffering, and at the end of the following class approached the directress with my tale of pain.

"You've been having a lot of ailments lately," she said, looking at me with a glint of suspicion.

The danger sign flashed clearly, but compulsion overrode it.

"There . . . there." I hurriedly opened my mouth and stuck a finger into it to point to a tooth. "That one . . . the last on the left."

She mulled it over and then let me go.

"Tomorrow bring me the name of your dentist!" she called after me, no doubt wondering how anyone so sick could run so fast.

In the locker room, I quickly slipped into my coat and valenki (boots made of processed felt), wound the shawl around my head and neck and sprinted to the entrance hall. Lisa was already there, tapping her foot impatiently.

"Hurry, hurry!" She waved me on, and I followed her down the stairs at breakneck speed.

Out in the street, however, we had to slow down. Walking was hazardous. City maintenance was a thing of the past, and the accumulating snow had reshaped the streets into white roller coasters. More snow was massed into pyramids on the sidewalks, leaving only a small margin for pedestrians, and that surface was buffed into ice by the continuous traffic. It called for great dexterity to remain upright. Yet it was rare to see anyone fall; people balanced precariously, waved their arms like tightrope walkers, went through weird contortions, but they kept going. Given enough practice, the human body can adjust itself to almost anything—it's the mind that is the troublemaker and has a mind of its own.

Transportation was near zero. A few emaciated horses were pulling sleighs or carts, and on the larger avenues trolley cars were still functioning, squeaking along the rails and shooting off sparks where they touched the cable, but they were so overcrowded that the chances of getting on one were remote. People waiting at the stops fought their way in with the ferocity of savages, knocking each other down, and those left out hung onto the outside doors in clusters.

Most people walked in the middle of the street; some dragged small sleighs loaded with bundles; others carried bags or packages; and it looked as if everybody were collecting something. In truth they were—the populace was scavenging for food.

Most shops were closed, their windows boarded. The handful that had managed to survive displayed merchandise that no one wanted or could afford. Plaster and stone were falling from the buildings, and many doors were sagging and on the verge of falling off. The face of the city had changed completely. Only the elements remained faithful—the same frost was stinging one's skin, the same lavender dusk was creeping into daylight, the same puffy clouds were promising more snow.

We walked as fast as the slippery ground permitted. Lisa talked incessantly, and I listened without much interest, my thoughts centered on our objective.

"Oh, look . . ." Her voice broke. "There's one again. . . ."

But I had already seen it. Near the corner a dead horse lay on its side. The gasses blowing up its belly had split the skin and forced the legs to spread and stick out grotesquely into the air. The exposed guts had attracted two hungry dogs; they were circling and sniffing the body, undecided where to begin. Then one of them lunged forward, buried its muzzle in the opening and pulled out a bloody entrail.

It was not an uncommon sight. Starved horses fell all over the city and were allowed to remain in the streets for days, to be partly devoured by dogs or sliced up by hungry humans.

Without a word passing between us, both Lisa and I took a deep breath and broke into a trot as if the physical effort could erase what we had just seen. But no matter how fast we ran, the picture of the dead horse stayed right in front of our eyes, and only at the teacher's door did it begin to fade.

Lisa's teacher was of no spectacular stature—perhaps a step or two beyond the corps de ballet—which didn't diminish her in my estimation, for, to me, anyone who even waltzed across the Maryinsky stage was a colossus.

This particular colossus, wrapped seductively in a Spanish shawl, met us in the hall and, having greeted us blandly, retired into the depths of her apartment to let Lisa get ready for the lesson.

The studio was a converted dining room stripped of its furniture and embellished with such professional items as a short barre—barely sufficient for one person—and a narrow Victorian mirror in a fancy frame. Lisa disappeared behind a screen into an improvised dressing room, and I sat down on a stool by the window to wait for the lesson to begin.

It was getting dark. A multicolored Victorian lamp hanging on a chain from the ceiling shed most of its light on the center of the room and made one wonder what this place had looked like when the dining room table stood under it. It was quiet and musty, and the air was enlivened from time to time by whiffs of cooking cabbage.

Lisa came out dressed in a homemade tutu and leggins. She picked up a watering can that stood by the wall and began sprinkling the floor. Rosin was not known then and saturating old wood with water was supposed to prevent slipping.

The teacher reappeared and the lesson started.

Poor Lisa—she wasn't very good. Her wild energy, so effective in ordinary clothes, now made her seem awkward and disjointed, especially in comparison with the teacher, whose gestures were soft and graceful. The lady even used her Spanish shawl to advantage, making the fringe wiggle with every movement. She conducted the lesson in an offhand manner, admiring herself in the mirror and showing no interest in her pupil. I watched them with intense concentration, and though I remained seated on the stool, every muscle, every fiber, danced with them. And when Lisa would make a mistake, I felt anger rising in me, for I was sure that, given a chance, I could do exactly what the teacher wanted.

The hour flew by; in seconds it was over. Lisa curtsied, and the teacher, obviously relieved, beat a hasty retreat.

Now came the best part, the part I'd been waiting for. The minute Lisa vanished behind the screen, I quickly kicked off my boots, tucked the hem of my skirt under my belt and flew to the barre. Tightening my body like a string, I began faithfully imitating all the exercises I could remember. I went through every step, every movement, imprinting them in brain and body.

"One, two, three, four . . ." I counted under my breath, pointing my toes so that my instep hurt. "One, two—one, two . . ."

The teacher returned, glanced at me, shrugged her shoulders, plainly indicating that what I was doing was too idiotic to warrant comment, and turned out the light. She went out, leaving the room in semidarkness, the only light spilling over the screen, but it didn't dampen my enthusiasm.

"One, two, three," I continued stubbornly. "Point . . . stretch . . . Ouch . . . it hurts. . . . Never mind . . . try again . . . slowly . . . slowly. . . ."

There was no need to hurry; Lisa always took a long time to cool off.

131

28

After the lesson, Lisa and I walked together to the first inter-section, and there we parted, taking different routes to our respective homes. My head was still reeling with ballet terms, and the possibility of this being a day of reckoning never oc-curred to me. But when I turned the corner into our street, the first note of alarm jolted me. In the distance, I saw Fräu-lein Rosalia pacing nervously in front of our entrance door. Momentarily, she would stop pacing and peer into the dis-tance. Was she waiting for me? Why, and why downstairs? Thrown off balance by this unusual sight, I paused, my mind somersaulting to find an answer and a defense. But just then she spotted me, and I had no alternative but to go on walking toward her.

"Where have you been?" she asked evenly.

"In school," I answered, trying to appear nonchalant, mean-while edging my way toward the door to avoid further ques-tioning.

She blocked my way.

"You're lying," she said.

"Truly," I insisted, "we had an extra lesson . . . and the—"

"You're lying," she interrupted, raising her voice to me for the first time since I'd known her. "Don't get in any deeper. Today I went to fetch you and was told that you had left more than two hours before. You had missed your last class because of a toothache. Apparently you have been doing it quite often."

I must have looked terrified, for her tone softened.

"Naturally, I have to tell this to your parents. However, before I do, I want you to give me an explanation for your behavior, to tell me the truth. I came downstairs to wait for you, to prevent you from making a fool of yourself in front of your parents, as you were about to do with me. You see, I still believe in you, and I'm hoping that there may be a justifiable explanation for this chicanery. Now, suppose you tell me the truth."

The clear eyes looked into me and my defenses toppled. Swallowing tears, I told her everything—how I suffered watching Lisa run off to her lesson, how I couldn't resist the temptation, and I even confessed that often I didn't want to come home. At the last disclosure, she drew me to her side, reflected for a while and then opened the entrance door.

"We can go upstairs now," she said.

I doubt if walking up the steps of the guillotine was harder than mounting those familiar stairs. Up there an unknown, undoubtedly terrifying chastisement awaited me, to wipe out my hopes forever. In the vestibule Fräulein Rosalia stopped me and sat me in a chair.

"Wait here until I call you," she said, and disappeared behind the door connecting the vestibule with the corridor.

I waited, cold with trepidation and hating everyone responsible for this torment. A seed of defiance popped up in me, grew, and with it my brain launched on a project of elaborate schemes and plots. I was not going to buckle under . . . never. . . . If they won't help me, someone else will . . . I'll run away . . . and find someone. . . . There must be some understanding people in the world. . . . If I run away, where will I go first? A soothing vision of finding a bag full of money was interrupted by Fräulein Rosalia's voice calling me, and my schemes crashed.

My jury of three waited for me in the dining room, assem-

133

bled around the table—Father with a crumpled newspaper in front of him, Mother nervously tapping the edge of the table, and Fräulein Rosalia standing by the window, her overcoat still on, and her face wearing an expression of insecurity. I was met with ominous silence. Father was the first to speak.

"I hear that you have been sneaking away from school to attend somebody's dancing lessons."

I paid them back with what they gave me—a dead silence, and it made Mother lose her control. She jumped up and let go with a volley of accusations.

I was an ingrate . . . a cheat . . . I had no appreciation of the love they wasted on me, or the sacrifices they made to give me a good education . . . no punishment was severe enough for me.

"Please." Father raised his hand wearily in an attempt to subdue her. "You promised to be calm."

"I know I did, but I can't help it!" she shouted back. "She is a liar who thinks of nothing but running around the streets to other people's lessons. That's how criminality begins. God only knows what she might do next. Steal or kill somebody. How would you like to have a jailbird for a daughter?"

Father interrupted her again, this time with a harshness so alien to him that it made her shut up.

"Please stop! That kind of talk will get us nowhere. Fräulein was right—we are dealing here not with mischief but an obsession. Punishment will only antagonize her and lead to more conniving, although I doubt that the consequences would be as drastic as you predict." He smiled one of his rare smiles and addressed me directly. "I bet you've already been thinking of running away."

His clairvoyance so startled me that my mouth fell open.

"Don't be surprised that I know it," he hastened to explain.

"A thought like that occurs to many children in distress. I, too, wanted to run away when my parents insisted on sending me to military school. But don't misunderstand me; I do not condone your behavior. Deceitfulness is deplorable. However, in this case I am prepared to meet you halfway. Obviously, you have set your heart on dancing. Before, when I objected to it, I was able to offer you a lot in its place. Now I can give you nothing—not even partial security or a decent living. So I may as well help you in your chosen profession. You will need one to survive. However, before I do anything about it I want you to promise that you will never lie to us again."

"I promise," I whispered, not quite believing my ears.

"All right then," he said. "I'll see what I can do, but don't expect it tomorrow; it will take a little time."

Mother's blood pressure rose again.

"Why do you always listen to her?" she fumed, pointing at Fräulein Rosalia. "This is the stupidest decision ever made." And she stomped out of the room.

"It is better so," Father said quietly, and Fräulein Rosalia smiled and took off her overcoat.

I still stood on the same spot, nailed to the floor.

What I expected to be a dead end turned out to open on the path I had been seeking, and I was not sure that I was awake.

29

I kept my promise. I abandoned my excursions to Lisa's teacher, and I observed all the rules of the Gymnasia, behaving faultlessly and attending all my classes. It was unthinkable to give Lisa the satisfaction of having been right in predicting that I would be caught one day, and so I pretended that I had lost interest in her lessons. This, I thought, made me somewhat of an enigma. She, naturally, found the explanation inadequate and was constantly probing for the truth. But she never got it, for I was determined to save face.

I trusted Father, and I waited patiently. When, in a few weeks, he got work with the Theatrical Archives, which paid him a certain salary, a portion of that was allotted to me. By then, my entry into Theatre School was out of the question. By the time the next exams were held, I would be nearly eleven, which was overage, but, being the kind of man he was, Father looked into all the other possibilities. He finally decided to send me not to a third-rate dancer like Lisa's teacher but to a famous old ballerina named Madame Sokolova. There was one hitch, however; the old lady was cranky, temperamental and selective in her choice of pupils, insisting on a trial lesson.

Madame Sokolova's studio was very professional—not large but equipped with all the necessary paraphernalia, including a parquet floor and a mirror covering one entire wall. An armchair stood to one side of the mirror where Madame sat for the better part of the lesson, her knees under a coverlet, teaching with her hands more eloquently than Lisa's teacher did with her whole body. Madame was quite ancient, but the fire and vigor were still there, flaring up frequently, and the cane she carried tapped out the rhythm against the floor with the force of a twenty-year-old.

Sometimes, in anger, she would throw the cane at her pupil, not caring where it landed, and if it hit you, it was your mistake too—you hadn't ducked properly.

The trial lesson was a near-disaster. Madame inquired if I had any previous training and I replied that I had not. The lesson began peacefully enough with a few exercises, but when she told me to stretch at the barre, the cane flew up in the air, scaring me out of my wits.

"The devil take you!" the old voice squealed with unexpected volume. "Who do you take me for? Do you think you can fool me? Liar! I hate liars! You had lessons before! Look at your extension!"

I swore that I had told her the truth, but she ranted on. Her wrath was climbing to the point of throwing me out when something made her change her mind. She rose from her chair, came to the barre and taking my outstretched leg by the ankle began lifting it higher and higher, simultaneously rotating it from the front to the side to the back. When it went above my head with no effort or resistance, her knotted eyebrows loosened and she simmered down.

"Well, well," she muttered, still eying me suspiciously, "maybe it is natural."

And I became her pupil, which was the greatest bit of luck I've ever had. She gave me a brilliant foundation, a first-rate classical base, teaching me unhurriedly, and paving the road to correct development when the muscles grow long and pliable and coordination settles into the body to stay.

The sense of pride and superiority I felt when I reported the news to Lisa was beyond description. Moreover, according to Madame Sokolova's stipulation, I had to take lessons every day—she would not waste her energies on any amateurish nonsense—and the seriousness of this approach lifted me even further in Lisa's estimation.

My new routine required a lot of stamina. Madame's apartment was far away, at Maryinsky Square, but buoyed up by my enthusiasm, I trekked the three miles each way without noticing the distance and gave in to weariness only when I was back home.

That winter was brutal. By the middle of November the fierce cold and the lack of wood forced us to close off most of the apartment and move into three bedrooms. A small black stove was installed in the center bedroom—a combination of an Adam's stove and a cooking range. It had a long crooked funnel that went up to the ceiling and then turned toward the window, where an outlet for it was cut in a pane boarded up on the sides and stuffed with newspapers. Beds were pushed sideways along the walls, and a table and chairs were placed near the stove. It all gave the room the appearance of a set for *The Lower Depths.* Everything on the other side of the corridor was sealed off with strips of cotton wool and adhesive tape, except for the door in the vestibule leading into the museum. Despite the temperature Father would occasionally still go in there to work, but he had to wear his overcoat and his fur cap, and when he came out, his hands were purple and his teeth chattered.

The typhoid epidemic hit its peak and a new sight invaded the streets. Carts and carts piled up with coffins, one on top of the other like pieces of wood, were dragged to their final destination, usually a common grave, for there was no time to bury anyone singly. The carts traveled in caravans of two or three at a time, and one could seldom walk two blocks without encountering the grim processions. The effect of it was devastating. Fear of the disease, coupled with the constant reminder of one's mortality, was taking its toll of my nervous system, and my nights were filled with nightmares. I dreamed of dark and fearsome streets where coffins fell out of windows and broke open, releasing the dead who then came back to life, and of tiny coffins like candy boxes, that were delivered to me and that I was forced to open, and of green people caked with earth who chanted like priests. I would wake up screaming, and for the rest of the night I would hang on to Fräulein Rosalia for dear life.

Grandmother Sofia was the most affected by all the upheavals. Her advanced age and the violent changes damaged her mind. She had locked herself in her bedroom upstairs, and for a whole month no one had been able to penetrate that fortress. Tatiana would take her meals upstairs and leave them on a table in the boudoir next to the bedroom, but Grandmother would hobble out to nibble at the food only when she was sure that nobody was around. When the food remained untouched for nearly a week, there was no choice but to break down the door.

I had just come from Madame Sokolova and was warming myself by the stove when she was brought down. Father carried her fragile frame, and Fräulein Rosalia held up her head, which was dangling on the stem of her neck. One look was enough to know that Grandmother was already on her way to the angels. She looked ghastly. Her dry, yellow skin was pulled tight over her bones, and her vacant eyes, that still retained a remnant of vision, were sending out a final SOS. She was falling into a coma.

"My God," Fräulein Rosalia cried out, "she is covered with lice."

Indeed, black specks were crawling all around Grandma's hairline. Disinfection began at once. A kettle was put on the stove, and a mass of towels appeared along with bottles of iodine and alcohol, and everybody rushed about bumping into each other in the small space. Grandmother's condition made it impossible to follow the normal procedures for destroying the vermin and the most primitive methods had to be used.

The last thing I remember before I was chased out of the room was Fräulein Rosalia with Grandmother's head on her knee, washing the strands of gray hair with a piece of cotton soaked in some solution and picking out the vermin one by one with her fingernails. It was hideous and funny all at once.

A spasm of nervous giggles shook me.

"We are monkeys," I thought. "That's what we are now. Not people. Monkeys, monkeys in a zoo."

30

Grandmother Sofia died two days later. At Fräulein Rosalia's insistence, I was spared the funeral by being dispatched, as usual, to Aunt Pauline. It was a Saturday, and Nina was home, which helped immeasurably. Economic conditions had relaxed the rigid rules of Theatre School, and now the pupils were encouraged to spend weekends at home; it saved the school a lot of food and fuel. Ever since I had begun to study dancing seriously, my relationship with Nina had become more or less equalized, though she would never let me forget that I was a "private" and therefore niches below those in Theatre School. Still she spoke to me with a new tolerance, often inquiring about Madame Sokolova's methods, for Madame Sokolova was held in high esteem on all levels of the dance world. Madame had been invited to teach in Theatre School several times, but she always declined because, in her own words, "she couldn't abide the hordes of brats."

When I returned home, every vestige of Grandmother's existence had been removed and her upstairs apartment locked up. I felt no sorrow. Grandmother had never made any true contact with me, flitting on the periphery of my life, a strange old lady, a walking ancestor, out of an era I was born too late to enjoy. My only reaction to her dying was a growing puzzlement at the mystery of death, but soon that, too, disappeared under the pressures of living. The sole reminder of the old lady's presence was the legacy she left us in the person of Tatiana, who came to live with us. The addition of another human being to our already packed quarters required the opening of another small room, formerly a sewing room near the kitchen, and Tatiana brought herself, her few possessions and her questionable character in there.

I said earlier that Tatiana was Grandmother's ward, and there is nothing I can add. Perhaps Father knew of her origin and how she happened to fit into Grandmother's life, but he chose to avoid the subject, and Tatiana herself was a master at slithering out of any questioning. If her background was to remain a closed book, at such close proximity her true nature could not forever hide behind those shifty eyes.

She was a nymphomaniac and a pervert, so saturated with sensuality that it obliterated the line between right and wrong. Nothing was too amoral or too low so long as it satisfied her. When she became secure in her position with the family, she appointed herself my secret sex educator. Seeking out opportunities to be alone with me, she would involve me in conversations dripping with suggestive innuendoes, which in turn led to recollections of her own sexual experiences. And one day, having decided that I was sufficiently instructed, she stuck a pornographic picture in my hand.

"Look at it later," she whispered. "And don't tell anyone or we both will be in trouble."

And she vanished, leaving the incriminating object in my hand.

Sex fascinates all children, and it takes a picture of exceptional crudeness to produce revulsion. I took one look at it and was instantly disgusted. My only wish was to get rid of it, but to my dismay I found that was easier wished than done. It is no simple proposition to destroy something when there are only three rooms and people are apt to walk in on you at any moment. Tearing it up was no solution either, for what was I to do with the pieces? The garbage can stood outside the "black walk," where I was forbidden to go, and were I to be caught there, it would arouse immediate suspicion. The thought of the picture being exhumed and patched together brought goose pimples. At last, a brilliant idea struck me. Burn it! There is the stove, right handy! Again the execution of this plan presented complications. Each time I lifted the red-hot lid, I would divert the smoke from the funnel and it would shoot up into my face; blinded for the moment, I could never hit my target. In three attempts, the picture landed on the floor three times. Meanwhile the room was filling with smoke, and finally, interrupted by approaching steps, I had to give up my foul deed.

For the rest of the day, I kept the picture stuck in my bosom, walking stiffly and holding on to my stomach to prevent it from slipping out. This prompted inquiries about a bellyache, which I nervously denied. In distress, as the evening progressed, I pushed the picture under my mattress.

Next morning, in the rush of dressing for school, I forgot all about it, and when I returned, Fräulein Rosalia was sitting on my bed, the picture lying next to her on the bedspread.

"Where did you get this?" she asked, with no emotion or anger. It was an ordinary question like asking, "How did you get those spots on your dress?"

I disclaimed all knowledge of the article, which didn't fool her for a minute, and as usual she soon had me confessing the truth. Still, there was no anger, only a nod acknowledging the story. By this lack of any emotional response, she robbed the picture of its importance.

By chance, Tatiana entered the room at that moment.

"Speak of the devil," Fräulein said nicely, indicating her with a nod of her head, and Tatiana, thinking it a joke, smiled back.

"I believe this is yours," said Fräulein Rosalia, handing her the picture.

Tatiana stood aghast, the picture limp in her hand.

"What you do with your own life is not my business," Fräulein Rosalia continued very quietly, "but leave her alone. I'm warning you. If I ever catch you at anything like this again, I'll crucify you. Remember that—I will crucify you. And now—out!"

Tatiana backed out of the room, still staring stupidly.

"And now, young lady," said Fräulein Rosalia, "sit down. The time has come for us to have a talk."

We sat across the table from one another, and she stretched out her hands and took mine. There was regret on her face.

"In a way it is my fault," she said. "I should have spoken to you about these matters before. Then you would have been to some extent forearmed against anything like this. But I did it deliberately—I wanted to keep you innocent as long as possible, and it was bad judgment on my part."

She paused for a moment, arranging her thoughts.

"Life is like a medal that swings," she said then. "It has two sides, and it is up to us to choose by which side we will live. Tatiana lives by the wrong side, and she should be pitied because she misses a great deal. I doubt if she knows what love is. Love and sex are united, but she cut love away, and when you chop away an important part of a whole, the part that's left gets sick. That sickness makes Tatiana do what she did. And now let's see what love is. Love is when you want more for the other person than you want for yourself. Love is when you feel empty without that person. Love for a man is when you are drawn to him by an inexplicable force, wanting to be near, to touch, to get closer and closer until you are like one person, and that's when sex takes over."

Delicately she went into the details of a sexual relationship, making it an expression of surrender, normal and gratifying, holding two people in healthy excitement.

"And more than anything," she concluded, "love is rare."

I listened, and I think I understood, for my mind went back to the man in the white shirt.

31

Whenever I hear anyone announce that the days of miracles are over, I at once begin to wonder what kind of sage this man can be. How did he manage to avoid what cannot be explained? Has he lived with his senses anesthetized, or is his ego so immense that it denies any phenomenon that may cast doubt on his omniscience?

Rejecting what soars beyond human understanding does

not disprove it. For miracles do happen—they're all around us. Sometimes they burst upon us with startling suddenness— when a bullet imbeds itself in a medal instead of heart or lung—but more often, at least in my experience, the miracle occurs so imperceptibly that we don't become aware of it until it's all over. Some smaller miracles are labeled "lucky coincidence," but then again whose invisible hand sets the perfect timing, and why does it bestow its gift on one person and not another?

My life has been full of miracles, large and small, and if it were not for that blessing, I doubt that I would be sitting at this desk.

What I am about to describe began on a wintry morning at the Gymnasia. I wasn't feeling very well. I found it hard to concentrate, and my head was aching with the memory of what had happened the previous afternoon on my way to Madame Sokolova's.

It had been one of those days that has no light in it—when everything, the sky, the ground, the buildings, even the people appear to be of no color. Part of my route took me along the Fontanka Canal toward a bridge I had to cross to get to Maryinsky Square. This narrow stretch of road was below even the usual standards. Huge lumps would break off the mountainous snow banks piled high against the buildings and roll down like avalanches. On the opposite side, the waves of frozen snow overflowed the canal railing and spilled onto the embankment. Pedestrians were forced to the middle of the street, and it was from there that I saw a single cart loaded with coffins come out of the side alley and cut right in front of me. Flanked by walls of snow, and with the bridge less than a block away, and, moreover, pressed for time—Madame demanded punctuality—I had no alternative but to follow a few feet behind the grisly vehicle.

It presented a sorry picture. The wooden coffins, clumsily nailed together and with no ornament, not even handles, could have been taken for ordinary boxes if it were not for their unmistakable shape. Stacked up crisscross like children's blocks, they were tied to the cart with a serpentine arrangement of rope, the end of which dragged on the ground dangerously close to the left wheel. Swaying and creaking under its cargo, the cart proceeded at a snail's pace, and it looked as if the flimsy structure would fall apart at any moment. Those caught behind it walked slowly and reluctantly—captive mourners to the unknown dead.

We came to the bridge. The driver took a sharp turn, the cart swerved, and one of its back wheels cut deep into the snow bank, bringing it to a halt. There it stood blocking our way, tilted sideways, all the weight of its load against the ropes on one side.

The driver showed no alarm. He slid down from his perch, shuffled around the cart to the sunken wheel and squatted by it. For a while he poked the snow with his finger, then scraped some of it away from the wheel and blew at it, raising a gust of white dust. Having apparently concluded that the cart could be extricated from its predicament, he walked back to the front of the cart and took out the whip. The horse jumped forward under the blow, but the cart only rocked and fell back into the groove. Repeated whippings brought no improvement, each one sinking the cart deeper into the track.

And then . . . I thought my eyes were deceiving me, but there it was—in front of me—sliding. . . . One of the coffins was sliding from under the ropes.

"Stop!" I screamed, but the cry never came out.

Irritated by his failure, the driver blew his nose by pressing a finger against one nostril while emptying the other. Then

Deborah

from

he changed his tactics. Grabbing the horse by the reins, he began yanking and pulling it forward. In the back, the coffin continued to slide.

Oh, Lord, my dream . . . ! My dream of coffins falling out was coming true. . . . It will fall, it will break, and the dead will step out. . . .

The driver gave the horse another yank, and I slapped the palms of my hands over my eyes. Simultaneously there was a thud.

In the darkness behind my hands, I held my breath, expecting the howls of horror I fancied would accompany the rising of the dead. None came. The street noises remained unchanged. Still I waited, chained with fear, until I marshaled enough courage to spread my fingers and peer through them.

The coffin lay on the ground, bottom side up, and where the fall had loosened the nails a plank stuck up toward the sky like an arm reaching for help. I thought I saw a thin ribbon of vapor spiraling up the plank and disappearing into infinity.

Perplexed by this unforeseen development, the driver stood by, scratching his head and staring gloomily at the coffin. He was, indeed, faced with a dilemma. One man alone could not possibly lift the coffin back on the cart, and after some consideration he did the only thing left for him to do, asking help from the passing pedestrians. Clapping his hands and injecting a humorous lilt into his voice, he shouted, "Come on, it's good for your muscles," or, "Hey, don't be afraid, he won't bite you," or, "How would you like me to leave him here to stink up the street?" His performance brought no volunteers. Deaf to his appeal, people circled the cart at the farthest possible range. Some even climbed over the snow banks on all fours, and no one would take the chance of touching the box that held the mortal remains of a typhoid victim. In disgust, the driver kicked the coffin with his boot.

"You are not listening," said the teacher. "You seem to be looking at me, but you don't hear me. I have asked you the same question three times."

The voice snapped me out of yesterday. I jumped up to answer the question I hadn't heard, in the hope that she would repeat it again, which she did not.

"What is the matter with you today?" she asked instead. "You are acting most peculiarly. Your face is flushed and you seem to be somewhere in the clouds." Dismissing me, she turned to another girl. "Luba, you answer."

The girl stood up and rattled off the answer, and I sank back on the bench. Soon the bell rang, and we all moved into the dining room for lunch.

The china bowl was in front of me. Porridge and glycerin berries . . . glycerin berries and porridge . . . it will be the same forever . . . and ever . . . and ever. . . .

My fingers were barely holding on to the spoon. It went twirling around the bowl, seemingly of its own accord, while I watched the kernels turn pink, liquefy and become a mush that I had no wish to put in my mouth. A strange heat was thumping under my skin and my head was empty of any coherent thought. Round and round went the spoon, making designs in the mush—a moonface . . . a heart . . . a coil, unwinding and menacing the center. . . .

An uneasy feeling of being under surveillance made me look up. From the head of the table, the directress was observing me with stony concentration. The expression on her face gave me a start; she was glaring at me as if I were not the girl she knew and saw every day, but something foreign and a little frightening.

My eyes skimmed over the rest of the table. Some of the girls were staring at me too, and I saw one of them nudge her neighbor to attract her attention. Disturbed, I looked back at the directress. Her eyes were still on me, but now her body was retreating from the table, pushing back until her shoulder blades touched the back of her chair, and then her hands gripped the edge of the table, and she pushed herself up.

"Come with me," she said dryly.

Not comprehending what had happened, and what I had done to be thus selected, I obeyed. She walked briskly, always a few feet ahead of me, past the classrooms, all the way down the corridor and across the entrance hall into the adjoining alcove. Fumbling with her key ring, she picked a key and opened the door to her office.

"Go in," she said, "I'll be back."

No sooner did I cross the threshold than I heard the click of the door being locked behind me. So unexpected and startling was this sound that it made me doubt my own hearing. To reassure myself, I turned back to the door and attempted to turn the knob, first gingerly, and, when it resisted, with increasing force. I twisted and rattled it, pushed and pulled with no success: the doorknob would not budge. There was no more doubt left—I was securely jailed within the confines of the office. What was the reason? What crime had I committed to deserve this?

My thoughts tore in all directions, frantically seeking a clue, but my aching head refused to provide any explanation. "Never mind," I said aloud, trying to calm myself. "She'll be back soon and I'll ask her what this is all about."

The directress, however, was in no rush to return. Instead, and to my growing unrest, I heard the voices of the girls filling the entrance hall, an excited chirping chorus, and then there was a stampede of footsteps running down the main stairs. Here was another puzzle. Why were they being dismissed so early? I calculated that it must have been about one o'clock, and we always had two more classes after lunch.

The stampede continued, departing into the distance, carrying the voices with it, and then all sounds broke into fragments and it was quiet again.

Still no sign of the directress. I sat down on the window sill, biting my lips. On the desk, a clock was mercilessly ticking away time—a half-hour—an hour—another twenty minutes . . . and as the hand passed the hour of three, reminding me that I'd been locked in for over two hours, adrenalin shot into my veins and sent me pacing the room.

I wanted to shout, to pound the door, yet I only paced, from the window to the desk, to the filing cabinet, and back again, and as I walked by a small mirror on the wall, I inadvertently glanced into it.

And there I stopped—and so did my heartbeat.

The face that looked at me out of the frame was splashed with blotches of an ugly rash that ran down the neck and crawled under the collar of the uniform. The girl in the frame lifted a hand to her cheek, and I felt a hot, slightly scaly surface under my fingertips.

Mirror, mirror on the wall was telegraphing the answer.

I was sick . . . it must be something contagious . . . are they waiting for a doctor . . . or maybe they have called home to have someone come for me. Or maybe I'm just dreaming. I began to shake.

People were coming. I heard the footsteps of more than one person in the hall, and presently the door opened, letting in a man. The directress remained outside, at a respectable distance. The man's coat was unbuttoned, exposing a stained white smock and a linen surgical mask that hung loosely on an elastic band around his neck. In his gloved hands, he held my coat, boots and shawl.

"Come on, little lady," he said without preliminaries. "We've got to go."

The top of my head came off and out of it, like a jack-in-a-box, a word sprang out, jumping around in fiery letters: "Typhoid . . . Typhoid . . . Typhoid . . . !"

He was coming toward me. I dodged him and darted toward the open door, but the directress slammed it in my face. He was after me again, now slightly crouched, his hands spread out to block my escape. Terrified, I ducked under his arm and, falling to my knees, crawled under the desk, where I huddled out of reach.

"Don't make it difficult," I heard him grunt. "Come on, girl, you have to go. That's all there is to it."

His hand went under the desk groping for me, and I hit it with all my strength, ripping off his glove with my clawed fingers.

"Hey, you! Stop that!" he yelled, snatching the fallen glove and withdrawing his hand. He squatted down in preparation for the next attack.

In the commotion I didn't hear the door open again, but now Fräulein Rosalia's voice rang out clearly, shouting at the directress. "Why did you do it? Why didn't you wait until I got here?"

The reply was unintelligible, and immediately Fräulein's feet stepped into my view next to the squatting man.

"Sir, please . . ." she said. "Won't you let me take her home?"

"Can't be done," he snapped. "Regulations. There was a call, it's on the ledger. Have to deliver." He had a common voice, flat and coarse.

"But, sir . . . please listen to me." Fräulein Rosalia renewed her plea. "You know as well as I do that you could easily say that it was a mistake and nobody will be the wiser. They have enough on their hands as it is. . . . I promise you that if you let me take her home, we'll call a doctor and if he agrees with . . . what you think it is, I'll bring her in myself. Please . . . have a heart."

But his heart must have been out on loan somewhere, for he responded coldly with the same set phrase. "That's what I hear from everybody. No. Can't be done. Must follow rules. Must deliver."

He raised his voice to a shout, calling out to the directress, "Hey, lady, tell the other man to come up here. . . . And bring me a broom . . . I'll get her out."

"No! Please!" Fräulein Rosalia topped him. "You can't do that. She's not an animal! You can't use a broom on her!" She paused, apparently mapping out a new strategy.

"All right, then," she said, "I'll make a bargain with you. If you will let me come with her, I'll get her out—right away, and quietly."

The man was adamant. He would not depart from instructions. If he was an intern, he was a very stupid one, angry with his lot and totally lacking in compassion. More likely, he was just a driver, calloused by his job, a "deliverer" of souls, as he himself unconsciously implied, to whom the human beings he collected were nothing more than so many head of cattle to be carted away.

Refusing to be defeated, Fräulein Rosalia persisted. She threatened him with repercussions from political figures she claimed as friends. She appealed to his better nature and, when all persuasions failed, resorted to the Bible. With fanatical fire, she quoted Christ's reference to children and reminded him about the Good Samaritan to whom Christ promised a reward in heaven for his good deed. Did he not see that he was being given the chance of a similar reward? Was he going to flunk this opportunity for redemption? It was a stroke of genius, for on that superstitious note he capitulated.

"All right, lady. It's your funeral," he said, not without a touch of morbid humor. "I'll take you to the 'receiving room' and then it's up to them."

She was on her knees at once, her face almost touching the floor, her eyes seeking me out under the desk.

"Come out, darling. We'll go together. There's nothing to be afraid of." But the reassurance in her words was forced and not quite believable.

Still, there was nothing else for me to do. Somehow, I was wrapped in my clothes; somehow, holding on to Fräulein Rosalia, I stumbled down the stairs; and though by then I knew that I was really sick, somehow I didn't care any more.

Downstairs, a wagon resembling a Black Maria awaited us. I remember its being long and narrow and having slits for windows, and a door in the back, which, when opened, released collapsible steps. We climbed in, the door closed, and death caged us in. The wagon jerked forward and began to roll.

It was dim and damp in the wagon, and the air, what there was of it, was thick with the smell of carbolic. The last rays of the afternoon light, filtering in through the window slits, met in the center and blended into a yellowish mist with an eerie light of its own. From the corner came a rattle of instruments carelessly tossed into an enamel basin. Two narrow bunks were nailed alongside the walls, and across from where we sat a woman's figure lay under a dirty blanket. Our knees were almost touching her. Sporadically the woman's body shook with a tremor that started at her feet and traveled up

153

to her shoulders, and then she would lift her head and moan dolefully, like a wounded animal forsaken and forgotten. Her sweat-drenched face was a mask of resignation. Over her bunk, a coil of some medical equipment was swaying with sinister regularity—a noose. . . .

We bounced over the hilly street, and at one turn the woman was thrown toward us, her hand falling over my wrist and smearing it with the moisture of her skin. Swiftly, like a cat, Fräulein Rosalia snatched my hand away and quickly wiped it off with the hem of her dress.

On and on we rode, three voyagers and a presence. He who feeds on human breath was traveling with us. One could feel him in the foul air that tore at the lungs, in the stench that emanated from the spittoon standing by the woman's bunk, and in the woman's glazed eyes. He was watching, waiting, considering.

The wagon jolted to a stop. The door opened, the steps fell down, and we got out into a large yard. Several wagons similar to ours were waiting there, and a few people were milling around carrying bundles and talking to each other, all in a slow-motion, lethargic manner. Our man called to someone to bring a stretcher for the woman, and then told us to follow him. I don't remember all the details of that walk, for by then I was only half-feeling and half-seeing, but it must have been the back entrance to the hospital because we walked through many wards and halls, and everywhere there were bodies, in beds, on stretchers and sprawled on mattresses thrown on the floor. The place vibrated with hollow sounds mixed with whimperings. Flies must have found refuge here before the frost fell, for there were swarms of them circling the air, which was unusual for this time of year.

Our "deliverer" deposited us in the "receiving room" and

left, closing a heavy double door behind him. In contrast to the rest of the building, this room was entirely empty and quiet. There was no one behind the desk and not a soul on any of the rows of benches. The silence was further emphasized by the soft buzzing of flies dying in black clusters on spirals of flypaper suspended from the ceiling.

We sat down to wait. I looked up at Fräulein Rosalia. She sat straight and still, and her eyes, though half-closed, were focused on some point way beyond the walls. I think she was praying. Whether it was her prayer, or the soporific buzzing of the flies, or an emotional collapse, my lids suddenly grew heavy, my body gave up, and, supported by her arms, I dropped into a deep sleep with my face against her shoulder.

I was awakened by the pressure of a thermometer being thrust under my tongue. A man in a wrinkled white smock was leaning over me.

"Keep your mouth closed," he said and turned to Fräulein Rosalia. "When did it begin?"

"Sometime this morning. I couldn't tell exactly. . . . I was not there." Her answer was barely audible. He unhooked my uniform down to my waist and lifted up my undershirt. "Nothing there," he said. "Chest and abdomen clear. I don't understand this. It never starts on the face." He took a magnifying glass out of his pocket and began examining my face. He peered at my skin and I peered at him, and I saw that his beard was matted and that perspiration had glued his thin hair to his forehead, and that exhaustion had painted blue circles around his eyes. Sleep seemed to have refreshed me and I saw everything much more clearly than I had in the wagon.

"Funny," muttered the doctor, his magnifying glass still over my skin. "It doesn't seem right."

I had not eaten all day and my stomach chose that moment to announce it with a grumble.

"Excuse me," I said, embarrassed, "it's because I'm hungry."

"That's even funnier," said the doctor, putting down the magnifying glass. "You should be vomiting by now. Well, we'll soon know." He took the thermometer to the desk, where he examined it under the lamp.

"I'll be damned," he exclaimed. "It's normal. Just as I thought." Then his tone changed into angry agitation. "Someone there must have been really hysterical. What a rotten trick to play on a kid. How I wish those stupid interns would learn to recognize the symptoms."

His anger subsided just as quickly as it had flared up, and when he returned to us, he spoke gently and a little sadly.

"There is no reason for me to hold her here. And I must be honest with you—I have no idea what this rash is. One thing is certain—it is not typhoid. Perhaps it's a manifestation of some nervous condition. Our knowledge of skin diseases is still in its infancy." He put his hand on my shoulder. "Something troubling you, girl?"

So many things were troubling me that I could not possibly condense them into a single answer. So I kept silent. It was just as well, for he was speaking again. "Take her home. Go quickly. You've been here much too long already. This is not a healthy place to visit. Hurry! I'll show you out."

He guided us through a short cut to the exit, and when he opened the door, he gave us a penetrating look.

"Good-bye," he said gently. "And may God . . . help you."

We were out in the street, we were free, and we were running. Hand in hand, we ran stumbling, tripping, slowing down for breath and running again, as if afraid that the hospital would extend its tentacles and pull us back. When we had put enough distance behind us, we had to stop because, suddenly, Fräulein Rosalia was crying and laughing all in one, and she had to press her handkerchief to her mouth to silence herself. Only then did we realize that we had no conception where we were and in what direction we were running.

We reached home way after dark. Everyone was waiting for us in a state of high agitation. Fräulein Rosalia was alone when she received the call, and in her rush to get to me she didn't think of leaving a note, never expecting the crisis she was to find in the Gymnasia. All efforts to locate us proved futile, and even the Gymnasia would not give any information other than to say that we had left at the usual time.

The sight of my face provoked gasps of dismay, and when all the facts were known, a true pandemonium broke out. I was tucked into bed and fed innumerable pills washed down with hot tea and some liquid that passed for soup. A hot-water bottle was applied to my feet and a cold compress slapped on my head. Fräulein Rosalia took no part in this feverish activity for she knew well that our fate was in the hands of God and that no amount of medication would alter what was or was not to be. Father, too, was conscious of the gravity of the situation, and he looked at me with concern. When he left the room, out of nowhere there appeared a stack of medical books. Hands grabbed them, and in no time I was surrounded by a forum of savants who, with their heads bent and their fingers leafing the pages, were engaged in a loud argument on the interpretation of Latin terms, descriptions of symptoms, and cures not only of typhoid but of other diseases, including Asian flu and trench foot. They had learned a lot that night—at my expense. I dozed off to a hot debate on arthritis.

By morning the rash had paled. The family doctor arrived

with his inevitable satchel of herbs, raspberry tea and leeches, but he, too, was unable to diagnose the case.

Improvement came rapidly, each day wiping off more of the rash, and soon I was as good as new.

Psychosomatic illnesses had not yet been explored in that country, but as I look back from this more enlightened time and place, I think my case could have served as a perfect example of the power of the psyche. Misery and fear, those termites of the mind, had whittled away at my nervous system and produced the symptoms of the disease the way I understood it, for I had heard repeatedly that a rash was an integral part of it.

And what of the miracle?

I think it is shining with a soft glow.

For several hours we were exposed to one of the deadliest, most contagious diseases, in direct contact with a victim and, in the contaminated setting of the hospital, at the mercy of the worst of typhoid carriers—flies—and neither of us contracted it.

If that is not a miracle, I'll have to wait until the skies split open and angel Gabriel comes down dancing a jig.

32

About two weeks later, when it became absolutely certain that I had survived the unfortunate incident with no ill effects, Mother paid a visit to the Gymnasia for Young Girls. What made her choose that particular moment, which might have seemed more suitable for rejoicing than revenge, she would not disclose, and her only comment on her return was a curt "Well, I showed them," which turned out to be no exaggeration.

From what we heard later, she descended upon the office unannounced and pretty nearly attacked the directress bodily, punctuating her indictment with random destruction of whatever caught her angry eye—one inkwell, thrown at the wall, one picture frame broken, several school records torn up and strewn upon the floor, and several other items damaged. The commotion reverberated throughout the school, since the directress, terrified out of her dignity, picked up her skirts and, pursued by Mother, in full view of the astonished students, fled the battlefield, to lock herself in a bathroom.

I fully believe the story. Mother's temper had to be admired —it was monumental. At its peak, it ceased to be an emotion and acquired the attributes of an elemental force, like a tornado or a volcanic eruption. No one in his right mind would venture to tangle with it. One did exactly what the directress had done—became scarce.

In normal times Mother probably would have been brought to justice for assault and destruction of private property, but during that period any dealings with the government or any of its representatives—even if justified—were so feared that the school board had considered it wiser to overlook the whole matter, and Mother got off scot-free and pretty proud of herself.

I never went back to the Gymnasia that year. It was not because of Mother's onslaught, but simply because all the school closed. Conditions hit rock bottom, and even Theatre School, which was subsidized by the government, had to lock its doors, turning its pupils out into the world to fend for themselves. This created a great deal of hardship, for many of the pupils came from out of town and had no means of getting back to their families.

I continued my lessons with Madame Sokolova. She was growing fond of me, encouraging me in her gruff manner, and often extending the lessons beyond the time paid for. I think it amused her to watch my greed for improvement. My energy was inexhaustible, and no matter how long and hard she drove me through my paces never, to my best recollection, did I ask for a breathing spell or complain of fatigue. Thanks to the Maker who had provided me with a body made to order for dancing, I was advancing rapidly. Reflecting on my progress, Madame Sokolova sometimes remarked that she had seldom seen a youngster who was such a slave to her ambition.

She was absolutely correct in her observation. Ambition was there, deep-rooted—and blind, for I had no idea where it was leading me.

As a "private" my future was far from promising. The avenue to a career of any distinction was blocked to me forever, and the view from Madame's studio was a consistent reminder of this sad fact. Below the window at the far end of the square loomed the Maryinsky Theatre—a baroque fortress, a temple, all glory and tradition, the unattainable goal. Left alone after the lesson, I would stand gazing at it, my eyes going over its every curve, every angle, and despondency would twist my insides. Why was I working so hard? Where was I going?

Yet the next day, when I had put on my dancing clothes again, everything would be forgotten, and I would work as hard as ever.

I walked home slowly, postponing my arrival. For me, the day was over, and there was little to look forward to. Family life was disintegrating in the squeeze of cramped living.

Nerves frayed, tempers warped and tension gripped the household. With the exception of Fräulein Rosalia, it seemed that everyone hated everyone else. Moments of friendliness were rare and passed quickly. Father was seldom home, recoiling from this atmosphere of discord, and when he joined us for the evening meal, he would sit in silence, deaf to the chatter around him. Not a gregarious man by nature, he was withdrawing more and more into himself and his private world. Also, an asthmatic condition had recently developed that interfered with his breathing and depressed him generally. But above all, I think, it was the political scene that contributed to his distress. An ardent advocate of free expression, a champion of individuality, a man who had not flinched when his wealth was taken away because he believed it to be for the good of his country, he now saw his dream of democracy slipping away and his land turning into a police state. Still, despite his disappointment, his basic faith in his people never wavered, and when the invariable complaints began, he would cut them off.

"Come on," he would say, "it isn't really that bad. Maybe this is retribution. Maybe we are getting a taste of what eighty-five percent of the country endured under the Czars. This will pass. Mark my words—one day we will be a great nation again."

And he would leave, often without finishing his food, and if we heard the squeak of the hanger in the corridor, it meant that he was putting on his overcoat to retire into the museum for the rest of the evening. Mother would mumble something about his not giving a damn about anybody and her being sick and tired of it, and Irra and Tatiana, ever ready to delight in trouble, would side with her, adding fuel to the conflict.

By now, Tatiana was getting bolder, and she had developed

the charming habit of bringing men to her room when the rest of the household was asleep. This diversion went unnoticed until, one morning, she was discovered prostrate on her bed with a bruised and swollen face—a token of affection left by her transient lover before he made off with her gold earrings. The incident was hushed up and the truth kept from Father by inventing a vicious fall down the "black walk." The experience sobered Tatiana, but not for long, and soon after the bruises cleared up, she was at it again, though with a little more finesse.

There were many chores to be attended to: carrying water, emptying the refuse into the nearby canal, washing dishes and trying to keep oneself at least partially clean. And, of course, we all took turns standing in line for the rations which were never distributed at the appointed time. A bored clerk sat waiting in an empty store while a line of people blocks long clapped their hands and stamped their feet to keep from freezing. Sometimes, when the provisions arrived, there would be an announcement that extra rations like salt (the rarest commodity) or rice would be handed out, and then a roar of near-rapture would rise from hundreds of throats, traveling like a wave all along the line.

But famine has its inevitable counterpart, and it was a-borning—the black market. Rumors began to circulate and everyone's ears were tuned to whispers about such and such an address where, it was said, one could get some potatoes or cabbage or even a soup bone. A race to that address would start immediately, and if you were early and lucky enough, you came out with some provisions and an empty purse.

Amid these tribulations, Anatol was growing like a weed. He was a serious, almost solemn-looking child, with dark hair and skin and eyes—a tiny replica of his father, with an even more aloof personality. His favorite pastime was to sit crouched on a bed in the center room, silently observing the activities around him, his eyes full of adult sorrow and his little face set in an expression of scorn, as if he already foresaw and resented his tragic destiny. In her spare time, Fräulein Rosalia showered him with affection and tenderness which were never reciprocated. Love had no place in Anatol's nature. The world was already his potential enemy.

Winter was giving way to spring. The river ice cracked and big chunks were carried by the churning waters down toward the sea. Winds blew, snow melted, and the black market flourished. Very soon it would be warm enough to open the rest of the apartment, and we would be free of one another. Oh, what a lovely thought. I would take the blanket off the piano in the living room, and maybe, if the cold had not damaged the instrument too badly, I could practice a bit.

With the approach of spring, small quantities of decent food began to appear intermittently on our table, and since the black market prices were exorbitant, there was a good deal of speculation as to where it was coming from. Mother, when questioned, would lift her eyes to the sky and say, "God will provide." It became obvious that no other explanation would be forthcoming, and "God will provide" was accepted as an answer. Why question the hen when she's laying the eggs?

Good Friday came. That year, Mother had decided that I was sufficiently grown up to be taken to the evening service of the "Four Gospels." This ritual, lasting more than three hours, demands endurance from the congregation as well as the clergy, and Father objected to my going. It resulted in a long argument. Mother accused him of being a heathen in partnership with hell, and denounced his godlessness as the primary reason for all our hardships. He replied that if that were the case, the whole nation must be composed of Satan's partners since everyone was suffering similar hardships. It ended nowhere—and I went to church.

On Good Friday, in commemoration of Christ's agony on the cross, the church is left in darkness. The only shaft of light comes from the open street door, near which, at a counter, two black-robed monks sell candles. Having made their purchases, the worshipers move into the interior, and, as the church fills, tiny flames puncture the darkness, multiplying and uniting finally into a gently flickering field of light. Faces made beautiful by the glow rise above this sea of candles, and overhead the dome of the church is lost in black shadows. There are no pews in Orthodox churches; people either stand or kneel, depending on their degree of reverence or fatigue.

Mother and I came early and were lucky enough to find places near a lectern that stood a few feet below the altar steps. A huge Bible already open to the proper place lay on top of it, and two thick candles still unlit stood on either side.

The worshipers were quiet, their eyes on the iconostasis that screened the altar, the candles flickering in their hands.

Presently, the doors of the iconostasis opened and the priests, deacons and acolytes appeared. They walked to the lectern and fussed there for a while. Then one of them lit the two candles and the service began, each priest reading a certain number of chapters of Matthew, Mark, Luke and John, ending each Gospel with Christ's death on the cross. The glad tidings of the Resurrection were left for the Easter service the next night, when the church would be ablaze with light.

The priests intoned the Slavonic text in a flat chant, their voices, rising and falling within a limited range, hypnotizing the listeners. One bearded face succeeded another, yet the voice seemed to be the same, always nasal, emotionless and mesmerizing. By the end of the first Gospel, I began to itch; in the middle of the second, I was on my knees; by the third, which was two hours later, I was sitting on my heels ready to keel over. On my left, a pious soul, also kneeling, attempted to touch the floor with his forehead, which resulted in a collision between his head and the heels of the person in front of him. The church was packed to capacity, and the heat generated by the candles and our bodies was closing in. Everything swayed.

On and on it went, mystic, awesome and exhausting, with only one interruption—when someone fainted.

". . . and he bowed his head and gave up the ghost."

The last words vibrated through the hollow dome, and it was over. A deacon blew out the two candles, picked up the Bible, and ceremoniously they returned as they had come. The doors of the iconostasis closed.

A sigh of relief swept the congregation, and immediately the church was filled with crackling sounds as if a gust of wind were whirling dry autumn leaves. Paper appeared in people's hands—newspaper, tissue paper, brown wrapping paper, colored crepe paper—and they shaped it into protective shades around their candles. Occasionally, the paper caught fire, but it was quickly extinguished, barehanded. The stakes were much too high to worry about a little scorched flesh. The belief was that if one could bring the Sacred Flame into one's home and with it relight the wick before the icon there, one would be blessed for the rest of the year.

Mother had brought pink crepe paper, and after wrapping it around our candles, we edged our way into the street.

Never before had I seen the city look so beautiful. In all the churches, the services ended within minutes of each other, letting out the worshipers at approximately the same time, and now the streets were rivers of tiny shivering flames, ravines filled with fireflies. People moved cautiously, protecting their candles with hands and bodies. Some failed to block the wind, and I saw many a face weeping over a dead candle. Mother found herself in that category only a block away from our house. She shed no tears, but her distress was characteristically expressed: she let out a wail, swore like a trooper and threw the dead candle into the gutter.

I fared better. My candle reached home. In my room, I climbed up on a stool, snuffed out the votive lamp with my fingertips, and cautiously tilted my candle to the wick.

"Don't go out now," my brain begged, "please don't go out."

The wick caught the flame. The new light shone gently on the face of St. Nicholas, who was my personal protector because his supposed assignment was to look after those born in the month of March.

"There you are," I whispered. "There you have it. Now see to it that it all comes out right."

I had no specific request in mind, only something vague yet badly needed, and I was sure that He, who was listening, would look into my thoughts, sort them out and get to the essence of my plea.

33

"Who is he?" I was referring to a man who had just left the room.

A few minutes earlier, when I had come in, I found him leaning against the wall, his feet wide apart, his thumbs stuck inside his belt, and his whole body expressing the relaxation of someone who has the right to feel completely at home. I had never seen him before.

He was tall and muscular, with sandy hair, a blond mustache, wide-apart green eyes, and a short upturned nose set cockily in a flat and bony face. I noticed that his hands ended in knotted, callused fingers. His whole appearance was common but not unattractive.

He was talking to Irra and Tatiana. "Yeah . . . and what's more, I told him so. . . . You bet your crooked soul, I won't take that crap from anybody. . . . I'll break his ass and—"

Language of that sort was not used in our house, and my entrance must have reminded him of it. He stopped abruptly. His glance went over me from top to bottom.

"Hi, youngster." He greeted me without straightening up, an arrogant grin on his lips.

For a moment, there was silence.

"So long." Abruptly, he pushed himself away from the wall, cutting our meeting short. He waved a lazy farewell and walked out of the room, his heels scuffing the floor.

I repeated my question. "Who is he?"

A surreptitious look passed between the two witches, but I caught it, and could plainly read in it "Shall we, or shall we not?" "We shall" prevailed.

Irra's cheeks puffed up with a laugh she could no longer hold in. It burst forth with a force that shook her whole body. Tatiana joined the merriment.

"So you'd like to know," Irra said, recuperating from her outburst. "All right, I'll tell you who he is." She stopped significantly. "He is god."

"God?" I was dumfounded. . . . Obviously, she was mocking me.

167

"She is right," Tatiana corroborated with affected seriousness. "He is god."

"What do you mean?"

"I'll explain." Irra's voice took on the tone of an instructor. "You have been eating potatoes ... and at times even meat. ... Correct? And last week we had herring. True? Where does it come from? Didn't we all ask your mother? And what did she tell us? Think. She told us that God provides."

I was completely lost in her dialectic. She paused to relish my confusion.

"And if she tells us the truth," Irra resumed, coming to the point, "then *he is* god, because he is the one who provides."

I was relieved. It turned out to be so simple.

"Oh, how very nice of him," I said. "What a good man he must be."

"Very good, very good indeed." Irra nodded with exaggerated approval. "But—" she lifted her finger—"even god must be paid. ... That's why he is here, to collect."

Tatiana provided the finishing touch. "And he always gets paid," she said. They both studied me, smiling.

We were in the dining room. Spring had moved in, and all the windows had been unsealed and flung open to welcome it. Freshness poured in, soothing the senses. A lush sprig of lilac on the window sill trembled gently, exhaling its heady fragrance. All was well. All except those smiles.

From past experience, I knew the implication behind them.

Tatiana decided to elaborate on the subject.

"Of course, you wouldn't know," she said. "You were a tiny tot, and besides, you didn't live in this house in those days. Before the Revolution, he was a butcher—he had a shop around the corner. We used to buy our meat there. But your grandmother—now there was a lady—she wouldn't ever think of letting him into the house. And look at him now. My, how times have changed." She assumed a pious expression.

"What's his name?"

"Stepan."

The smiles broadened.

Pretending not to care, I walked casually out of the room, following the course he took. Since he had left by the last door on the side of the corridor, I deduced he was heading for the kitchen. I walked calmly and resolutely, yet with no clear awareness of why I was trailing him and what I intended to accomplish.

The kitchen door was closed. Behind it, I heard voices—his and Mother's. I paused. An old-fashioned iron latch nailed to the oak door guarded the privacy of the kitchen. I pulled it down and waited to make sure that my maneuver had not been observed from within. Then, hoping that the hinges wouldn't squeak, I pushed the door open a few inches.

Mother was sitting on the edge of the table in the middle of the kitchen. He must have been somewhere to her left, out of my sight, for her face was turned that way. What I could hear of their conversation was ordinary enough—something about Thursday, and about the opera singer who had recently moved upstairs into the apartment left empty by Grand-mother's death, and other everyday talk.

Without bothering to close the door, I retreated and walked away reassured and lighthearted. If those two witches were silly enough to waste their time on foolish talk, it was their business.

In our room, Fräulein Rosalia was sitting at the Singer sewing machine. I was growing out of my clothes, and when-ever she came across a piece of usable fabric, she would turn it into something I could wear. Right now, she was making me a nightgown out of a torn linen tablecloth. Anatol was also in the room, curled up as usual in the corner of an armchair, engrossed in the picture book on his lap.

I sat down on a stool beside her. The machine was noisily knocking out the stitches while her hands skillfully manipulated the linen under and around the needle.

She had not been looking well lately. Her cheeks were sunken, her skin, normally translucent, had lost its opalescence, and, watching her work, I thought her fingers were slightly swollen.

"Fräulichka!" I used her pet name. "You're very tired, aren't you?"

"No, not really." The machine stopped and she pressed her hand to her forehead. "Just a little headache—that's all."

"Can I get you a glass of water?"

"No, thank you, dear. I'll be all right." She leaned back and took a deep breath.

"Do you know Stepan?" I asked. There was a beat of hesitation.

"Yes, I do," she said then.

"I have just met him."

"Oh!" she said. The tone was noncommittal. Her hands went back to the cloth and the machine resumed its noisy knocking.

34

He came often—always during the day, when Father wasn't there. He never stayed long—maybe an hour or more, but he made himself felt. He strutted about with a proprietary air, talked and laughed loudly, played cards with the two witches, and told jokes that must have been smutty for they were cut short by a look or wink whenever I was within hearing distance. Recalling what Tatiana had said about his background, it was plain that he relished having conquered what was formerly forbidden territory and enjoyed being able to dispense small favors according to his fancy. His whole personality seemed to shout: "Here I am and what are you going to do about it?" Yet with all his swagger, there was one old rule he wasn't able to violate. He couldn't bring himself to use the front door; he always came and left by the servants' entrance—the "black walk." In his heart, the underdog wasn't quite dead.

Familiarity was his keynote—no doubt a slipcover for that still wiggling dog—and he imposed it on everyone except Fräulein Rosalia. Their relationship was simple—there was none. She treated him with acid politeness, and he was wise enough not to tackle that barrier.

Insolent as he was with other people, he made it a point to be solicitous with me—a strategy that didn't get him very far. Intuitively, I shrank away from him no matter how honey-tongued his speech. I couldn't figure out why Mother not only tolerated his vulgarities but seemed to descend to his level, slapping him down only when he got too far out of bounds. It all had an undertone of raucous camaraderie.

Stepan's emergence had worsened the relationship between Mother and Fräulein Rosalia. There were no open clashes, for Fräulein would not allow herself to express any opinion of him, but Mother, sensing her silent disapproval and being weighed down with guilt, watched Fräulein's every step with angry suspicion, ready to pounce at the slightest provocation.

Father was not even remotely aware of Stepan's existence. In accordance with some telepathic pact, nobody ever mentioned Stepan's name in his presence. The improvement in the food also failed to attract his attention. At least, he never mentioned it, perhaps attributing it to Mother's sharp dealings on the black market. He was a small eater, who hardly noticed what was placed in front of him, and now, what with his asthma and a new job that absorbed him completely, he ate less than ever, gulping it on the run.

He had recently been appointed director of the Theatrical Museum, and it gave a lift to his spirits. He was transported from the dusty archives into the active life of the arts, for his assignment extended beyond the walls of the museum. He was in charge of assembling and supervising various exhibitions, and of organizing experimental theatrical groups in the city and the nearby provinces. It brought him in contact with new talent and he was back in his element. Financially the gain was fractional, but morally it was invaluable.

Father's job kept him away from home for days and sometimes weeks at a time. This played right into Stepan's hands. He would make himself very much at home, and it was not unusual to find him dozing on the living room sofa, his boots unceremoniously on the upholstery and his hair staining the cushions. One night I was surprised to find him at the dinner table. Fräulein Rosalia was not there, having excused herself because of an attack of nausea.

The conversation was giddy and strained, and right after the meal Mother and Stepan got up and left. Irra, Tatiana and I remained at the table, lingering over our tea. Irra's fingers were drumming out a rhythm on the table. Then she began to sing in time to her tapping. The tune was a gypsy ballad.

"There'll be guests at the opera singer's tonight," she caroled. "Tra-la-la, there'll be guests, there'll . . . tra-la-la—"

"Don't be silly," Tatiana interrupted her. "The opera singer isn't there. She went out."

"Ah—" Irra wagged her finger in front of Tatiana's nose—"but the key is there . . . to the left of the door . . . under the mat. . . . I saw it."

"Now isn't that lovely and convenient?" Tatiana said, in apparent admiration.

The mention of the opera singer made my mind flip back to the conversation I had overheard when I was eavesdropping at the kitchen door. Now, with the witches bringing her into their weird dialogue, she was beginning to acquire significance. I resolved to discuss this with Fräulein Rosalia and find out all there was to know about the opera singer. But when I got to our room, I found her lying down, her eyes closed and her face damp with perspiration, and I couldn't bring myself to disturb her rest.

Whenever Father had to leave town, he would entrust me with the keys to the glass-enclosed cabinets of the museum.

"Go browse around," he would say. "It will do you good."

And I would spend hours on the sliding ladder looking at books, old programs and photographs of celebrities, some contemporary, others already swept into eternity.

Three top shelves of a certain cabinet were dedicated to translations of foreign literature, and I was sitting on the top rung when I made my acquaintance with Louisa Alcott's *Little Women*. Until then, America was nothing more than a distant name, seldom heard, like Zanzibar or Kyoto, a shape on the map, marked by a certain color, and visually connected with Fenimore Cooper's Indians. The novel opened up a new world full of promise, with different and fascinating standards and customs, where a girl could be called Jo and anything was possible.

I fell in love with the book. Perched on top of the ladder, I read and reread it, refusing to bring it down to earth, determined to keep it in my private treasury of dreams, together with Theatre School and the Maryinsky Theatre. The thought that I could ever really leave Russia never occurred to me. The country was closed in tight, the borders patroled, and no one had a chance of getting out except, of course, those who risked their lives to slip out on the run. Moreover, Father was not the man to desert his country in a time of trouble.

Spring ripened into summer and the first soft heat filled me with new energy. Lessons with Madame Sokolova no longer satisfied me, and at the end of the hour I was raring to start again from the beginning. I wanted more work, more practice.

I was restless. And there was very little recreation available. Nina had a lot of time on her hands because of the summer vacation, and she came to see me often. We would take long walks to the Summer Gardens, an enormous park at the outlet of the Fontanka Canal into the Neva River. Beautifully landscaped, but neglected and overgrown with weeds, the paths wove around ponds and deserted bandstands and gazebos, and then straightened out into wide alleys lined with stately trees and dirt-stained statues. We paraded around for hours, ogling people who in turn were ogling us or watching platoons of the Red Army, drilling on an adjoining field.

But our goal lay across the canal, where a flat building stood with bright banners flying from its roof. Circus Chinizelli! From all over the land the very best acts collected there for the spring season. Intimate, all velvet and gilt, containing only one ring, it projected a magic I never again experienced at any other circus.

On matinee days, Nina and I hung around the lobby. Neither of us had any money for tickets, so we had to devise more imaginative ways of getting in. We either tried to sneak in unnoticed with the crowd or, if that failed, waited until the performance was well under way. Then we would choose the attendant with the kindest face and approach him with our pleas to be let in. Sometimes we succeeded and were allowed to watch from the back of the amphitheatre. Just as often, we were thrown out.

No matter what we did or where he went, Nina's conversation eventually reverted to the following spring, when she would graduate from Theatre School and become a full-fledged member of the Maryinsky.

"I wonder what pas de deux they'll assign me," she murmured, looking ahead to that glorious night when the Maryinsky Theatre, symphony orchestra and all, is turned over to the graduating class for their exam performance.

I listened to her and my frustrations grew. Despite the uncertainty of my future, I was determined to catch up with Nina and the other lucky ones.

A few blocks away from our house, there was a private dancing school run by a soloist from the Maryinsky, who taught character dancing in addition to ballet. Though I fully recognized the futility of my move, my feet carried me to that school one day and I found myself in front of a desk in the reception room inquiring about the tuition fee. A young woman told me, and I thanked her and went out feeling a fool. What did it matter how much it cost? If it were one kopek or a ruble, there was no money to pay for it anyway. Madame Sokolova was already taking a sufficient share of Father's salary and further expenditures were unthinkable.

Foolish though I felt, I told Fräulein Rosalia of my expedition, pouring out all the ferment inside me. She listened intently and, when I had finished, crossed to her desk and picked up a pencil and a sheet of paper.

"How much did you say the tuition is per month?" she asked.

I repeated it. She opened her personal drawer, took out a small brown notebook and, after studying a certain page, wrote down some figures, her hand moving very slowly. The harsh light of the overhead lamp fell directly on her hand, and I suddenly saw how swollen it was and how much difficulty she had in holding the pencil. Absorbed in what she was doing, she leaned forward under the light, and I was struck by something else I had not noticed before. The contours of her face had changed. The clean-cut lines of the cheek and jaw were gone, and where before her skin lay close along her bones, it was now puffed and doughy.

For a second, the room vanished leaving me in empty space, and somewhere between my heart and my brain, a voice said clear as a bell, "Fräulein Rosalia is going to die."

The room came back. Fräulein Rosalia was still at the desk. After a while she lifted her head.

"Don't despair," she said. "We'll make a try at it."

35

Fräulein Rosalia was always the first one up in the morning. She took care of Anatol, put the tea glasses on the dining room table, and then busied herself in the kitchen brewing tea and preparing what was available that day for breakfast. Normally it consisted of rationed black bread sliced thin to make it more palatable and small cakes that she baked out of leftover coffee grounds mixed with fat. Lately, since Stepan had come into our lives, there might be an occasional egg or even some goat cheese and honey. Things were looking up. The traditional samovar was not in use; the coal it required was hard to find, and tea was made in an enamel teapot.

It was a lovely morning, pale pink skimming over blue, and I distinctly remember a faint smell of tar floating in through the open window because, below it, two workers, seized by an unheard-of compulsion for public service, were filling a hole in the street. So unique was this spectacle that it had attracted a sizable audience that was not only expressing its admiration but hopefully suggesting that the good labors be extended to other holes on the block—a hope that never materialized. Having leveled that one hole, the workers picked up their tools and left without a backward glance.

I was nibbling on my coffee cake and wondering why that particular hole got such priority when Father came in. He waved good morning, sat down and took a magazine from his pocket. Fräulein Rosalia had already finished her breakfast and was now polishing the sideboard, but she interrupted her work to pour him a glass of tea. She was major-domo, cook, seamstress, general organizer, and she did it all so unobtrusively that one was hardly aware of her efforts. The witches, naturally, took advantage of her and deliberately stayed in their rooms until they were reasonably sure that most of the morning work had been done.

Mother came in a while later. Her hair was hanging loose and her face was dull with the tag ends of sleep, and from the way she shook her head and yawned it was obvious she wished she were still in bed. She looked around lazily, dipped her spoon into the honey pot and slowly licked it clean. Little Anatol, his face cupped in his hands, was studying us with his unwavering gaze.

Nice stillness. Spring breeze and inertia. The smell of tar fading in the warm wind. A rare moment of quiet and peace.

Father folded his magazine, put it in his pocket and stood up to go.

Fräulein Rosalia swung away from the sideboard.

"Sir," she said, "I should like to talk to you and Madame before you leave."

Mother looked up in annoyance; she disliked any verbal exchange with Fräulein Rosalia because she wasn't equal to it. Father, who suffered no such handicap, took it in his stride.

"Indeed, Fräulein Rosalia," he said and sat down again. "Indeed. What is it?"

"It's about your daughter," she said tentatively.

"What about her?" Father asked.

Fräulein Rosalia waited. When she spoke, her words were carefully chosen.

"I'm sure you know that she's been making great strides in dancing," she said. "Madame Sokolova told me so herself the other day. She's a great old lady and a great teacher, but there comes a time . . ." She hesitated.

"Go on," Father urged her.

"What I mean to say, sir, is that Madame Sokolova's lessons alone are no longer sufficient. . . . They are important, indeed, and should be continued, but the girl is badly in need of more practice. She has reached the point where she needs to expand . . . to branch out, so to speak . . . her energies are bottled up. We were discussing it the other day, and I took it on myself to do some investigating. Near here, only four blocks away, there is a very good dancing school. . . . Perhaps she could take lessons there . . . after dinner, in the evening. . . . The teacher is a soloist at the Maryinsky . . . very respected. . . ."

She paused, uncertain of their reaction.

Father was playing with the lock of his hair, his gaze steady on Fräulein Rosalia's face. He sighed.

"I quite agree with you," he said sadly. "It would be helpful, if it were possible. Unfortunately, it is not. The state of my finances won't permit it. I simply haven't got the money."

Mother chuckled sarcastically.

"It is the stupidest thing I've ever heard," she said looking at Fräulein Rosalia as if the latter were one foot away from idiocy.

"Believe me, Madame, it is necessary," Fräulein insisted.

"Necessary, necessary," Mother aped her with open hostility. "It's easy for you to say it. Words don't cost anything. Go on, be grand and magnanimous. If it is that necessary, why don't you do something about it?" The word "you" was stressed with insulting harshness. "Why don't you send her there?"

"That is precisely what I am asking to be permitted to do," Fräulein Rosalia replied calmly.

If the ghost of Napoleon had flown into the room singing the Internationale, it couldn't have produced a more startling effect. It was not silence that followed—it was a gap in time.

Father studied Fräulein Rosalia with new interest, and Mother's mouth fell open with no breath going in or out of it.

"You . . . you . . ." she finally gasped.

"Yes, Madame." Fräulein Rosalia reaffirmed her statement. "I would appreciate it if I were allowed to do it. You see, I have a little money—it is what's left of my life's savings. I've kept it for an emergency, and I think that emergency is here."

"You . . . you have money . . ." Mother jumped in before the last word ended, "and you never had the decency to offer it to me? It's unbelievable! You live here, you eat here, you are treated like one of the family, and you never thought of contributing anything."

Fräulein Rosalia grew pale. "Contributing? . . . I think I have contributed to the best of my ability. . . . I work as hard as I can."

"Everyone works!" Mother lashed out. "What makes you so different! You don't do any more than anybody else!"

"And, Madame . . ." Fräulein tried to defend herself, "forgive me for saying this, but I've worked for years without remuneration . . . just as Madame says . . . like one of the family."

"Family!" Mother was getting worked up. "You are not family and never will be!"

"Easy now!" Father cut in sharply.

It had no effect. She went on, intent on finishing off her victim.

"Don't you know how hard it is to get food? You must know that every morsel counts—that every mouth counts! And you, my dear, have been here at every meal! I wonder if you know what it costs to buy anything on the black market?"

The words fell hard, brutal, humiliating. But Fräulein Rosalia matched them. Suddenly cold and detached, her voice controlled, she played her trump.

"Yes, Madame, I know how much it costs . . . other people. But I have noticed that Madame has her own methods of dealing with the situation."

She spoke with exaggerated clarity, each word a distinct warning that everything was in jeopardy—Stepan, Tatiana's whoring—and that she was prepared to use and risk anything to gain her point.

And Mother understood.

Father's face darkened.

"What do you mean by special ways, Fräulein?" he asked.

"Nothing, sir, nothing." Fräulein Rosalia's voice softened. "Except that Madame really has a wonderful knack of getting things cheaply. It's a gift, and I admire it. There is no question but that my money would have helped us get a trifle more food over the years, but the amount would have been insignificant . . . and it would have brought no dividend. If you allow me to invest it in your daughter's future—who knows, it might bring her food for life. After all, she started late—she has to catch up with the others. And she wants so badly to make you proud of her one day."

Mother was silent, her mouth tight and angry. Father's fingers were working on his lock of hair and his face was a picture of concentrated thought.

"Haven't you any relative to whom you could leave that money?" he finally asked.

"I have a brother. But we've never been close and I hardly ever see him. He has a job that pays him well. No, I wouldn't leave it to him. I'd like to spend it on someone who, in my opinion, has a future."

Father stood up and slowly strode the length of the room, mulling over Fräulein's request. Then he stopped in front of her. "You are an amazing person, Fräulein Rosalia," he said and then turned to Mother. "What do you think? Don't you agree that we should accept? If we cannot meet this need ourselves, we should be grateful for Fräulein's generosity."

She only shrugged her shoulders.

"All right then," said Father. "We accept, Fräulein Rosalia— accept with deepest gratitude."

He smiled at me. "Well! You must have been born under some special star. Now work hard and become one."

He looked pleased when he left. Mother waited until his footsteps were heard no more and then she walked over to Fräulein Rosalia. They stood face to face. A vein was throbbing in her temple and her fists were clenched so tight that they were white.

"I'll never forgive you for this," she hissed. "You'll be sorry. Just you wait and see. You'll be sorry."

36

Together we went to the school, and Fräulein Rosalia put down on the receptionist's desk a small pouch that made a lively, clinking noise. It was filled with "chervontzi," the colloquial name for five-ruble gold pieces. Paper money had changed several times since the Revolution, repeatedly becoming worthless, but gold remained what it always had been.

The receptionist looked dumfounded as she watched Fräulein Rosalia spill out the gold pieces and count them in front of her to make sure there would be no mistake in the total.

"This will cover a year and two months of tuition," Fräulein Rosalia said to the receptionist, who just sat there, gaping.

Rarely did anyone pay more than a month in advance, and

that sum of money, especially in "chervontzi," stupefied her. It was lucky for us that she was not an informer, otherwise Fräulein Rosalia might have been interrogated and, possibly, accused of illegal hoarding. That would have meant confiscation at best.

As it happened, the school was only too happy to receive the money.

"Please give me the receipt in triplicate," said Fräulein Rosalia, confusing the receptionist even more.

The poor girl got up and ran into one of the classrooms. Presently she returned with a teacher, Mr. Chekreguin, an attractive, trim man of about forty.

"Why do you want it in triplicate?" he asked Fräulein Rosalia, staring at the gold.

"Because it is a great deal of money, and one receipt might get lost," she answered with a simple logic.

It seemed to satisfy him, and he nodded and wrote out the triple receipt. Then, after a few routine questions about my previous studies, he left us with the understanding that I would begin my lessons the following evening.

Later, at home, Fräulein Rosalia handed me one of the receipts. "Take care of it," she said. "Make sure you have it safely hidden. You never know when you might need it." Then she dug three more gold rubles out of her pocket.

"For a new set of practice clothes," she said. "One set won't do—it will never dry out in time."

Dancing is hard physical work. Whether in class or on the stage, it is grueling labor. At the end of a lesson I was so sopping wet that my clothes clung to me as if I had just walked out of the sea. Those lithe, lovely creatures we watch on the stage, defying gravity with breathtaking ease, are, on close inspection, sweaty and panting and nowhere near as appetizing as they seem from the blessed distance of the auditorium.

So began my two-a-day lessons. Previously, having worked alone with Madame Sokolova, I had no yardstick by which to judge myself. That I was making progress was obvious, because I was slowly conquering technical difficulties, but I had no idea of my basic ability. Was I talented, average or mediocre? Madame Sokolova never volunteered any opinion, and I was too busy working to worry about it consciously.

In Chekreguin's school the situation was different. Seven girls, including me, and three boys were working in the same class, learning the same combinations of steps, all of us facing and reflected in the same mirror and seeing clearly how well or badly the others were doing. Competition and comparison were literally staring me in the face.

By the end of the first week I began to suspect that I wasn't bad at all, and by the end of the month I came to the conclusion that I was rather good. Confidence in myself began to sprout.

Summer rushed by busily, marred only by a noticeable increase in the swelling of Fräulein Rosalia's body. No bright light was necessary any longer to see that her bone structure was disappearing under the puffiness. Even her ankles were thickening and slowing down her walk. Finally, although she always minimized her illness, she went to a clinic for help. Some pills were prescribed, together with a diet that was laughable, because in our circumstances it couldn't be followed.

Mother hardly spoke to her, ignoring her illness. She restricted herself to giving orders, which were often absurd and always fatiguing. She would send Fräulein Rosalia out on long errands, sometimes more than once a day, and, considering the lack of transportation, this was an arduous task even for a healthy person. Or she would pretend to have lost a trinket and make Fräulein Rosalia crawl on her hands and knees looking for it, until, her vindictiveness satisfied, she would produce the missing article from nowhere. If I tried to intervene and help, Mother would shout at me to stop.

"Save your strength for those 'dancing lessons,' " she would say cuttingly.

Fräulein Rosalia showed no resentment, serving Mother in quiet obedience and concealing as best she could the strain those extra jobs imposed on her. Having challenged a woman who couldn't stand contradiction or criticism, she knew she would have to pay for it.

Stepan was still around, the time of his visits depending on Father's whereabouts. If he was there in the evening, one could be fairly sure that Father was out of town. On one such evening, the mysterious opera singer descended from her apartment upstairs and joined us. She turned out to be a very fat lady with a crude countenance and one out-of-kilter eye. It was disconcerting, as though someone invisible were under her constant surveillance. After dinner, she was persuaded to sing. Throwing her head back as far as her fat neck permitted, she hit the keys and let go with a rendition of "Les Filles de Cadiz" in a voice so shrill that it shook the walls. Mother and Stepan were ecstatic. They cheered and applauded, and Stepan picked up the opera singer and whirled her around so that her petticoats flew up to reveal a fat bottom.

I was getting used to Stepan. Not that my dislike of him lessened, but because of my concentration on my dancing, his very existence dwindled to second place. Until one evening when our lesson was called off at the last minute, because of Mr. Chekreguin's sudden indisposition, and I returned home an hour and a half ahead of schedule. Disappointed, I was slowly climbing the stairs to our apartment in the dimness of the falling night. The electricity was out of order, which was its normal state, but the shapes of things were still visible, and on the landings between floors the windows shone with the silver luminosity of the sky behind them.

I was about to press the button of our bell when my attention was diverted by voices on the floor above, where the opera singer lived.

"Damn it! She must have left the wrong key."

It was Mother speaking.

There was the rattling of a key in a lock and then Stepan let out a few obscenities.

"She never made this mistake before," Mother tried to placate him.

A few more tries at the door and I heard them descending the stairs.

My hand was glued to the wall next to the bell, and I myself turned into Lot's wife. They reached the landing between floors. There he grabbed her roughly and pulled her down on the window sill, dropping down beside her. From where I stood, their silhouettes were clearly outlined against the luminous windows, and I saw him press his body against her and squash her mouth with his. His hand traveled from the nape of her neck down her body and then got lost in her skirt. She didn't resist. There was a whispering and a squirming and a suppressed groan.

A sinking feeling came over me, but my eyes were riveted on them.

Irra—her words—God! . . . he who provides . . . the opera singer upstairs . . .

The pieces of the puzzle fused into a hideous design.

Night was falling fast, darkening the window, and in a few minutes I couldn't see them any more.

Unsteady and afraid of tripping, I gripped the banister and held on to it as I tiptoed downstairs and out into the street.

The house next to us had a low brick wall that once upon a time had enclosed a flowerbed. I sat down on its edge, feeling stripped to the skin. I didn't know how to go home.

37

It was past midnight, yet sleep wouldn't come.

"Fräulein Rosalia . . . Fräulichka," I called softly, almost hoping she wouldn't hear me.

"Yes?" came the answer.

"I saw them."

"Saw whom?"

"Mother and Stepan."

"Of course, you saw them. What is so unusual about that? You see them often."

"No . . . no . . . I mean . . . I saw them together . . . on the stairs . . . they had the wrong key . . . they were on the window sill . . . they didn't see me . . . it was dark . . . they . . ."

The light of Fräulein Rosalia's bedside lamp flashed on. She sat up quickly. Her face bore witness that no further explanation was necessary. She gave herself a few moments to reflect, then she dropped her feet to the floor and slid them into her slippers.

"I saw them . . . I saw them . . ." I kept repeating stupidly.

She came to me, and pulled me up until I was sitting.

"Now, now . . . quiet . . ." she said soothingly.

She sat on the edge of my bed. Neither of us spoke. Then she took my hand.

"We can do nothing about it, can we?" she asked quietly.

"Oh, yes, we can," I said defiantly. "Father doesn't know that Stepan comes here."

"No, he doesn't. And you are not going to tell him." The quiet strength behind that command, and the calmness of her tone, astonished me. I felt betrayed by this lack of compassion, but now I realized that one drop of it would have made me fall apart, and her object was to teach me to hold myself together.

"Let me ask you a question," she said. "Whom in your family do you love best?"

"You and Father."

"In that case, I'm sure, you would not want to do anything that would hurt him."

"But I must—"

"Oh, no, you mustn't," she cut me short.

"Listen to me, dear heart," she said tenderly, lifting my drooping chin. "Listen carefully. Life will always offer you a choice of action. In every situation—bad or good—there will be several roads for you to take, and one will look like the obvious choice. However, it may not be the wisest. Weigh each choice carefully. Ask yourself many questions before you come to a decision. First of all—will your decision bring pain and misery to anyone? And will it achieve what you hope to achieve? What if the trouble it creates will be worse than what you are trying to correct?"

"But everybody is lying, and you told me that lying is wrong."

"Yes, I did say that and I will not retract it. But there are exceptions to every rule. That's why we have words such as 'excuse' and 'reason.' And there is one excuse for lying. Can you tell me what it could be?"

"No, I can't. I don't know."

"Protecting someone else. If you lie to protect someone from a hurt, then lying is not only justifiable but honorable. It is very hard to do, because in that case you transfer the burden of that hurt to yourself. Wouldn't you be proud if you had the strength to carry that burden instead of inflicting it on your father?"

"I don't want to hurt him," I said, on the verge of tears.

"Of course you don't. And you will not. Stepan will go. He won't be here forever. Till then, we'll disregard him and protect your father as best we can. Shield him from hurt. Remember, he is the most important person. He is sensitive and vulnerable."

"I hate Mother."

"You must not say that either. I told you once that life is like a medal. It twirls. Sometimes people get caught on the wrong side. It happens to the best of them."

I fell back on the pillows. "Then I mustn't do anything."

"You're quite wrong," she said. "You must do a great deal. You must marshal your forces to exercise self-control. It won't be easy. And then, after your father, you must think of yourself. Don't allow evil forces to destroy you. Learn how to brush them off. Selfishness, at times, is a necessity and a virtue."

She got up. "And now to sleep. Remember the old proverb: the morning is wiser than the night."

She kept her bedside light on until I became drowsy.

38

It wasn't easy. Pretending in an illusory world of your own making is a joy and a delight. You cast yourself in a role you have invented, you let your imagination guide you, you change scenes at will, and when it gets out of hand, you wipe it all out with a flick of a thought. Pretending in a world of reality is another matter. The scene is set. Stripped of your magic powers of transformation, you trail along with the sickening plot, you adjust yourself to what you abhor, you fake your reactions and hate yourself for it, and throughout you can't believe it is happening to you.

It was a strain to look at Mother. Between us stood the picture of that woman being mauled on the window sill, backed by the shining night, and that image became so powerful at times that in order to control my feelings, I had to avert my eyes and concentrate on some other object. Her behavior made me cringe. How could she, in view of the treachery to which I had been a silent witness, be so easy, so normal, as if she had nothing on her conscience?

I lived in misery. The sight of Stepan nauseated me. Whenever I saw him come in, I would slink away to my room—I thought, unobtrusively. This presumption was proved wrong when, in the middle of one such escape, he stopped me with a smack on my behind.

"Hey, there," he bellowed, "why do you run away from me? Don't you like me any more?"

I could not fathom what gave him the impression that I had ever liked him.

"It isn't that," I managed to squeeze out, "it's that I don't feel very well."

Surprisingly, I wasn't lying. His touch brought bile into my throat, and when I got to my room, the bile refused to subside.

Hardest of all was to be with Father. I wanted to run to him, throw my arms around him and free the tears that, in his presence, welled up behind my eyes. To conquer that compulsion, I would go to the opposite extreme. I would giggle and act foolishly, which made him wonder aloud if dancing had gone to my head. Though he said it in jest, it hurt me deeply, intensifying my resentment of the whole affair, and I barely restrained myself from spilling out the truth.

Fräulein Rosalia tried to help me by keeping me out of the house or out of sight on various pretexts; it might be a date with Nina, or an errand, or something she would invent that I had to do alone in my room, with the door closed.

Luckily, autumn was upon us, and with it came the announcement that the Gymnasia for Young Girls was reopening to resume normal activities. It couldn't have come at a more appropriate time. Of necessity now, I was out of the house most of the day. I was the first to leave in the morning, and would not return until five in the afternoon, after Madame Sokolova's lesson. At seven, I was out again, on my way to Mr. Chekreguin's school.

Still there was suppertime. The family was united around the table, and it was painful to listen to the talk, for in my mind everything that was said took on a double meaning.

Bits of decent food continued to trickle to our table, but knowing that they were Stepan's donations, I refused to eat them. For a while Fräulein Rosalia observed this protest, and then she took me aside.

"Don't you remember what I said to you? Think of yourself. Good food is hard to come by. You are working strenuously; you need energy. By refusing to eat, you hurt no one but yourself. No one." Her words were hammered out with force. "Your behavior will only arouse suspicion. And that's the last thing you want to do. So, eat. A long life is ahead of you, and you'll need strength to live it. Remember that when I am gone."

"Where are you going?" I asked, panicked.

"Nowhere," she said. "It's a manner of speaking, to make you listen."

I listened and I began to eat. I ate ravenously, feeling that with every mouthful I was revenging myself—getting even with Mother and Stepan and everybody else concerned.

In the very first class at the Gymnasia for Young Girls, we were met with an innovation. As we sat waiting for the teacher, the door opened and the directress paraded in with three young boys in tow. The teacher trailed behind them. The whole group got up on the teacher's dais, and the directress began her speech.

"Ladies," she said, "these young gentlemen are assigned to your class. A new government ruling has changed our educational system. From now on, boys and girls will study together." She wrinkled her nose, unable to hide her distaste for what she was saying. "So far, we have these three young gentlemen, but there might be more coming."

It was said with funereal gravity. She was obviously embarrassed, for she was twitching her shawl and looking somewhere over our heads. Nor did the boys feel any better; they stared at their shoes, picked their ears and generally looked as though they would rather be whipped with a cat-o'-nine-tails than endure twenty-two little females glaring at them in silence.

The directress added something about friendliness and togetherness, and then the boys were assigned to their places among the girls.

This break with tradition created a furor among the parents of the girls. They were sure it would result in wild orgies, the boys seducing the girls under classroom benches. Nothing could have been further from the truth. Instead of interest, the imposed togetherness aroused hostility on both sides, and the boys hadn't a chance since they were outnumbered. The girls invented tricks to torment them; glued tacks upside down on their seats, spilled ink over their books, ganged up on them, ten to one, during recess. Many sadistic incidents occurred, with the result that one of the boys gave up and vanished.

Autumn was taking hold. Rains washed the city, collecting dirt in the clogged gutters. And the sadness of fall was accentuated by the more and more evident deterioration in Fräulein Rosalia's health. Now a respiratory congestion was added to her other symptoms. By the middle of October she took to her bed.

The family was sympathetic in a polite, superficial manner —and no more. Mother's attitude didn't soften an iota; she saw to it that Fräulein Rosalia was fed, inquired through other people about her health, and that was all. I think she and the witches were secretly relieved not to have her around, for they must have felt her presence as a reproach. Little Anatol alone seemed to be genuinely concerned, sitting by her side and watching her for most of the day. He seemed to appreciate her more now that she was unable to take care of him. Father would drop in occasionally to cheer her up with a few encouraging words, until the day he had to leave town to organize an exhibition somewhere in the provinces.

I wanted to quit my dancing lessons to take care of her, but she forbade me to do so.

"For you, every day counts," she said. "Besides, all I need is rest, and I am getting it."

Rest, despite her optimism, was not proving to be a healer. The luster was fading from her eyes, and the swelling increased to such an extent that if a finger was pressed into her flesh, the indentation remained long after the finger was removed.

Mercifully, the great law of the universe that sustains and balances our existence had obliterated the memory of that voice I had heard the day Fräulein Rosalia consulted her little notebook, and I still looked forward to her recovery.

39

At the end of an exceptionally good lesson with Madame Sokolova, she announced, as a bonus, that she had asked one of the teachers from Theatre School to come and look at me.

"Not that it will do any good," she said. "You are twelve and way overage to get in there. But I want to show him that even though I'm old, I'm still a better teacher than any of them."

The old lady was proud of herself, and of me, and it lifted my spirits to the sky.

In a rush to share the news with Fräulein Rosalia, I kicked my boots under a chair in the vestibule and threw my coat down without bothering to hang it up. Yodeling, I ran into our room.

Her bed was empty. The sheets were rumpled and the shawl she usually wore around her shoulders lay coiled on the floor.

I ran out. There was no one in sight. I ran from room to room calling, down the corridor and into the kitchen, just as Tatiana, dragging Anatol and carrying a bundle, was coming in through the "black walk."

"What happened?" I asked, getting cold.

Yes, she knew what had happened. By noon Fräulein Rosalia had become so ill that she had to be taken to the hospital.

"What hospital?"

She didn't know. Somewhere nearby, at the crossing of Nikolayevsky Prospekt and "what's the name of that street?" Anyway, didn't I see the note under the paperweight on my desk? The details were on it.

It was a small ward—only nine people. Walls stained by leaking pipes, the plaster cracked. Iron bedsteads standing at assorted angles as if they'd been shoved into this room on the way somewhere else. Harsh light falling from two unshaded bulbs dangling from the ceiling.

Her bed was pushed into the corner, the foot of it stuck out toward the center of the ward. There was an empty triangular space next to it.

She was lying propped up high on the pillows to help her breathing; it came in soft gasps, like the breath of a child about to cry, and her hands lay limp on top of the rough blanket. With each breath, her head moved mechanically up and down a few inches. She was obviously in pain and barely on the edge of consciousness. She smiled at me only once.

I didn't know what to do. Across the room a kitchen chair stood by the door, and I dragged it over to her bed and sat down. I sat rigid, everything in me at a standstill, waiting for something—perhaps a sign of recognition, or a human voice to give me a drop of hope, or a shudder to ease the constriction of my body. My lips were parched, curled under the gums.

Around us were incongruous, ordinary noises: the sound of scraping coming from the hall, where someone must have been plastering a crack; a sneeze; a fit of coughing; a piercing ring; and the shuffling feet of an old lady who was slowly progressing toward her bed with the help of a cane. Even a laugh. All so improbable and discordant in the face of her lying there.

Sometime later, the doctor came, making the rounds. He gave me a sickly smile, and bent over Fräulein Rosalia with his back to me so I couldn't see what he was doing. But I caught a glimpse of the syringe he whipped out of his bag. Then he turned to me.

"You a relative?"

I nodded, not being sure that I could speak.

"She's suffering," he said. "God, I wish I could give her some morphine."

"Why don't you?"

"It isn't that simple," he chuckled sadly. "We don't have it in the hospital. We could get it on the black market, but it's expensive and we haven't got the money."

"You need money, Doctor? Is that it? You could help her then?"

"Yes," he said, "I could. At least, a little. Ease the pain."

I didn't wait for him to leave. I was on my feet—running.

"Mama!"

She was wiping the dishes and stacking them up neatly on the table in the center of the kitchen.

"Ah, you're back," she said offhandedly, not interrupting her work. "Tatiana told me you went to the hospital." There was a note of caution in her voice as if she were uncertain of what the next minute would bring.

A pot was steaming on the stove and Irra was concentrating on stirring it. There was a pile of rubbish in the corner and next to it, resting against the wall, a broom sported a towel on its handle like a flag. Under the window, a pair of men's galoshes were partly concealed by an ironing board. Stepan must be here, probably snoring on some couch inside.

"Mama, I need money!"

"What?" The surprise nearly made her drop a dish.

"Please, Mama!"

"Why do you want money?"

"Mama, it's for Fräulein Rosalia. . . . The doctor said he could help her. . . . Please give it to me."

"What nonsense." She dismissed me and picking up a stack of dishes carried them to the cupboard. I followed her.

"Mama, he said it would ease her pain . . . morphine . . . but the hospital has no money to buy it. . . ." I was talking to her back. "If I bring him money, he'll be able to get it."

"I have no money, and you know it," she said, her hands distributing the dishes in their proper places on the shelves. "She had money, but she gave it to you, remember?—not to me. You could have bought tons of morphine with her money." Her voice was brusque.

My head was swimming. "Mama . . . don't be like that . . . help me . . ."

"Too late for help," she said. "Besides, I told you, I have no money."

"But you can get it!" I cried.

"How?"

"Ask Stepan! He'll give it to you!"

She swung around. "How dare you?" I thought she was going to hit me.

"Yes . . . yes . . . he will . . . just ask," I went on relentlessly, despite the threat. "He will give it to you . . . he will!"

"Why should he?" she screamed.

"Because . . . because . . . because . . ." I was beside myself.

"There's no because, and I won't ask him, you brat!" She advanced toward me, and I backed away.

"Where's Father?"

"What a stupid question. You know perfectly well he's out of town."

"Yes, yes, but where? What's his address? Give it to me!"

She eyed me, carefully calculating her reply.

"I don't know the address; he hasn't written to me yet," she said finally, and went back to her dishes.

I made one more desperate try. "You won't give me the address?"

"I told you, I don't have it. And I don't have the money. All the money is in your dancing school."

A second later I was stumbling down the crooked steps of the "black walk" because it was the nearest exit and because time was hanging over me. "All the money is in your dancing school."

I stood in front of the receptionist's desk. In the four months that I'd attended classes she had gotten to know me well.

"Say, you missed your lesson," she said. "It's not like you. It never happened before. But don't worry. I'll ask Mr. Chekreguin to give you credit for it. You're a good girl."

"It isn't that," I said, my voice shaking, "It's that we paid in advance and I need money. Can you, please, give me back some of it?"

She frowned. "Sorry, dear," she said, "it is the policy of the school not to refund money. As I said before, if you can't attend for a while, we'll credit you, and extend your enrollment."

"No, no, you don't understand. It isn't that," I repeated desperately. "It's that I have to have money. Twenty rubles, maybe?"

"Oh, that's a lot," she said. "But even if you asked for five rubles, I couldn't give it to you. We can't return anything. It's the policy."

The tinkling of a piano was drifting through the closed doors of one of the studios.

"Is Mr. Chekreguin in?"

"Yes, but he can't be disturbed."

"I have to see him . . . please . . ."

"Not right now," she said, getting up and going to the door, prepared to block my way should I make a try for it. "He is rehearsing with his partner. You'll see him tomorrow, in class."

"Yes, of course . . . of course . . ." I mumbled, not knowing what I was saying.

I was back, in the same kitchen chair, by her bed, reduced to a pulp by my failure to help her.

She is beyond help now. She doesn't recognize me any more. I sit and watch her sink away.

Her skin is drawn tight over the swelling, and her eyes, peering out between the puffed lids, have that look of childish bewilderment that comes to the eyes of the dying—a silent cry for explanation, forever unanswered. Slowly, her agony is being absorbed by the coma.

The nurse comes in and as a matter of routine takes her pulse. When she was here before an hour or maybe two hours ago—I can't remember—she suggested that I leave, and finding me still here, she again presses me to go.

"Go away, girl. Go home," she insists. "It isn't pretty to see."

Her words fly somewhere around my head, missing me. She puts the wrist back on the blanket, shakes her head and walks out, zigzagging between beds. And I remain in the same spot, in a trance. My mouth is struggling to form Fräulein's name, but the letters don't jell—the name, too, is dying. She is strange, she is alien, she isn't Fräulein Rosalia any more.

A twitch, a faint gurgle, but the eyes still hold a flicker of life. I have a feeling that the ward is expanding into space—a gigantic balloon inflating itself into a universe . . . giving us a chance to fly out. . . .

Her gaze searches the air and settles on me. I think she sees me . . . yes, she does.

The gaze is steady, but withdrawing, like the tail of a train disappearing into distant mist. . . . The mouth falls open . . . a bubble of foam spills out of one corner . . . and the eyes lose life.

Now you see me . . . now you don't. . . .

It was midday. I knew it because as the nurse pulled the sheet over her face, there was a rattle of trays. They began serving lunch to the patients.

The rest I remember in spurts, in vignettes, in between passages of time blotted out by amnesia. For instance, I know there was a church service, and I know that I was present at it, but I was not aware of being there at the time, and I have no recollection of it now.

What I do remember is vivid, isolated pictures, branded into my memory, as alive as if it were all happening right now.

A drizzly rain . . . streets nearly deserted . . . penetrating dampness . . . a clickety-clack of horses' hoofs on the wet cobblestones . . . a cart with a plain pine coffin on it. The horse is dragging its legs, an undernourished creature whose head hangs low. Someone has stuck an ostrich plume into the front of the bridle, following the old custom, but now the ornament looks grotesque and pitiful dangling in the rain. On top of the coffin three chrysanthemums, lavender, and tied with a limp, rain-soaked ribbon that clings to the coffin. The curved petals collect raindrops like tears. . . . Ironic: I think I heard somebody say that it is Stepan who brought them.

Clickety-clack . . . clickety-clack . . . an endless, monotonous sound . . . We walk with appropriate solemnity, each step a dip in the slush. . . . I am the first behind the cart. Next to me a man. It's her brother. He appeared out of nowhere for the funeral. I saw him, but I don't know what he looks like. He is just somebody who happens to be walking beside me.

The others are farther back. I feel lost and cold, and I glance back over my shoulder. There is Tatiana with a piece of newspaper over her head, and Aunt Eugenia all wrapped up in a cape and a heavy shawl, and Irra huddled with Mother under a communal umbrella, and a few other shapes that I can't distinguish because my eyes are trapped on Mother.

She is eating an apple.

The cart has stopped. An argument is going on. Most of the mourners want to turn back—the cemetery is too far and it is raining. Apparently I have expressed the determination to continue because Aunt Eugenia, holding on to Mother's coat, is outraged.

"But you can't let her go alone," she says excitedly. "I would keep her company, but Armin is waiting for me . . . he'll be worried. . . . You just can't let her go alone. . . ."

"She won't be alone," says Mother, indicating the man next to me. "You are going, aren't you?"

The man nods.

Mother bends down, and as her face comes closer, I see it enlarging, until there is nothing but two large lips with words flying out of them.

"All right, you can go. But be sure to get back early. Hoodlums climb over the walls after dark to rob fresh graves. So come back before dark . . . before dark . . . before . . . dark. . . ."

The man and I resume the journey.

We must have reached the cemetery, and they must have buried her in front of me, but that, too, is blotted out.

Then . . . the next picture swims in.

I sit on a tombstone. It's dark and the drizzle has stopped. There is nobody around. The brother left a long time ago.

In front of me a fresh mound, the heaped-up earth black and soft, and crowned with three chrysanthemums, now free of the ribbon, that has been washed away. The flowers are flat, almost like dried flowers pressed between the pages of a book, only these are wet.

It is still—very still.

I am numb. I wonder if anyone has ever been here, but I doubt it. I've been sitting here for years.

The sky is opening to a milky moon, seeping through the clouds, fighting the haze. Raindrops are dripping from the tree branches, plucking some celestial tune out of the puddles. I am trying to hum it, but I can't—the sounds dissolve before I can catch them.

My eyes are dry, and the emptiness in me is heavy. Its weight keeps me rooted to the tombstone, and I can't move. I am scoured of all feeling.

"Hoodlums climb over the walls after dark to rob fresh graves"—that's what she said.

Ghosts and vapors rise from the teeming ground and wrap themselves around the naked branches like wet towels. They hang and shimmer, but they don't bother me. . . . Nothing bothers me . . . maybe I'm dead. . . . Otherwise I'd feel my fingers.

"The hoodlums are coming. . . ."

No matter . . . They can't harm me because I am not here. Someone else is sitting on the tombstone—I'm only a pair of eyes, looking.

A breeze whips through the trees, sending a downpour of raindrops, and the puddles respond with a series of crazy chords.

Through the haze, I see a figure approaching from the direction of the chapel. It must be a hoodlum.

No, it isn't. It's a nun. A black vestment billows around her stout figure, a hood is pulled snug around her head, and she carries an umbrella. She stops by the grave and surveys me for the longest time. She wears glasses and her face is kind. Not a bit like the nuns who came that Christmas morning, long, long ago.

She gestures at the grave.

"Your mother?"

"Yes," I say.

She sighs, comes to me and lifts me off the tombstone.

"It's late," she says. "You must go home now. There is nothing you can do any more."

Her touch is warm; it transmits love and sympathy.

"Is there anyone at home, waiting for you?"

"Oh, yes," I say. "Sure, there are a lot of people."

She takes my hand and leads me out of the cemetery.

I walked home as if a moving ramp were under my feet; faces passed me, corners turned, and streets opened by themselves while I trod the same spot.

There was a thickening inside my skull. I climbed the stairs, entered the apartment and, without taking off my coat, walked through the vestibule and down the corridor, printing dirty blotches on the carpet with each step.

Lively voices were coming from the dining room. I walked to the door.

Mother and Stepan were sitting at the table, a bottle of wine and two glasses between them. When she saw me, she reddened.

"I told you to come back early," she snapped. "Where have you been? How can you do this to me! Look, you're soaking wet. Take off that coat!"

A wave of insanity swept over me and shook me from head to toe. Nerves cracked, blood pumped in my ears, and I had to hang on to the door to keep from falling.

"You killed her!" I screamed. "You killed her! Killer! Killer, killer!"

Terror contorted her face, and then she was next to me, her arms engulfing me like steel bands.

I was too exhausted to fight her off.

40

I think that the most significant measure of time is the split second. Most of the important events in our lives are compressed into that tiny capsule of eternity.

We die in a second when the valve closes; a newborn baby becomes alive when he utters his first cry; love comes in an instant, and though we have often heard about "slowly falling in love," I don't believe it is true. The "slowly" is a preparation, the climbing up to the peak where love, like a streak of lightning, becomes reality. We waver over decisions until the decision, right or wrong, comes in a flash; and in the ring it's the last count of ten that makes the man still on his feet the champion.

In that split second when life flew out of Fräulein Rosalia's eyes, I lost her forever.

That moment at the door, when I screamed at Mother, I rejected her forever. Both irreversible. Life flipped a somersault and changed color.

There was no hatred in my heart for Mother. What I felt was indifference—the most efficient of knives, severing the connection with surgical thoroughness. I removed myself from her and she stepped down from being a mother to being someone who lived in the same house and was in charge of it. I obeyed her, helped with the house chores, followed orders, remained polite, and there it ended. She, on the other hand, underwent a different transformation. Whether it was brought on by a belated sense of guilt or by the shock of my outburst, she became softer, more solicitous, making halfhearted attempts to get through to me. My lack of response was not deliberate—I simply had nothing inside me, nothing to give. The emptiness that had filled me in the cemetery remained, a void so immense that it drowned any other emotion.

Of course, there was Father, but that was affection of a different kind, based on respect but without much communication—felt but never expressed.

When he came back from his trip, he made a gesture foreign to his nature; he put his arms around me, picked me off the floor and held me pressed tight against him.

"That's how it is, honey," he whispered in my ear. "Life is made up of losses—and a few gains."

I don't recall his doing anything similar before or after.

Irra and Tatiana expressed maudlin condolences, and then, like the Roman soldiers, drew lots for Fräulein Rosalia's clothes.

I was alone again, a thousand times more so than in my early childhood, for now I was consciously aware of it. I functioned automatically, wound up in the morning by restless sleep, unwound at night by weariness. Fräulein Rosalia's bed against the opposite wall brought on spells of insomnia, but no one was sensitive enough to think of removing it, and I would not ask.

Yet underneath the weight of grief and loneliness grew a subconscious resistance to destruction. Fräulein Rosalia had planted that seed the night of our discussion about Mother and Stepan. I knew that from now on I'd have to fend for myself physically and emotionally, and it made me grow up almost overnight. The girl who went to the cemetery was no more—a woman came back, bypassing adolescence with its dreams and gradual discoveries. I had learned the meaning of love, hate, loss, duplicity, idealism, and the rarity of love and understanding. Life lay raw and open in the palm of my hand. I had to survive, and the channel to it was work. Except for the first two days after the funeral, when I literally couldn't get out of bed, I went back to school and never missed a lesson, unless it was for reasons of health.

I would often stay after class at Mr. Chekreguin's school, practicing by myself in an empty studio.

And to keep my mind on the work and away from self-pity, I figured out a device that made dancing more difficult. Through a girl at the school, I bought strings of lead weights, sewed them into two ribbons and tied the ribbons around my ankles underneath the knit leg-warmers. This added two pounds to each foot. At first, it slowed me down, and both Madame Sokolova and Mr. Chekreguin were puzzled by this setback. But as I got used to the weight, my agility returned and later, when I took the lead weights off, I discovered that technically I had taken a terrific leap forward. My legs seemed to have grown wings.

On Sundays, when there were no lessons, I would wander off by myself. I didn't want to see anybody—not even Nina. It was easier to bear it alone. Much of that time I would spend sitting on a bench in Catherine Square where I used to play as a child, and then I would walk up and down Theatre Street, passing Theatre School over and over again. Some Sundays I would go to a certain spot on the Moika Canal where stone steps led down to a platform barely above the water level (an anchorage for small boats in ancient days), and I would sit there for hours on end.

For weeks, I didn't speak to anyone unless spoken to. I lived in a vacuum until, with time, the vacuum slowly began to fill with Fräulein Rosalia's presence. Invisible, she returned to live inside me for the rest of my life. Even today, in moments of crisis or despair, out comes the inevitable cry, "Fräulein Rosalia, help!"

41

Winter returned; the right wing of the house was sealed off again, the little black stove reinstated, and I was forcibly thrown into closer contact with the family. I had no privacy, even in my own room, for the door had to be left open to draw heat from the stove in the center room.

Tatiana's room absorbed heat from the adjoining kitchen, but besides that comfort, she had her own methods of keeping warm. With Fräulein Rosalia gone, the morality of the household sank even lower, and now Tatiana was unashamedly bringing in her partners in sin even during the day and locking herself in her room with them. No amount of knocking would make her open the door. Mother knew they were not making taffy, but she just laughed it off, saying that it didn't hurt anybody and therefore was nobody's business. In truth, she was in no position to censure it. Having taken Tatiana into her confidence and used her often as a watchdog in her affair with Stepan, she had lost the upper hand. Favor for favor. The freedom of "action" was balanced.

In the Gymnasia for Young Girls, the battle of the sexes continued. Three more boys were brought in, to the dismay and anger of the girls, who fought back with the skill of an experienced underground organization. During one recess, a boy whose hands had been tied behind his back was thrown into a tub of cold water and locked up in the bathroom. That brought down the wrath of the authorities.

"Ladies," the directress announced, "this cannot go on. You have to curb your hostility. The male sex will play a big part in your lives, so you might as well get acquainted with it."

Her voice rose to a whining, rage-filled pitch. "I want you to know that you are behaving in a preposterous manner, bringing shame and disgrace upon this school, and I want you, at once, to stand up and apologize to the boys."

A less likely action couldn't have been suggested. Nobody moved.

"I shall repeat it once more," squealed the directress. "Get up, all of you! Get up and apologize." She looked quite wild.

No effect; the boys were beginning to fidget in embarrassment. Infuriated, the directress swept out of the classroom. Then stern letters were dispatched to all the parents, demanding their cooperation in correcting the girls' behavior. When Mother got the letter, she burst into hearty laughter.

"What fools!" she said contemptuously. "That's what comes from having spinsters in charge of a situation they don't understand. Don't they know that everything has its own time? The girls will get acquainted with 'the male sex' when they feel like it—when the time comes. Till then, let them have fun. This kind of war has been going on since time began." And she threw the letter in the trash basket.

Not all mothers felt the same, and the letters had their effect. Many girls were punished at home, and the persecution of the boys subsided.

Meanwhile, more and more notice was being taken of me in Mr. Chekreguin's school, and several times during the lessons I would be singled out to do steps alone for the benefit of the others.

It gave me a lift—temporarily, until time to go home. Then, deflated, I would dress in slow motion, finding any excuse to postpone the moment of leaving.

If Father was home, working in the museum, then the others would be home too, sitting by the black stove, playing cards or gossiping, or mending clothes. If he was out or away, the center room would be less crowded, with one or more ladies missing.

I would bid them good night and go straight to my room, where Anatol was tucked into Fräulein Rosalia's bed. Later he would be moved to a bed in the center room. If it was snowing, I would leave the draperies partly open so I could see out, and then crawl into bed and pull the blankets up to my nose. Isolated by loneliness, I would gaze into the opening between the draperies and wait for sleep. There is peace in falling snowflakes, a white lullaby that anesthetizes the nerves, and I needed it.

The black market flourished. For reasons of its own, the government loosened its grip, and some of the speculators were boldly opening shops in certain sections of the city. Nonetheless, it was of no benefit to most people, since only a very few could afford the astronomical prices. The food on our table improved only slightly, but I had a suspicion that at lunchtime, when neither Father nor I was present, it was a good deal better. Some nights, when I was already in bed, Mother would bring me a leftover from the earlier meal. Remembering Fräulein's words about thinking of myself, I ate it.

"Why don't you talk to me?" Mother would inquire sharply as I devoured the tidbit. "After all, I am your mother."

"Yes, Mother."

"Yes, what?"

"Yes, you are my mother."

"Damn it, you have to stop this. So she died . . . so I'm sorry. We all have to die sometime."

"Yes, Mother."

"Don't 'yes' me. Say something."

"I have nothing to say, Mother."

And she would stomp out of my room, and I'd be glad that she was gone.

42

One afternoon when I returned home, I was greeted by horrifying noises coming from the master bedroom. I heard gasps and cries in Father's voice, interrupted by sounds of choking. I dashed toward the bedroom, but an iron hand held me back.

"Don't go in," Irra said. "The doctor is in there."

I felt a cold draft and saw that the unsealed upper part of the window was wide open. At the stove, Tatiana was hastily putting out the fire.

"What is it? Tell me."

"Ssss . . ." Tatiana pressed her finger to her puckered lips. "He needs air."

Irra dragged me into my bedroom, leaving the door open so she could follow any developments. She pushed me into a chair and lowered her face to mine.

"I'll tell you what happened," she whispered, not without gloating. "Your father never comes home during the day—you know that. Well, today he did. I met him in the hall, and he said he wasn't feeling well. My, was I scared, because Stepan was sitting by the stove, carefree as all get out . . . legs stretched out . . . and his boots off."

She paused and raised her eyes as if expecting a benediction and then continued. "I followed your father into the room, and do you know what he did? He stood looking at Stepan without a word. But, believe me, I wouldn't want anyone to look at me that way. The poor bum . . . he sort of shrank, picked up his boots and crept out. And then she came in. Stepan was gone and your father was standing there like a statue. She knew she was in trouble. . . ."

Though we had never exchanged a word about Stepan, she was taking it for granted that I knew the situation.

" 'Who is that man?' your father asked," she went on enthusiastically. " 'I don't like him,' he said, 'I don't want him in my house.' And then she attacked. God in heaven, what didn't she say to him! She said that Stepan was a friend who did more for the family than he did. She accused him of being a bad provider, and of being selfish, and interested only in his own silly notions . . . she said she was tired of everything, and that he was a fool who thought himself brilliant . . . she even called him—" She caught herself. "No, I better not say it."

"What did she call him?" I was fighting hard not to yell at her.

"She called him . . . impotent."

The word was new and meaningless to me, but it had to signify something terrifying and obscene. I kept my ignorance to myself.

"All the time she was talking, his breath kept getting shorter." Irra was winding up her story. "And then he gasped, staggered to the bedroom and fell across the bed. It's an attack of asthma."

Having finished, she turned her attention to the next room. The cries and gasps were abating, and presently the doctor came out accompanied by Mother. He spoke to her reassuringly, promising that Father would soon be well. She was pale, but there was a challenging look in her eyes.

"Where is Anatol?" I asked, suddenly realizing that the boy was nowhere to be seen.

"Tatiana locked him in her room when the trouble began."

I flew out and raced to Tatiana's room.

Anatol was sitting on the floor under the window, his little figure rolled into a ball, his hands clasped around his knees. In the dimness of the late afternoon he looked pathetic. Taking him under the arms, I tried to lift him, but he resisted and, defeated, I sat down on the floor next to him, our bodies touching. He didn't move. After a while, he shifted, so that there was space between us.

"I don't like them," he said. "When is she coming back?"

"Who?"

"Fräulein Rosalia."

It was the first time he had referred to her.

"She isn't coming back," I said. "She died. And when you die, you don't come back."

"Oh," he said and dropped his forehead to his knees.

Father stayed in bed for a few days. What more transpired between him and Mother I wouldn't venture to guess, but when he got up, the estrangement between them was glaring.

43

Stepan was never seen again inside our apartment, though I had well-grounded suspicions that his relationship with Mother didn't end. Several times, from my window, I saw him cross the backyard and vanish into the cavity of the "black walk," and I would rush to the kitchen to see if he would come in. He never did, which left me with one conclusion—he had gone upstairs to the opera singer's. Considering that Mother was always conveniently out on these occasions, it didn't require any sleuthing to deduce what was going on. I would get agitated and fret, and wish that Father would catch them, and then I would reverse my wish for fear that he might get another attack, which could kill him. He was no longer the giant I had once thought him to be; he was a weak man, who capitulated to her, and whom I loved still—with a love now diluted by pity.

Mother's outburst had an effect. Disregarding his physical condition, Father took on another job—reorganizing some library. This kept him away in the evenings. Thus I saw even less of him than before; sometimes at dinner (he preferred to eat out, or to take a tray into the museum) or early in the morning, at breakfast, when we were both gulping our tea and nothing much was ever said.

The opera singer no longer visited us. Why should she bother when all the fun was concentrated in her apartment? In the evenings I would generally find only one of the ladies at home, baby-sitting with Anatol. I suspect they tossed a coin for that vigil.

And so home ceased to be home. It became a place where an assortment of people congregated to eat and sleep. There was nothing to bind us, no mutual affection or common interest, and what dutiful concern for each other still existed was too fragile to constitute a family tie. We stayed together because we had no other place to go.

Later that winter, Konstantin came to live with us, unchanged and debonair as ever. He had been transferred from active duty (drills and maneuvers) to a desk job. It pleased him. He was not much of an activist. His nonchalance and his slightly high-hat sense of humor were a welcome relief. His presence wrought an improvement in the atmosphere.

"My, how you have grown," he said, sizing me up. "You're a young lady. Not bad, not bad at all." A glint of approval in his heavy-lidded eyes endorsed this statement. "But you look sad. Why?"

The only space available for him was the first room off the vestibule. It was isolated and cold, but it had a corner fireplace that was never used because of the shortage of wood. Konstantin soon saw to that. Through some undisclosed manipulations and his personal charms, he contrived to get enough wood to keep it burning every evening, which not only heated the room but added an Old World "Gemütlichkeit." Everyone teased him about the high-ranking lady Communist he must have seduced to get such a lavish supply of logs. He only grinned back enigmatically.

Irra was all in a dither. No persuasion was necessary now to make her stay home in the evening. She was there waiting for him, and when she was sent on an errand, she accomplished it with the speed of a champion runner lest she miss his return from the job.

He took her wooing as he took everything—with an amused

smile, responding with a suggestion of interest to fan her infatuation. He thrived on admiration, and he had no intention of altering this condition. Subtly, he nurtured that feeling in every female in the household, and they all responded. All except me.

I was in my fourteenth year, scarred by Fräulein Rosalia's death and its aftermath, and too withdrawn to pay him much heed. That did not correspond to his idea of a relationship with the opposite sex. He would not be ignored. Age meant nothing to him—I was a female, therefore to be conquered.

He embarked on this project with the skill of an expert.

I became uneasy under his continuous stare. He didn't look at me head-on, but from an angle, his face slightly averted. A stealthy look, full of meaning, as if we shared some sort of secret. The smile underscoring it was faintly suggestive, a kind of "you'll come around" smile, assured yet gentle. He scored the first point—he made me conscious of him.

"Does it embarrass you when I stare?" he asked me once, point-blank.

"Not at all," I answered much too quickly to disguise the truth.

He took his time replying, meanwhile observing me with interest.

"I'm glad," he said then, putting his arm around my shoulders. His other hand touched me under the chin and tilted my face up. "I like pretty things, and you, my dear niece, are pretty, very pretty indeed. Has anybody told you that?"

I shook my head and whispered, "No."

It was the truth. At home, no one ever commented on my looks. The only attention paid to me was at Mr. Chekreguin's school, and that I attributed solely to my dancing. This was a revelation.

"What a shame," he said. "When a young lady is lovely, she

should be complimented. And so I compliment you. Shall we be friends? Agreed?"

I nodded, flattered.

"Now go and take a look at yourself in the mirror," he called as I walked away. "Make sure you look at yourself," he repeated emphatically.

Haunted by his words I did—later that night. A hand mirror lay on my table amid piled-up books, tights and school papers, but it was too small to accommodate my whole face—either the top of my forehead or part of my chin would be missing. I threw the mirror down in disgust. Everyone was out except Irra. She was in Konstantin's room, no doubt trying to seduce him. I tiptoed across the center room, past sleeping Anatol and into Mother's bedroom.

Cold patches of moonlight fell through the lace curtains, tracing a shining design on the carpet. Otherwise the room was dark. I switched on the top light and crossed to one of the mirrored armoires against one wall. To my left, fitted between the windows, the mirror of Mother's dressing table also reflected me. I peered at myself from all angles, without getting any specific reaction.

In a dreamlike state, I untwisted my braid and let my hair fall loose around me. Then I unbuttoned my dress and stepped out of it.

The underwear I saw in the mirror was shabby and not too clean, and the stockings had long runs. The girl who wore this finery had pale beige skin, ash-blond hair, blue eyes—much bluer than I thought—regular features and a body that didn't show any visible defects. In my search for self-discovery, I studied myself intensely.

Who was I? Was I really pretty? Was there anything unusual about me? Would people notice me? Was he lying?

Seeking an answer, I stepped so close to the mirror that my

nose touched the cold surface of the glass, which didn't bring me any closer to a conclusion. The girl in the mirror looked painfully frustrated. Then she whirled gently and stopped in a graceful dance attitude. My heart leaped with joy. Now, that was pretty, very pretty! Slowly, I melted into another pose and, feeling a warm glow, without further ado picked up my dress and flew back into my room with noiseless ballet jumps.

To Irra's dismay, Konstantin was quite open about his interest in me. He treated me as a young woman and not as a child. When she objected, he fed her jealousy by telling her that in a couple of years I would put them all to shame, and she had better start improving herself. All this said with humor and charm. In the presence of others there was nothing in his attitude toward me that could have been considered improper.

When we happened to find ourselves alone, it was a different matter. An intimacy in his tone and manner suggested a special understanding between us, and his questions gently probed my private thoughts and feelings. There would be moments of silence when he would fix his eyes on me, and his hand would clasp mine so stealthily that I wouldn't realize it until I felt the warmth of his skin. It was very unsettling yet mesmerizing, and I would let him keep my hand.

I was doing very well at the Gymnasia for Young Girls, except in one subject. Algebra was anathema to me—a collection of unfathomable symbols and digits that my mind couldn't digest, and no amount of concentration and effort brought me closer to understanding those hieroglyphics.

Konstantin immediately volunteered to help with my homework. At first those evening sessions were conducted in my room, and then for the sake of quiet and privacy they were switched to his.

I would return from Mr. Chekreguin's lesson wondering if he would be waiting for me, and he always was. As soon as I entered the vestibule, I would hear him calling me from his room and I would go right in. He would help me with my coat and boots and then suggest that I relax for a while before starting to work.

The logs were always ablaze in the fireplace, casting trembling shadows on the walls and scenting the room with the pungent smell of burning pine. He would turn on the lamp on the carved desk held up by four Napoleonic lion claws, and I would curl up on the green velvet sofa and gaze into the fire, aware every moment of his presence. We would keep silent and then I would bring out my homework, and settling down at the desk, side by side, we would begin the exploration of mathematics. I am sorry to say that it didn't help me very much. The mere sight of an algebraic problem was still enough to befuddle me. Konstantin was very patient, explaining each problem in simple terms and treating it all lightheartedly to ease my tension.

"Don't be desolate," he would say, "everyone has his 'bête noir.' I have a notion that your life will not depend on algebra."

And his arm would curl around my shoulders, or he would give my cheek a light peck, but his eyes weren't laughing—they looked straight into me. Our intimacy grew.

It was the day before the quarterly exams. One of the three problems marked in my book would be given us the next morning and we would have to solve it in fifteen minutes. I couldn't make head or tail out of any of them. Konstantin met the challenge. Knowing that I had a good memory, he himself solved the problem, and then made me memorize the progression of all three. In no time at all I could rattle them off from beginning to end.

A weight fell off my shoulders, and I relaxed.

"Now they can't trip you up," he said, grinning. "You see, there is always a way out of anything." Suddenly serious, he took my hand, turned it palm upward and pressed his mouth to it in a long kiss.

A sensation like an electric shock shot up my arm and through me. When he let go of my hand, I was totally flustered.

The smile returned to his face. Under his amused gaze, I collected my homework, not knowing where to look, and disturbed by a premonition of something more about to happen.

I muttered a good night and was on my way out when he called my name. I turned and watched him come toward me with slow, confident step. His hands cupped my face, raising it up, and his lips came down on mine, brushing them lightly, feeling them out, and then taking them over in an all-consuming sensuality.

A quiver ran down my spine, the pit of my stomach dropped, and I was dissolving in a whirlpool of hitherto unknown heat. He held me in this kiss of full possession for what seemed hours. When he released me, I was trembling.

He backed away. I must have looked as though I had been struck dumb.

"Oh, I see," he said. "So it's the first time. Good! Now I will never be forgotten."

Again, he took my face in his hands and planted a tender kiss on my forehead.

"Good luck with the exams," he whispered.

I may not have gained much in algebra, but I certainly had the door thrown open to sex.

44

One leg held up high like a branch springing upward from the trunk of the body; it is kept in balance by the other leg, the foot firmly gripping the ground. Muscles taut, knees straight, toes pointed. The upthrust leg begins to glide in the air around the torso, from the side to the front, and the arms move into a new position. A momentary pause. Now the torso is turning away from the floating leg until the leg is in back of the body in an arabesque that arches the torso. The body is now slowly pivoting around, once, twice; the leg on the ground begins to tire, the ankle shakes. . . .

It goes on and on—adagio—a grueling exercise in muscle control and stamina.

Nine girls are standing in the center of the studio, facing the mirror. Tonight they are trying especially hard, because of a man sitting on the bench by the mirror. Before the lesson he was introduced to the class by Mr. Chekreguin. He is the famous Semenov, a dancer from the Maryinsky, who, it is said, can jump as high as Nijinsky, and is, rumor has it, as mean as a cobra.

"Second group!" commands Mr. Chekreguin, and we retire to the barre, letting eight other girls step forward and go through the same exercises.

One of the girls loses her balance on the first turn, and Mr. Chekreguin yells, "Hold in your side! How do you expect to stay up if you are as wobbly as jelly? Tighten up!"

No reaction from Semenov. His expression is that of a fish,

and his watery eyes watch the girls sleepily. If it weren't for an intermittent crossing and uncrossing of his legs, one might suppose him to be either asleep or doped. He is slight, with nondescript features and mousy hair.

I was leaning on the barre, trying to imagine what he looked like in a costume, on the stage, when the door of the studio opened and the receptionist, carefully circling around the dancers, tiptoed over to Mr. Chekreguin. She whispered in his ear, and he nodded and waved her away.

He let the girls finish their turn, and when our group moved forward for the next exercise, he beckoned me to approach him.

"Your mother is here," he said. "She wants you. She says it's important. So go! You're excused."

In the hall, outside the studio, Mother was pacing the floor. Anxiety throbbed in her every move; she clasped and unclasped her hands, chewed at her lips.

"Get dressed," she ordered brusquely. "We have to go somewhere. There is no time to lose."

"Go where?" I asked, my only desire being to return to the studio.

"I'll explain later. I told you there is no time to lose. Get dressed. Hurry." And she pushed me toward the dressing room.

No visitors were allowed in the dressing room, so she had to wait for me in the hall.

I didn't rush. I was angry at being interrupted. Drying myself with deliberate slowness, I wondered what kind of emergency could have prompted this unprecedented behavior and if it wasn't just an outburst of emotionalism caused by something very minor. She had never before bothered about Mr. Chekreguin's school on any count; in fact, I was not sure if she had ever asked me for the address. And now . . . all of a sudden . . . God, I hope it isn't something about Father!

That thought put high speed into my dressing, and I ran out to the hall. She stood tapping her foot.

"Anything wrong with Father?" I called before reaching her.

"No, no," she answered impatiently. "Are you ready?"

"Yes," I said, relieved, throwing a shawl around my head.

She led me to the nearest tram stop, and we waited with the throng until we managed to squeeze ourselves into one of the overcrowded cars. At the end of Nevsky Prospekt, by the railroad station, we pushed our way out, and started walking up one of the side streets to a part of town I didn't know. We walked for blocks. It began to snow. Through the thickening white curtain I could see we were in a poor section of the city, its two- or three-story houses badly dilapidated.

"Where are we going?" I asked, keeping in step with her hurried walk.

She looked straight ahead, silent. I was surprised to see that she was wearing her oldest coat, one that had hung unused in the closet for years.

I repeated my question.

"We are going to Stepan's house," she said. "Something went wrong. I don't know what he did, but the Cheka is after him. . . ."

I was startled. . . . The Cheka, the Russian Gestapo of these years . . .

"He had to escape, to run," she went on nervously, "but he came by to tell me that he has hidden quite a bit of money between the logs in his kitchen and that he wouldn't be able to retrieve it all. . . . He said that I should go and take what's left."

Her steps slowed down. "We're almost there," she said. "I don't think the house is being watched. Anyway no one would suspect a girl. There are three youngsters living on the second floor, so you might be one of them. Thank God for this snow-fall . . . it makes it easier. . . ." She stopped. "Here we are. See that house across the street? I have the keys to the kitchen. It's the first door to the left under the archway."

She forced the key into my hand.

"I don't want to go, Mother."

"Nonsense. It's perfectly safe." She spoke irritably. "I would do it myself but they know me in that house. . . . Here is a box of matches . . . use them when you get in. . . . The logs are in two sections on the far side of the kitchen."

"I don't want to go!"

She grabbed me by the shoulders and shook me. "Stop that! Go, do you hear! I told you there's nothing to be afraid of." She pulled me across the street. "I will be right here, by the archway, watching. If anything suspicious happens, I'll get you right out. Go on!" And she pushed me forward.

Key in hand, I walked under the archway in obedience to the force of her will. The door opened easily and I stepped into the darkness of the kitchen. I dropped the key into my pocket and, clutching the matches, edged myself along the right wall. I immediately bumped into something which my hands discovered to be a table. I lit a match and caught the outline of a row of logs ahead of me. The match went out. I moved forward in the darkness, feeling my way toward my objective until my fingers touched the rough surface of the bark. Heart pounding and ears attuned to the smallest creak, I let my fingers inspect one log after another, dipping into the crevices between them, going systematically from right to left. There was nothing. Splinters pricked my skin, but I kept go-ing to the left, examining every irregularity in the logs. My shoulder bumped into something heavy . . . and movable. As I bumped it, this object swung away and then returned, hitting me on the shoulder again. Quickly, I pulled a match from the matchbox and lit it. The tiny flame searched for the object and found it.

A boot . . . no, two boots, in the air . . . I raised the match . . . the flickering light climbed up. . . . Legs . . . and a torso . . . and limp arms . . .

The match was burning my fingers, but, galvanized with horror, I kept raising my hand and my eyes.

Stepan's body was hanging from the beam by a rope looped around his neck. His head was drooping forward and his dead glassy eyes were looking down at me.

The match went out.

I swallowed so much air that I strangled, and then, reeling and banging into the walls, groped my way toward the door and out.

45

Mother told me later that I ran past her into the snowstorm waving my arms like some crazed bird, and that it took her a good many blocks to catch up with me and pin me to a wall. In a paroxysm of hysteria, I must have thrown my head far back for I remember gulping down the snow that was falling into my open mouth. And I remember Mother's face above me, trying to quiet me down.

She took the whole event stoically, after extracting from me a solemn promise never to mention what had happened to anyone. Eventually, Irra and Tatiana were let in on the secret, but they, too, had to swear on the Bible that they would never divulge it to a soul. Father, of course, had no inkling of it.

There was no sleep for me that night. In the morning, when Father and I met at breakfast, he noticed my pallor and nervousness, and I had to call on all my strength to keep to my promise.

The mystery of Stepan's death was never solved because no one was foolish enough to make inquiries and associate himself with what might have been a shady business. There were several possible explanations: he might have been ambushed by the Cheka and hanged himself in fear of what was in store for him; he might have been observed while he was collecting his money, robbed, killed and then strung up to make it look like suicide. That, too, could have been done by the Cheka, as well as by ordinary bandits.

Immediately after Stepan's death, there was a purge of the speculators. Hordes of them were arrested and, from what we heard, ruthlessly eliminated. It seemed probable that Stepan had been a victim of that policy.

Thus ended the saga of Stepan. Though I hated him, I felt sorry for him and I was shaken by his death. The picture of his rag-doll body hanging from the rope stayed with me for months, and I had to sleep with my light on.

With the suppression of the black market, conditions worsened, and for a while we had to depend entirely on government rations. Most of the speculators who escaped the purge went underground, operating so secretly that only a few totally dependable old clients had access to them. This condition didn't last very long, however. Need and greed give birth to ideas and make people take chances. Soon the black market was reborn, this time under the legal guise of barter. The government, having made its kill, allowed it to operate, and soon open markets were being constructed all over the city. They contained rows of stalls with awnings over them to protect the merchandise and the vendors, who exchanged their produce for such items as the purchaser had to offer. Actually, the most successful deals resulted when money was passed under the counter, a porcelain cup or a piece of cloth placed on top of the counter as part payment or only as a blind.

Intermittently, the markets were raided by the militia, and people caught handling money were thrown in jail. But as soon as they were let out, they went right back to their trading.

Sundays were the best days to get results. Mother would bring out Anatol's old perambulator and fill it with whatever hadn't been confiscated. There were linen sheets and napkins, a lot of table silver, Dresden statuettes and lace shawls, and feather boas and other remnants of past glory. She always made me come with her. The nearest market was in an empty lot across the alley from the church where I had gone for the service of the "Four Gospels." We would wheel the perambulator there early in the morning. It was an incongruous sight: on one side of the alley people piously crossing themselves as they climbed the church steps for morning Mass, the church bells ringing; on the other side, a milling crowd, shouting, swearing, haggling. No thought of God or manners here.

We would circle the periphery of the market pretending indifference, but hoping that someone would stop us to inspect our merchandise. Many did. There were still people who had money. They would stop us and finger our wares and make ridiculous offers, and it took hours before we would make a decent sale. Linens were the best sellers. Luxury items were much harder to dispose of.

Armed with currency, we would wheel the perambulator inside the market and approach a stall. Mother would start a low-voiced negotiation with the merchant, trying to get him to take only part payment in money and the rest in whatever he fancied in the perambulator. The sense of danger was ever-present. The militia stood around, looking on lethargically, but one could never predict when they would get bored and start a raid just to liven things up. Mother was caught a couple of times, but, flashing her eyes and her smiles, she laughed her way out of it.

If we were lucky, we would return home with some salt pork, cabbage, potatoes, groats and, possibly, a few eggs, our precious acquisitions hidden under the remaining merchandise in the perambulator. They would have to last us till the following Sunday; it was not wise to be seen at the market too often.

Besides the black market, there was a flowering in other fields; small theatres and concert halls were beginning to come to life. They presented performances that were part recital, part vaudeville—with comedians, singers, jugglers, dancers, concert pianists all flung together in one show. Some theatres had single performances, others operated on a weekly basis. The pay was either in money or in produce, and there was no shortage of available talent, for everyone was eager to earn extra money or food. Performers called these slapped-together entertainments "halturas." The word had neither root nor meaning, but it caught on, stuck and entered the vocabulary. Father's theatre, confiscated a long time ago and managed now by some man who had "connections," also followed the vogue for presenting "halturas."

But the most striking development was the opening of a movie house on Nevsky Prospekt near Nikolayevsky Street. A gaudy marquee advertised American pictures, and the first attraction featured an actress named Pola Negri. Lines to the box office would form early in the morning, though the movie didn't begin until seven at night, and the flow of people never stopped.

How I yearned to see it! I had never seen a movie. But I had to wait until I had money for the ticket and a Sunday free of the black market.

Semenov came back twice to Mr. Chekreguin's school, stirring up the same anxiety and excitement among the pupils as the first time. He watched class as sleepily as before, not looking at anyone in particular.

On his second visit, when the class was over and we curtsied and scrambled out of the studio, Mr. Chekreguin and Semenov remained behind.

I changed into my street clothes, wrapped newspaper around my feet (good insulation against the cold) and pulled on my boots. All bundled up, I was about to walk out the door when the receptionist came running after me.

"Come back," she said. "Mr. Chekreguin wants to see you in the studio right away."

Boots were not allowed in the classrooms, and I sat down on a bench in the hall, took them off and peeled off the newspaper. I had no other shoes to put on to hide the holes in my stockings, and I walked back in my stocking feet, wondering what it was all about, and ashamed of the patches of bare skin around my toes.

Mr. Chekreguin and Semenov were still in the same place, sitting on the bench by the mirror.

"Come here, dearie," called Mr. Chekreguin. "I have something to tell you."

I approached, curling my toes to make the holes less noticeable.

"You have a big surprise coming," said Mr. Chekreguin, a big grin spreading over his face. "Mr. Semenov likes you very much. He wants you to dance with him—to be his partner in a haltura three weeks from now."

I was struck dumb.

Semenov lifted his eyes and looked at me without any sign of interest. I might as well have been a door, or a cucumber.

"And so," Mr. Chekreguin continued, "tomorrow, after class, he'll begin rehearsing you in the number you will dance."

I was standing before them, my mind gone blank.

Semenov's eyes dropped to my feet, and with a weary gesture he pointed to my toes.

"Then you'll be able to buy a new pair of stockings," he said with undisguised sadism.

46

The great Semenov and I—a pupil in a private school! Why did he choose me? Why not a dancer from the Maryinsky? Was I that good? Or were there other reasons?

The reasons were simple. If he had danced alone, he would have had to exert himself—men's variations are usually very difficult but short. One variation would not have been enough. He would have had to combine at least two variations, or else create a new number. With a partner, he could present an easy old number, divide the dancing burden, and then grab the glory with a few sensational leaps. However, if his partner was a dancer from the Maryinsky, he would have the unpleasant obligation of splitting his salary with her. In my case, both problems were solved; apparently I was a good enough dancer to share the stage with him—my extreme youth would predispose the audience in my favor—and he could pay me a pittance. Also, it created the illusion of generosity—the great Semenov giving a youngster a chance.

I resolved not to tell anyone at home about it. The time element helped me to this decision: The performance was scheduled for about the same time as Mr. Chekreguin's usual lesson, so no one needed to know where I was. And if it was destined to be a disaster, I could swallow the bitterness of failure in private without exposing myself to ridicule.

We were to dance to the music of Kreisler's "Liebesfreude." At rehearsals, Semenov drilled me with all the delicacy of a platoon sergeant. He was cold, condescending—no smile, no encouragement. Again and again fear and uncertainty almost drove me to beg off, and I had to steel myself to overcome that impulse. While we rehearsed, Semenov barely marked his steps, using his full strength only for the lifts so that I could get used to them. (Can't drop her yet—she might be valuable.)

In the second week, he sent me to an old lady who had a collection of ballet costumes (probably lifted from the Maryinsky wardrobe), and she outfitted me very prettily. A pink tutu, the top layer embroidered with pink and pale green sequins, a wine-colored bodice and a garland of pink flowers to hold my hair on top of my head in a coronet. She also gave me a pair of pink silk tights, something I had never worn before; my working tights were made of cotton. I had to supply my own ballet shoes.

Semenov and I were driven to the performance in a sleigh by the man in charge of the theatre. Dressed and waiting in the wings while a singer on stage was bellowing something from *The Merry Widow*, I could literally hear my heart pound against my bodice. So loud was the hammering that I fully expected my heart to drum a hole through the bodice and fall out. My ankles shook, my shoes were suddenly too small, my breath uneven, and all of me seemed turned to wood. I got up on my toes and couldn't feel them. Semenov was standing behind me, cool as a frozen fish.

The piano struck the opening chord.

My first move was a grand jeté (a big leap) across the stage into the opposite wing, where I waited while Semenov followed me with the same movement. The step was identical, but it came out quite differently; he rose into the air and glided through it arrogantly, held up by an invisible force, and the audience broke out into spontaneous applause. After this introduction, we ran out on the stage and danced together, and, near the finish, I fell on one knee and remained in that pose while he stepped forward and knocked the audience cold with his prowess. At the end he ran off the stage carrying me on his shoulder.

I was allowed to take a bow alone, and received a nice hand, and then he stepped out to face an ovation.

Back in the dressing room, still dazed, I couldn't believe that it was over—finished. So short, so fleeting. I tried to recapture the feeling of dancing on the stage, but it eluded me. The last half-hour had already passed into the cosmos of illusion as does everything that lies behind us.

It was time to get out of costume. I began the descent to earth by pulling the hairpins, one by one, out of my coiffure and laying them in rows on the dressing table. And I saw that the room was dingy, its walls marred by graffiti, and that the mirror was nothing but a big chip without a frame, and that the dressing room table was a kitchen table scarred by use. All this had escaped me before.

There was a knock on the door, and Semenov walked in. He gave me an imitation of a smile, placed some money on the dressing table next to my hairpins and put his hand on my naked shoulder. He kept it there for some time, looking at my reflection in the mirror, and then jerked his hand away.

"Nice going," he said, "very nice. We might do it again someday." He left without saying good-bye.

I was driven home alone. From the vestibule, I could see that a card game was going on in Konstantin's room. The four of them—he, Mother and the two witches—were so absorbed in the game that they neither heard nor saw me pass their door. I walked into my room, peeled off enough money for a ticket to the American movie with Pola Negri, hid it in my school satchel, and walked back to Konstantin's room with the rest of my pay in my hand. It was an hour later than my usual return from Mr. Chekreguin's school, but apparently nobody gave it a thought.

I came to the card table, and put the money down in front of Mother. She stared at it, mystified, and then lifted her head, her eyes round with bewilderment. The other heads followed suit.

"Where did you get it?" she asked. God only knows what thoughts flew through her head.

"I earned it," I said. "Tonight, I danced with Semenov and got paid for it."

The effect was electrifying. They all seemed to have lost the power of speech.

"Yes, I did," I reiterated, a sense of triumph welling up in me. "You can ask Mr. Chekreguin."

"You . . . you . . . danced with Semenov?" I thought Mother was going to faint.

"I did," I repeated. "What's more, he said we may do it again."

And I walked away, leaving them to digest this new twist of my fate.

47

Father congratulated me on my dancing adventure. He seemed pleased and proud. He put his hands on my shoulders and said, "We must think of Fräulein Rosalia. It is she who made it possible."

I didn't need to be reminded of Fräulein Rosalia, but it made me happy that his thoughts, too, had turned to her.

Konstantin, also, once he recovered from the initial shock, was pleased.

"Atta girl!" he roared delightedly. "I told you you would show them all, didn't I? And no more worries about algebra. Who cares!"

And he kissed my hand, openly, in front of the others, with a gallantry that positively screamed for a plumed hat.

Mother was reluctant to reveal her true feelings—or maybe they were so complex that she couldn't unravel them herself. I think this unforeseen twist threw her off balance. She treated me with new respect yet with a certain apprehension, on the alert to any trick I might pull next. It was not easy for a woman of her temperament to accept the possibility that Fräulein Rosalia might have been right when she invested in me, and even harder to admit that even at this early stage I was capable of bringing in a dividend on that investment. Mother didn't relish being proved wrong. Moreover, she must have sensed that her maternal grip on me had loosened a few more notches. At any rate, if she took any pride in my accomplishment, she did not show it. She concentrated on how the feat had come about, and her comment was: "Well, that's good. You should be happy, but don't get a swelled head."

I was so eager to see Pola Negri, whose sultry countenance was displayed on several posters outside the theatre, that I cheated on Mr. Chekreguin. I said I was ill, skipped a lesson and went to the movie.

What unfolded on the screen floated me into reveries far beyond those induced by reading *Little Women*. At the beginning Miss Negri played a nurse whose inner fire contrasted with the virginity of her white uniform. After a romantic involvement and a series of hot love scenes, she was transformed into a glamorous baroness dripping with furs and jewels. The decor, from the spotlessly hygienic hospital to the baronial castle overrun by liveried lackeys and surrounded by grandiose parks, meadows and lakes, was something I had never dreamed of. Was it true, or all cardboard? At any rate, Pola was real—I knew it—the personification of everything beautiful, loved, cared for—and clean! We were limited to one bath a week, washing daily only our hands and faces, which left a definite line of demarcation at wrists and neck where a slightly grayer skin began. And lice were still with us, stubbornly resisting extinction. Pola Negri bathed in a marble tub, attended by maidens, amid plants and flowers, in a room more elaborate than any living room I'd ever seen, and for nights afterward I dreamed of soaking in such a bath.

Semenov asked for me again. We were to repeat the same "Liebesfreude" in some remote concert hall, far-off on Vasily Island, and this time it was a disaster. The stage was a square platform open to the audience on three sides, thereby eliminating the effect of flying in and out of the wings, and making the whole dance look rather silly. The pianist added to our misery, hitting the wrong notes and playing in erratic tempi, as if his hands were suffering periodic seizures. At the end, running off with me on his shoulders, Semenov tripped on the exposed steps, somewhat hampering the illusion of ethereal flight.

He was furious with the management, with the pianist and with me—blaming me for failing to cover up the rough spots, though for the life of me I couldn't figure out what I could have done. Sadists need a scapegoat and I was it.

No one in the family witnessed this shambles, and I never told them about it. And in my heart, I carried the conviction that my partnership with Semenov was over.

The world of dance is small and gossipy. Within that circle everyone knows what happens, where, to whom and how. My dancing with Semenov didn't pass unnoticed. Nina told me that news of it had reached Theatre School and that considerable annoyance was felt there about the "private" upstart who had stolen a little thunder from the chosen. When they discovered that Nina knew me, she was deluged with questions. Was I dark? Blond? Tall or short? Did I really dance well? I emerged from the limbo of invisible private pupils, and became a "somebody."

I was wrong about Semenov. In less than a month he called me for the third time. This time the pay was to be in produce—thirty pounds of flour and two pounds of salt. At least, that was my share. Fearing that it might be another fiasco, I didn't tell anyone about it. To my surprise, we found ourselves in a real theatre, small, but with all the attributes—backdrop, wings, footlights and gels, even a suggestion of a decor that hung overhead and down the wings like wet moss, and a well-tuned piano in the pit. The lights went down, a young man attacked the piano with skill and verve, and, caught up in his enthusiasm, we ran out on the stage to give the best performance we had ever given. Semenov was superb, and the audience went wild.

236

Semenov was so pleased that he hooked his arm in mine and walked with me to my dressing room.

"Not bad, not bad at all," he kept repeating.

Inside the dressing room, he turned me around to face him, and his hand went to my shoulder and stroked it.

"I think I'll take you to my house for supper," he said, and his hand slid into my bodice and gripped my breast.

Jolted, I grabbed his hand, pushed it away and jumped back.

The great Semenov, the idol of the multitudes, repulsed! He didn't take kindly to it. Hatred shriveled up his face, his eyes narrowed and he sputtered his fury with the ferocity of a striking snake.

"Who the hell do you think you are?" He spat out his words, each syllable a slap. "A stupid kid from a private school. How dare you push me! You little tramp . . . I can see right through you! You should be grateful for what I've done for you. You should be glad I'm even willing to touch you! . . . Shit! Oh, pardon me, your highness!"

He bowed in mockery and stalked out of the room.

The turnabout was so sudden that I didn't immediately grasp what had happened. An evening of brilliance had abruptly ended in a catastrophe.

Crestfallen, I dropped into my chair. Mechanically, I took off my makeup, changed into my street clothes and, feeling doped, went out to look for the man who had driven us to the performance. I was informed that he had left, taking Mr. Semenov home, and would not be back again. On the stage, the last act of the evening was taking curtain calls to dwindling applause, and I could hear the audience shuffling out.

Finished—ended—the partnership was broken beyond repair. What's more I had acquired a powerful enemy.

I returned to my dressing room. The sack of flour and the

bag of salt were on the floor, by the wall. How was I to get home with this load of staples, plus my tutu, the satchel with the rest of the costume, and the shoebox filled with makeup?

And—no money.

A stage hand came to my rescue. He brought two empty burlap sacks, stuffed my paraphernalia into them, and tied them with a rope, looping a facsimile of a handle on top of each sack. He helped me to the street, and left me there to my own devices.

I stuck my hands into the looped handles and started for home through dark and empty streets, dragging the two sacks. I had to stop often to give my arms a rest, and to straighten my back. Weary and humiliated, I plodded along, my brain gradually clearing in the cold air, and introducing another painful disturbance—self-doubt.

So that was the reason for his picking me out . . . not my dancing. Am I deluded in thinking I can dance? What am I striving for? Have I any talent?

The light was on in Konstantin's room when I got home, and leaving the sacks on the floor of the vestibule, I walked right in. He was sitting in an armchair, reading.

"You're very late," he said, lifting his eyes from the book. "Where have you been? We've been wondering." A sly smile crossed his face, "Don't tell me you have sneaked another haltura without letting us know."

I didn't answer. I climbed up on his lap, threw my arms around him and hid my face in the shelter of his neck.

"What is it?" he asked, stroking my hair.

Trying to keep calm and with my face still hidden, I whispered the story.

He sighed. "Remember, I told you that you were pretty? And this kind of thing happens to pretty girls. You must be prepared for it, and not get hurt by it, because, believe me, it will happen again. Too bad he was so coarse. And forget your doubts about your dancing. The man is much too shrewd to jeopardize his reputation with a poor partner."

His hand was still stroking my hair. I pulled my head out and lifted my face to him.

"Kiss me, please," I said.

He did—softly, on the lips, with just enough fervor to help me regain some of my lost self-importance.

48

Konstantin took it upon himself to tell Mother about the incident, and she exploded in mother-hen indignation. There was also another angle to it: a female had been insulted and Mother was all female. She was going to kill him—she swore it—and then, having discarded that idea, she adopted a different attitude. Never mind the bum! Who needs him! She, who had never taken my dancing seriously, now turned to the opposite extreme.

Despite Konstantin's words, I was still haunted by spells of self-doubt. In class, anxious for signs of praise and confirmation, I watched Mr. Chekreguin's reaction to me more than I watched myself in the mirror. He noticed it.

"Hey, why are you looking at me?" he said. "Look at yourself. I'll tell you when you're wrong." And gradually I turned my concentration back upon myself.

On Sundays, we were still pushing the perambulator to market, but our merchandise was dwindling. Mother would part only with things we didn't need ourselves, and they were about exhausted. One day she exhumed six wine and six liqueur glasses of the famous gold and crystal set that had been stashed away in a crate behind the stove. Laid out neatly on a piece of green velvet that covered the less spectacular merchandise, the gold and crystal sparkled brightly, attracting a lot of attention. But there were no bidders. People would stop, glance at them and walk away. Because of the ever-present militia, they were afraid to buy objects of luxury that had no place in the People's Republic. And besides, what would one do with them? A towel, a coffee cup, that was different.

One brave soul came up, stared at the glasses, picked one up, examined it—and bought the piece of green velvet. The glasses remained, lying on top of several pairs of lace underpants.

The green velvet transaction caught the attention of a militiaman. He approached us and began questioning Mother. Had the glasses been stolen from a museum or a palace? How had they come into our possession? Nothing could persuade him that we were the rightful owners.

"Look," Mother blazed. "Look, you fool, here are my initials, on the side of the glass! They belong to me. . . . I've had them for years!" Defiantly, she stuck the glass under his nose.

"Now, you shut up, comrade!" he flared up too. "Hold on to that glass and come with me. We'll find out the truth." He grabbed her by the arm and started pulling her away, both of them yelling.

The crowd joined in, registering a few loud comments more for participation than to object, since it was well known that one didn't argue with the militiamen.

"Where are you taking her?" I screamed, trying to be heard over the hubbub.

"To jail, girl . . . to jail!"

My last glimpse, before they rounded the corner of the church, was of Mother hitting him repeatedly with her free hand.

Quickly, I packed the underpants between the glasses to reduce the chance of breakage, and made for home.

What jail could it be? The city was full of jails, and the fact that it was Sunday complicated matters. It took Father until late afternoon to locate her. Immediately, Irra was commandeered to take Mother some food, but she returned with her basket full, because she had arrived five minutes past the time for such deliveries, and the jail was about to be locked for the night. There was nothing to be done till morning, and then Father pulled all the strings available to him. Because of his position, he was able to get in touch with certain authorities and explain the origin of the glasses; they, in turn, brought pressure to bear on those directly in charge. By next nightfall, Mother was returned to Father's hands.

She was sizzling angry, not only with the militiamen and the regime but with us. It was for our sake that she was selling her beloved goods in the marketplace, and it was because of us that she had been thrown into a cell with thieves and whores. Father suggested that a little restraint might have helped, but she was too full of her own martyrdom to listen. What annoyed her most was that the militiaman had kept the crystal glass. "Breaks up the set," she said angrily. "Hope he drowns."

For a time we abandoned our excursions to the market, and when we resumed them, that particular militiaman was gone. Nonetheless, Mother kept herself in hand, and we never again peddled anything that would invite special attention. The glasses went back into their crate behind the stove.

During Stepan's reign, Aunt Eugenia, Mother's half-sister,

and Uncle Armin would invent excuses for not visiting us. Now they reappeared. Aunt Eugenia considered Mother a Jezebel, and tolerated her only because of the ties of blood, and for Anatol's sake and mine. They lived quite comfortably, and it was well known that Uncle Armin had not only his finger but his whole wrist in the black market—which he vigorously denied. Somehow, because of his German craftiness and a web of connections with the "upper" world, he sailed through all the purges.

They were a lonely couple, basically good, childless, with only a cat to love. One day they came to ask a favor. They wanted to "borrow" Anatol. A dacha, right by the sea, had been given them for the summer, and it would do the little fellow a lot of good to have some fresh air. They promised to give him care and love—which no one doubted—and it was agreed in a family council that they could take him right after Easter.

The skies were clearing, and spring was back again, bringing on its wings the most extraordinary event.

It was a bombshell! No one in his wildest dreams could have envisaged it. For two hundred years, Theatre School had adhered to its ironclad rule of keeping out everyone except those children carefully chosen at the age of nine who grew up to become the select group admitted to the Maryinsky. Now . . . all of a sudden . . .

It was inconceivable that such a reform would ever come

to pass, but there it was, on paper, a proclamation distributed among all the private dancing schools in the land. The new regime had looked into the matter, and come to the conclusion that the ancient system was a carry-over from the capitalistic era, that it created a privileged class, and that in the People's Republic everyone had to be given an equal chance. Hence, the old rule had been abolished and a new rule inaugurated.

From now on, every year, examinations for private pupils would be held at Theatre School and the Bolshoi School in Moscow, and those approved by a high-echelon professional jury would be admitted to a newly created evening course. At the end of a probation period (varying with the age of each pupil), those whose ability had been confirmed would join the regular ranks, thereby automatically becoming eligible for the stages of the two great theatres.

I couldn't believe it! I felt fate had snapped her fingers to produce this miracle especially for me. Delirious with joy, I whirled around my room, singing and dancing, fantasizing, bowing to a nonexistent audience, and generally behaving like a loon.

"Thank you, thank you," I chanted, "thank you, whoever you are . . . and thank you, Fräulein Rosalia—you must have had a hand in it!"

More soberly, the family was cautious in expressing its feelings. None of them had ever seen me dance, and having no clue as to my ability beyond Semenov's short-lived interest, they took a skeptical view, warning me of the possibility of rejection. I would have none of it.

Examinations at the Bolshoi were scheduled for late spring, a month away, and at Theatre School for early fall. Naturally, Theatre School was my aim.

A long application requiring endless information had to be

filled out, and Father and I completed it with dispatch: age, sex, hair color, education, state of health, how many years of training, where and with whom, if living with the family, how many were in the household, and many other superfluous questions. Father thought it silly, but it didn't bother me. I would have enumerated the cavities in my teeth if it had been necessary.

Meanwhile, the day of Nina's graduation was upon us. She had promised that I could go to the performance with Aunt Pauline (each graduate was given two tickets), and she had kept her promise. I spent days before the event trying to assemble an outfit suitable for the great occasion. I dearly wanted to look grown-up and sophisticated, but my wardrobe didn't lend itself to such an impression. Invention was required. In the end, I settled on a brown skirt too short for my purpose, but I took care of that deficiency by pulling it down and pinning it around my hips with two safety pins. The gap where the hooks wouldn't meet was camouflaged by a long sweater borrowed from Tatiana, who was slight in build. I tied my hair in a ponytail, stuck a sprig of artificial lilac in the ribbon and, as a final touch, threw around my neck a pink chiffon scarf that I lifted from the perambulator. I felt smashing—a real femme fatale, like Pola Negri.

Attired in this alluring outfit, and keeping close to Aunt Pauline, I entered the auditorium of the Maryinsky Theatre. Aunt Pauline was in a high state of nervousness, walking as if her path were strewn with eggs, her hands tearing at the program. She had reduced it to shreds even before the performance began. Her eyebrows were painted higher than usual and wisps of hair were falling out of her coiffure.

And I walked in with a new assurance. My awe for this temple of high art had not diminished, but my despair was gone. I already considered myself a part of this establishment.

The atmosphere was festive. Everything seemed more brilliant than usual—the crystal chandeliers, the gold cupids floating on the façades of the boxes, the polished red wood—and the air was charged with great expectation. This night was the crowning glory for the youngsters who had spent nine years in hard study.

The theatre was filled with the families of the pupils, dignitaries from all branches of the arts, and many government officials, including the one-eyed sailor who was credited with playing an important role in turning the navy to the revolutionary side. He sat in the front row, conspicuous in his sailor hat tilted over his black patch. Many a mother's heart felt apprehensive. Would he choose a girl? God, don't let it be mine! He was well known and feared for his ruthlessness.

The audience buzzed, the orchestra tuned up, and presently the chandeliers faded, silencing the chatter. The black and gold curtain parted to reveal an empty stage backed by folds of blue velvet, the conductor lifted his baton, and the performance began.

It was a conglomeration of pas de deux, variations, character dances and other ballet excerpts. Dressed in splendid costumes belonging to real stars, the students came out to perform their assigned dances. It was astonishing to see how much they varied in talent. Some danced with classroom precision, like little robots, others substituted temperament for ability, some were tense and apprehensive; only two or three exhibited the essentials: fluidity, assurance, beautiful body line and a sound technique. The performance was proving the wisdom of the new rule—not all the chosen ones were of superior mettle. A lot of equal or superior talent had been overlooked in the private schools.

I glanced at Aunt Pauline. Her face was frozen in frustration, and rightly so. Nina, though adequate, had not given any indication of extra endowment.

Good or bad, they all received ovations. I applauded till my hands hurt, and when, at the curtain calls, we all surged toward the footlights, my safety pins unsnapped, and I felt my skirt sliding down my hips. I didn't care. I was rushing toward the footlights that one day would be lighting me. Let the skirt fall.

50

Fate likes to play with people as a cat plays with a mouse—catch it, release it and snap it up again.

A week after Nina's graduation, my application for the Theatre School exam was rejected.

The reason for it was absurd. Under the category of "State of Health," we had, in all honesty, mentioned that at the age of six I had had a mild siege of TB which had left a scar on my right lung. I emphasized that I had never suffered any recurrence, that I was completely healed, and that the experience had never hampered me in dancing or any other form of physical activity. Nevertheless, it served as a pretext for turning me down. The die-hards of the old tradition weren't at all pleased with the new rule and were seizing every opportunity to turn down as many applicants as possible.

Father tried to break the news gently, but it didn't work. I was inconsolable; the old despair returned. Father, too, was indignant at the injustice.

"Please don't weep," he said. "We won't back down. It is unfair, and we have to find a solution."

With my application in his hand, he was pacing the room, his anger simmering and his mind working at high speed. Then he stopped in front of me.

"Young lady," he said, "go and pack. You are going to Moscow for the exam at the Bolshoi. This time we will leave out any mention of the lung scar. But even if we put it in, they would not dare refuse the man who will deliver the application."

The man he had in mind was Vladimir Mayakovsky, the great revolutionary poet and his friend. Father had helped him through the lean years of the Czarist regime, when Mayakovsky's poetry was suppressed and he himself stood in constant danger of imprisonment for his political views. Now Mayakovsky was revered, almost idolized, not only as a great poet, but as a hero who had never wavered from his ideals and, it was said, "had never lowered his voice before anyone."

Correspondence flew back and forth, everything went according to plan, and in due time, in mid-May, I was on a train heading for Moscow.

In an unprecedented demonstration of unity, the whole family came to see me off. Father alone looked cheerful—the rest wore dour expressions. I suspect they felt sorry for the star-crazy youngster.

The train was packed. People were squeezed in like sardines in a can, only with less order. Double bunks extended from the windows toward the center of the car, leaving a narrow aisle where late-comers squatted on the floor, shoulder to shoulder, crouched over their duffel bags or battered suitcases. I was lucky to find a space on an upper bunk, between a soldier and a cheerful woman in a bright kerchief who was holding on to a basket of radishes. Of necessity, our feet dangled down, which caused violent objections from those below us, but after a colorful exchange of the Russian equivalents of four-letter words, foot-dangling was declared unavoidable, and a truce followed.

Ordinarily, a train trip to Moscow should take overnight, but that timetable had long ago passed into myth. A delay of three to five hours, or even more, was to be expected.

The train crawled. It jarred to a stop in the middle of open fields, or on bridges, or in the thick of forests, presumably because of an overheated engine, or an obstacle on the tracks, or to let the engineer have a breath of fresh air and a smoke.

The passengers, resigned to a long trip, were set on making the best of it, and as evening fell they became quite lively. Whatever situation a group of Russians finds itself in, two things will inevitably pop up to gladden their hearts—a bottle of vodka and an accordion. Before long, a bottle was passed around, in a true spirit of camaraderie, and then they were all singing to the playing of a young man with a mop of yellow hair.

The soldier next to me was swilling his own pint. He was getting drunker and drunker, and I was increasingly in danger from his wandering hands. The woman in the kerchief noticed it.

"Change places with me, girl," she said. "I'll take care of him."

This stratagem required some gymnastics, but we managed it by a simultaneous two-way move—I crawled over her toward the window, while she edged herself under me to the soldier's side.

The soldier, drinking from his bottle, was oblivious of the change of partners; as he grabbed her thigh, she lifted her leg and kicked him in the ribs with such force that she dislodged him from the bunk and sent him sprawling down on the people in the aisle. They, being as drunk as he, received him with a loud hoop-la, and kept him there, with professions of undying friendship.

Now we had enough room to pull our legs up on the bunk. I nestled into the corner, my hands tight on my satchel, which I wedged securely between my body and the wall. The woman in the bright kerchief peacefully munched her radishes.

Darkness was moving in fast. The electricity was out of order, and soon it became pitch-black. Gradually the revelers succumbed to sleep. The woman finished her last radish, yawned a few times, and then she, too, fell quiet. Now there was only the rattle of the wheels, a few snores and the hush of the night.

I couldn't sleep. The air was fouled by alcohol fumes and the smell of unwashed bodies, and I was grateful for a bullet hole in the window that let in a trickle of fresh air.

Presently a greenish moon came peeping through the haze, outlining the passing landscape—bare, bleak, the earth patched with the white dregs of winter. I stared into the night, suspended between weariness and tension. When the first light peeked over the horizon, I keeled over my satchel and slept.

We arrived in Moscow late in the afternoon. I had been warned that there would be no one to meet me because the hour of our arrival was so uncertain. I was to hire an "isvoschik" and go to Mayakovsky's address. Elbowing through the throngs at the station, I came out on the street and found an isvoschik a block away. These small carriages were rare in Petrograd, but Moscow, already becoming the central city of the nation, was ahead of us in many respects.

After the architectural magnificence of Petrograd, Moscow surprised me with its ugliness. Massive, with no unifying style, it looked as if it had been slapped together by a million different hands indifferent to each other's work.

The carriage stopped in front of an unpreposessing-looking house. The written directions said second floor. I climbed up to a door with an old-fashioned bell above it and pulled the string to ring the bell.

A man in a leather jacket opened the door.

"Hello," he said. "Come in. Welcome. My name is Brick."

All I noticed about him was that he was stocky and wore thick glasses. My attention was instantly diverted to the far end of the room.

There, amid stacks of books piled up on the floor, potted plants, tools, boxes and other, unidentifiable objects, a man and a woman sat at a table. A samovar was puffing merrily, various dishes were set out around it, and a big bright bouquet of spring flowers was stuck in a pitcher.

The woman was of startling beauty. Her hair, copper-red and burning with highlights, was pulled back severely, accentuating the creamy pallor of her skin and the flawless structure of her head and neck. The face was classical—each feature perfectly cut—and heightened by almond-shaped eyes so dark they seemed black. Their glance was velvety.

The man next to her was naked to the waist. When he jumped up, I realized he was at least six feet four—and that his bearing was that of a king.

"Hello, little one!" he boomed, his voice resonant. "We've been expecting you. I'm Mayakovsky, and this is Lily, my mistress. She is also the wife of that fool there." He pointed at the man in glasses. "We three live here together. So you get the picture. Sit down. Glad to see you." He pulled a chair up to the table.

The man in glasses didn't seem to mind being called a fool, the beautiful lady took the outburst serenely, and I must have looked the way I felt—stupefied.

It prompted Mayakovsky to explain further.

"Nothing to it, girl!" he said. "It's very simple. I love Lily, and so does Brick. In fact, every man loves Lily. You have only to look at her and you are done for. And Lily loves us both, though I suspect she prefers me. Of course, he'd like to kill me, but he doesn't dare. Ah, why make anyone unhappy! We're rid of the old taboos, and we're free to love any which way we want. Understand?"

I nodded, understanding nothing.

"And now, eat," he said. "You must be hungry. Lily, fill the young lady's plate with delicacies not intended for the palate of the proletariat. Only the daughter of such a man as your father is worthy of tasting this ambrosia."

"How was the train?" Lily asked, but before I could answer, Mayakovsky burst out.

"How could it be? Dreadful, of course—perfectly terrible. Nothing is working in our country; the brew is raw, it hasn't aged yet. But pray, have patience. We're destined to be the first successful political alchemists."

A plate of noodles and black bread, and a side dish of cucumbers, were placed before me.

"Eat, eat," Mayakovsky urged. "You eat and I'll talk. I like talking."

"He certainly does," Lily said, smiling. Nothing seemed to disturb her. There was a charismatic calm about her, the tranquil consciousness of her power.

By then Brick had joined us at the table.

Comparing the two lovers, I felt Mayakovsky was correct in claiming first place in Lily's affection. His face was handsome, generous, alert. And if ever I have seen total fearlessness, it was in his eyes, clear, candid as a child's. Nothing to fear, nothing to hide, they seemed to proclaim.

Brick's face was in direct contrast. It was not ugly, but it was a stingy face: eyes hiding behind those glasses, mouth clamped shut, nose cut short at the tip, brow low under wavy hair. Also, inexplicably, he conveyed some hint of menace. My instinct was justified when I learned, later, that he was a high-ranking official in the Cheka.

Mayakovsky went on talking, and while I listened, my eyes scanned the room.

Two upside-down bicycles were resting against one wall, several dresses were thrown across a sofa, and two chairs were lying on top of the dresses. Suitcases and boxes were scattered about.

Mayakovsky's voice went on. "So you have decided to conquer the art of Terpsichore! Commendable, very commendable. Personally, I prefer the art of word weaving. Words are the heart of being—the children of thought." He dropped his flowery verbiage. "And how is your father? Now there's a wonderful man. I hope you appreciate him."

I assured him that I did, and told him of Father's asthma. He was concerned. Was there anything he could do? No, I said, it was all taken care of.

The noodles and the warmth of those two people, Lily and Mayakovsky, had relaxed me, and the ordeal of the long trip was catching up with me. I felt my eyelids drooping.

"What time is your exam?" Lily asked.

"Tomorrow, at ten," I said, my tongue barely responding to my thoughts.

"Then you must go to sleep at once," she said.

She took me into the bathroom, where I washed. Then she led me out of the room and rang the bell of another door on the same floor.

"Moscow is overcrowded," she explained while we waited for someone to answer the bell. "But this friend has a nice big sofa. You will be comfortable. We are sort of cramped ourselves. We've just moved to this apartment. Of course, Brick could get us a larger one, but Mayakovsky will have none of it. He says he is the voice of his people and will stay with them in all their needs."

A nice motherly woman opened the door, and Lily turned me over to her.

"Have you enough money for an isvoschik?" Lily asked before leaving.

"Yes, I do, thank you," I said, hoping I would stay on my feet until I reached the sofa.

51

A huge studio, the floor raked down to a mirrored wall. A long table; behind it, a row of people, the backs of their chairs almost touching the mirror. The faces are solemn, appraising their little victims. They don't like these young creatures who are encroaching on their exclusiveness, and they will judge them harshly.

They don't look real to me, those people at the table—more like cutouts in a shooting gallery. I don't know any of them, have never seen them, not even in photographs, and they don't know me, and I feel alien and a little afraid. The contestants have entered in groups of eight; each exam has lasted close to an hour; and since we are the third group, it means we have been waiting in the dressing room for a long time. On our way in, we passed the eight who had just gone through the exam, but their blank, sweaty faces revealed nothing, and no one had enough courage to ask them what it was like in there.

Now our group is in, standing against the walls, waiting.

The cutouts confer in whispers, barely moving their lips, their bearing regally stiff and their eyes going over each of us with razor sharpness. No compassion there for the plight of the young—no sympathy or understanding of their hopes and fears.

I am standing with my back pressed against the barre, using my elbows for crutches. My toes are twitching in my shoes and I keep digging them into the floor.

Bang, bang! Felled by a shot, one of the cutouts topples forward across the table. I shake my head and look hard.

No, no, it's only my imagination. They are all there, intact, upright, still conferring.

I swing around to the wall, throw my foot on the barre and start stretching, to loosen my tight muscles and bring some life into my frightened body.

Begin! Please, begin! This waiting is torture.

"All right," a man's voice says behind me. "We start. Get ready."

We spring to attention, our left hands on the barre and our right arms stretched out sideways at a graceful forty-five-degree angle.

"Plié, second position," orders the man, and we all go into a very slow deep knee bend, knees turned out.

Thank God, they are letting us warm up slowly. The exercise at the barre goes on and on. The man conducting the class walks from one pupil to another, scrutinizing each one, but there are no remarks, no corrections, no reactions whatsoever. The barre finished, we move to the center of the studio and are lined up four and four in a checkerboard formation so that every girl or boy can be seen clearly by the people at the table. I am in the second row.

Over the heads of the judges we can see our reflections in the mirror: tense faces, glassy eyes, most mouths slightly open. I feel a little better, knowing I am not alone in my trepidation. Incongruously, the sun is pouring in through the enormous windows, filling the studio with a golden light.

The teacher gives us an "adagio," an exercise in fluidity and control.

It was my forte! My legs could go up very high without much effort, my balance was solid and my backbone flexible.

After the first combination, the teacher clapped his hands.

"Come here," he said to me. "Change places with that girl in front."

I moved forward, and the other girl moved back to the second row. In the mirror, I could see her lips quiver.

My heart was beating fast as I saw the people at the table studying me. Oh, God, maybe they like me! Otherwise, why would he have moved me?

More exercises, more combinations. Then we were separated into two groups. When the time came for real dancing— that is, a combination of jumps and turns—I was called on to do it alone. Confidence began to bubble in me.

Last part—jumps and beats in the air. I was not a high jumper, but I jumped very softly, creating an illusion of lightness.

"That's all!" said the teacher.

We curtsied and were starting back to the dressing room when someone tapped me on the shoulder. I turned my head to find the teacher behind me.

"You stay," he said.

The other pupils walked out, unaware of my lingering behind. I was left alone with the long table, the cutouts and the teacher. The vastness of the studio suddenly made me feel like a speck about to be wiped away.

The teacher went back to the table, bent over it and spoke to the others for a considerable time. Standing where he had stopped me—not far from the door—I couldn't hear what they were saying, but from the tone of their voices and the rising inflections, I gathered that they were arguing.

The teacher beckoned to me, and I came forward to the center of the studio. He began composing the combination I was to repeat. It was an intricate composition, and I had to summon all my strength and concentration not to falter. When it was over, he smiled and dismissed me.

I was puzzled, but elated. Surely, they would not have singled me out if they didn't like me.

We had to wait in the dressing room for the results, and then the verdicts were handed to us on slips of paper. I glanced at mine.

Rejected!

For a second everything became blurred. It couldn't be! Rejected after all that attention?

When my eyes cleared, I returned to that piece of paper. At the bottom, in the space reserved for remarks, were the handwritten words, "Definitely talented, but the style strictly that of Petrograd, therefore not compatible with the Bolshoi." The words were underlined.

It was true—the styles differed. Petrograd was purer, more classical, less flamboyant, stressing the beauty of body line, whereas the Bolshoi emphasized technical effects and tricks. The two ballet theatres had been at odds for years.

This logic, however, didn't make it easier. The fact remained that I had been rejected, that I was not impressive enough to overcome the difference in styles. It was defeat, the end of my dreams. The blur came back to my eyes.

The train for Petrograd was not leaving until the following morning, and I dreaded the thought of enduring the long evening and night. How was I to live with this failure? How was I to carry the bad news to Father?

Lily and Mayakovsky were kind. They tried to console me and cheer me up by pointing out that all my life lay ahead of me, that no one could predict what might happen next and that I should not give up. Again we were sitting at the table with the puffing samovar, and again Mayakovsky was naked to the waist, and Lily looked even more beautiful in a green kimono. Brick didn't show any particular interest in my troubles—he sat on the sofa reading a newspaper, his stocky body squeezed in among new packages that must have been thrown there that morning.

Mayakovsky asked to see the rejection paper. He scanned it quickly and his fist hit the table.

"My girl," he bellowed in his powerful baritone, "you've won a great battle! Don't you know what these two words imply? Definitely talented! You were among your enemies. They didn't want you. And yet those relics of another time had to admit that you have talent. The argument you saw was over you. Your enemies were fighting over you, and that is not a rejection, that is a victory! Come, we'll celebrate!"

He got up and turned to Lily.

"My gorgeous, I'll go put on some clothes," he said. "You and Brick must consider yourselves abandoned for the evening because I'm taking my little girl friend out on the town."

Lily's eyes followed him to the door, and when he was gone, she dissolved into loving laughter.

"Isn't he something!" she said. "He was looking for it, and he found it."

Mayakovsky was truly "something" when he returned. He was wearing a dark suit that made him look even taller, his handsome face was shining from a fresh shave and his head was held high—a conqueror entering a vanquished territory. He offered me his arm, which was on a level with my head, while Lily picked up a pretty shawl and threw it around me. Brick lowered his paper, gazed at us blankly and returned to his reading.

We hired an isvoschik, and Mayakovsky took me on a tour of the city, pointing out the places of interest. On a second inspection, Moscow didn't seem quite so ugly. It had some wide streets and interesting buildings, a lot of greenery and masses of lofty lilac trees at the height of their bloom. We passed the Kremlin towering over its enclosing wall, its hundreds of gold and mosaic cupolas like mounds of jewels ablaze in the setting sun, and drove by the green waters of the Moscow River. Mayakovsky talked incessantly in his high-voltage vein, and when he decided that I had absorbed enough information, he announced that we were ready to go to a restaurant for dinner.

Moscow was indeed ahead of Petrograd. The government, eager to get foreign currency, had months before opened the ports to foreign ships, and merchandise was already flowing into the city. There were many shops, and kiosks, and street vendors, and the whole atmosphere was brighter than in Petrograd.

The restaurant was a combination of eating place and nightclub, with the astounding name of "Don't Sob." We went down a few steps and entered a dimly but pleasantly lit room below street level. Someone was strumming a guitar and most of the tables were already taken—Russians dine early. But the proprietor became so excited at the sight of Mayakovsky and so determined to seat us in a conspicuous spot that he pushed a table already occupied by two clients right into the corner. They didn't seem to object, but gaped at Mayakovsky and smiled, probably feeling lucky to be so near him. Everyone recognized him; ladies sent him inviting glances; men came to the table to shake his hand; and the proprietor was beside himself with pride. No motion picture star ever received more adulation.

He ordered Caucasian wine, and poured some of it for me, diluting it with water. I confessed that I had never had wine before, and he assured me that it was the proper day for my initiation. He gave me his undivided attention, discussing my situation, and persistently built up my courage and defiance.

Dinner was simple, but good—much better than at home—and then two gypsies came out, mounted a dais and began wailing their mournful melodies to the tune of a guitar. After a few songs, they took an intermission, and in that interval an old lady shuffled in with a big basket of lilacs. She came to our table.

"No, little mother," said Mayakovsky. "Thank you, but that's too easy. My little friend here deserves better." He gave her money, but refused any flowers in exchange, despite her insistence.

The old lady shuffled around the room. Sentimentality and a kind of primitive gallantry are deeply imbedded in the Russian nature, and the men were gladly buying the flowers for their companions. Soon the old woman walked out with an empty basket.

"Now we shall see," Mayakovsky said, rising. He went from table to table, and I watched him talk to people and extend his hand, and then the ladies, their faces melting with admiration, would hand him most, if not all, of their flowers. By the end of the round his arm was overflowing with the foam of lavender blooms. He carried them to our table and, while all eyes were on him, dropped them in my lap.

"A tribute to you, my girl," he said, and sat down next to me.

A ripple of charmed approval went through the room; people were smiling. I held on to the flowers, flustered yet gloriously the center of attraction. I was on the stage, even if it was not the stage I dreamed of, and with that giant sitting next to me, nonchalantly sipping his wine, I felt like a queen beside his majesty.

It was late when we drove up to the house. I jumped down first and stood by the entrance, my face buried in the flowers, waiting for him to pay the coachman.

There was a shot, and the horses reared and neighed.

My head snapped up from the bouquet. Mayakovsky was standing behind the carriage, the muzzle of his pistol aimed at the ground.

"Don't be afraid," he said, putting the revolver into his trouser pocket. "I test it every night, to make sure it doesn't jam." A shadow of torment crossed his face.

That moment sprang back at me when, years later, he shot himself. He left a note which was reprinted in a Russian paper, and Father forwarded a copy to me in America. The note said that the reasons for his act were personal. And then: "And above all, don't gossip. The corpse hated that sort of thing. And, comrades in the government, take care of my family."

There was more, but what saddened me most was the P.S. below his signature. Three words only:

"Lily, love me."

52

Carrying bad news home is hard enough—delivering it to people who act as though they were fully prepared for it is even worse. One feels not only a loser but a fool chasing a shadow.

Father scrutinized the rejection paper thoroughly.

"What a shame," he sighed. "How unfair and stupid." His reaction was the same as Mayakovsky's. Obviously, the two words "definitely talented" interested him.

"Well, that's that!" Mother said, without ever looking at the paper. "We might as well forget it." With this pronouncement, the whole distaff side evaporated, leaving Father and me alone.

"Papa," I couldn't help crying out. "Papa, I want one more chance. Just one more. Please give it to me—somehow—find a way."

He looked at me regretfully and patted my hand, but he didn't promise anything.

He found a way though. I don't know what means he used to reverse Theatre School's dictum, but when we sent in a second application for the exam, complete with a doctor's certificate and a few signatures, it was accepted. This time, I didn't jump for joy—the finality of this last chance weighed heavily on me. There was nothing more to be done, except work and wait through the summer months for this last tryout.

Mother had a new lover, or a "good friend" as she called him, which fooled nobody, for in her jargon the two words were synonymous. Besides, she had good friends only among women, and only two at that—Aunt Pauline and Marianne. The opera singer was simply used as a convenience in certain situations.

This new addition to her court was a great improvement on the last. His name was Karpenko, and he was a studious-looking young man whose spectacles could not conceal the glint of humor in his eyes. He was amusing, had a puckish sense of mischief and was fond of practical jokes. That particular characteristic alienated me, for I was his dupe more than once. His most redeeming feature was his profession. He was a pianist, not quite in the concert bracket, but a skillful musician in the pop vein with a great flair. He brought his own technician to rejuvenate our piano, and regaled us with his arrangements of different tunes.

Being an ingenious young man, he was his own impresario, arranging halturas in which he was the main attraction but including other artists whom he hired. They were very profitable because he also doubled as an accompanist and master of ceremonies.

His manner was discreet. Nobody would have suspected that he was anything but what Mother claimed—a friend. The opera singer reappeared, and the coincidental departures into her apartment were renewed. Afterward, Karpenko would drop in accidentally. In short, with a few mild variations, it went according to the old routine. Father didn't suspect him. They even met sometimes and exchanged a few words, but I suffered the same wrench as during the Stepan affair.

262

When Karpenko learned of my dancing ambitions, he suggested that I break the tedium of waiting for the exam by appearing in one of his halturas.

"I'll take a chance," he said, his face full of deviltry. No doubt he delighted in the prospect of turning loose on the audience an inexperienced student. "After all, you danced with Semenov. You can't be too awful. Dance something simple like—" he giggled—"like *The Dying Swan*. . . ."

I hesitated, not sure that he was serious. Mother joined in. "Come on, do it!" she laughed.

"You think you are good. So you must prove it," Karpenko urged. "And do *The Dying Swan* by all means. You will, won't you?"

"Of course, she will," Mother said gaily.

The undertone of ridicule infuriated me, and I agreed. I would dance—and it would indeed be *The Dying Swan*.

Minutes later, I was sorry I had consented, but my pride would not let me back out.

The Dying Swan is hardly the piece of choreography to be attempted by a schoolgirl. It requires superb toe work, endurance and mature emotion, and only the very best dancers had ever performed it. The minute I began rehearsing it, I realized I was not capable of dancing it in its original form, and I began to clip out little pieces here and there that would allow me to get off my toes. I also concocted a new ending whereby I would start dying earlier than the famous choreography prescribed. I would be dying for a long time, and emoting on the floor, but it was better than falling down.

I went to the old lady who dressed me for the halturas with Semenov and begged her to help me, and the dear soul gave me a white tutu and a bodice. Swan feathers, however, were not to be had. But Mother unearthed a box filled with white ostrich feathers (she had a variety of such items stashed away) and, with a total disregard for authenticity, pinned the feathers over my tutu and attached them to my headband. To her it was a lark, a bit of fun, a game.

The performance was a matinee, starting at two in the afternoon, in a large concert hall in the center of town. The dressing tables were behind a curtain in the green room, and I was surprised to see that there were only two of them. Consulting the program, I realized that one was for me and the other for the famous character dancer, Lopoukhova II.

The star came in with an entourage of three women and immediately evinced displeasure at my presence. I was putting on makeup, but under her hostile stare my eyebrows ended up on my cheekbones.

"Who are you, girl?" she addressed me in the tone of a guard questioning a new prisoner.

Gingerly, I explained myself.

"Well, well," she puffed, "I thought it was a professional performance." And I began to crumble.

Her friends reacted with a loud "Tch . . . tch . . . tch . . . ," plainly conveying their disapproval of me. Having arranged Lopoukhova's dressing table with crystal bottles and other beautiful objects, they left the room. Like all important performers, Lopoukhova would appear after the intermission. I was to be the third number on the program, after a comedian. A sorry placement for *The Dying Swan*.

Karpenko's voice called half-hour to the performance. I had finished dressing and, standing in front of the mirror and observing myself, I suddenly felt ridiculous. The ostrich feathers on my tutu made me look like a white cockatoo, and those on my headband drooped over my eyes like shaggy dog's hair. Holding on to the back of a chair, I began warming-up exercises, but my nerves were raising havoc with my coordination, and when I did a grand battement (a special high kick), my leg caught on Lopoukhova's table and brought it down with a crash. Everything on it scattered over the floor, and one of her crystal bottles splintered into fragments. I stared at this new disaster. What was I to do? I could not go on stage with the pressure of this guilt and fear. I had to find her and confess. I ran out to look for her and found her reclining in an armchair backstage, her entourage standing guard. Breath caught in my throat, I blurted out my apologies for the accident, promising to replace the broken bottle.

She froze me with a stare.

"Oh, go away," she said, "just go. And don't bother about the bottle. It would never match my set." And she turned her back on me.

I came out on stage shaken and stripped of all confidence. I went through the routine like an automaton, fear visible in every movement, knowing I was doing badly and incapable of changing. Lopoukhova was peering at me from the wings, which incapacitated me even more. Finally, the ostrich-feathered swan was dead on the floor, and glad of it.

There was polite applause—probably from the family. I took a bow. Walking back through the dark passageway to the green room, I overheard a heated dialogue.

"How dare you!" Lopoukhova was storming in a stage whisper. "Who do you think you are to let a girl, an amateur, appear on the same stage with me? It's preposterous."

"Please, Madame—" Karpenko was trying to placate her— "don't take it seriously. It was a joke—to amuse the audience— that's all."

A joke? That's what I was to them, to my mother and her lover. Something to laugh at, to ridicule.

I didn't wait for the family to come backstage to see me during the intermission. I got out of my costume, packed it quickly and walked back home by myself.

53

I am going up the stairs of Theatre School. Ahead of me and beside me, other youngsters are also climbing to the hour of judgment. Some are accompanied by relatives, and they talk excitedly, but most are silent.

I am alone—no one came with me, no one offered to do so, and I would not ask.

From my visits to Nina on reception days, I was familiar with the layout, or at least part of it. When we reached the landing, I knew there would be a long hall, at one end of which were two studios, back to back, with classrooms at the other end. The rest of the school was a mystery—no visitors had ever been permitted into the inner sanctum.

This is the girls' floor. Small groups of the regular pupils are clustered in the hall, watching us go by. It's an event for them too—nothing like this has ever happened before. Demure in their powder-blue uniforms, their hair drawn back severely, shyly observing us, they resemble figures of the Brontë era.

The procedure here is similar to that at the Bolshoi, with one exception: we are not allowed in the dressing rooms and are obliged to change in one of the classrooms. But we are separated into groups of eight, just as in Moscow, and made to wait until our turn comes. After sitting for over an hour, our group is ushered through the first studio into the adjoining one.

I walk straight to the barre, take my place right opposite the mirror and then glance around. The setting is identical: a huge studio, the floor raked to the mirrored wall, a long table and people sitting at it, their backs to the mirror. Here, however, I can recognize some of them, having seen them either on the stage or in the photographs that are sold in the lobby of the Maryinsky Theatre. One face belongs to the object of my passionate admiration—the lovely ballerina named Lukom, who interpreted lyrical roles so beautifully. My eyes follow the line of faces. At the end the man who is obviously going to conduct the examination stands leaning against the table, a baton in his hand, his head turned sideways, talking to the judges.

Semenov!

I feel a trap door open beneath me.

Run! Don't stay here. Spare yourself the humiliation of another defeat! He'll never let you win. What excuse can you give for leaving? Think . . . think . . . think.

Semenov looks at me but gives no sign of recognition.

Go, go, quickly! He is pretending—he's fooling you!

Too late. Semenov claps his hands and the exam begins. I try to pull myself together.

The exercises at the barre are going smoothly, and I begin to hope he may actually not have recognized me. It was nearly a year since we had danced together. He walks along the barre between the contestants, sometimes touching one with his baton, and giving suggestions or criticism.

And then I hear his voice behind me. He is so close that I feel his breath on the nape of my neck.

"Well, well," he says softly for me alone to hear. "You can do better than this. How about getting your leg a little higher? Or perhaps you are tired? Stayed up too late?" The voice is vicious, mocking me. Then his hand touches my spine. "How about straightening that back a little?" he says in the loud, stern voice of a teacher, and walks away.

I was right. He is going to torture me; he is going to make this as trying as his sadistic nature can contrive, and he will crush me.

When the barre work is over, we move to the center of the studio. Semenov places me in the front line of the checker formation, and gives us the first exercise. It is difficult, but possible. The following combination of steps is more intricate, the third still more so, and finally he makes us go through exercises and routines so complicated and unsuited to our age that some of the pupils begin to stumble and fall out. He doesn't care. Sacrificing others in the process of eliminating me doesn't touch his hard core.

I am unmistakably the target. Standing in front of me, a Mephistophelean smirk on his lips, he makes me repeat certain passages alone several times after I have already done them with the others. He is out to break me, to tire me out so that I will falter and give up like some of the others.

But neither of us has counted on the metamorphosis that suddenly comes over me. I know I have lost and so I lose the fear of losing. Nerves relax and a cold anger revitalizes my body. I don't care what happens any more, whether I lose or, by God's miracle, win—the contest is between two wills. I am not on trial any more—I am doing the best I can for my own sake. I feel my jaw tighten, and a new expression must have come to my face for I hear one of the people at the table say, "I think she'll bite." The others laugh.

The more he goads me, the more resistance I seem to pluck from somewhere, the more precision I am able to force into my body, hating him with all my being. The last combination is given us by my idol, ballerina Lukom—a beautiful routine full of dips and soft jumps. Relieved, I plunge into it with abandon. Here I am, in the studio of Theatre School, and if this is the only hour I am destined to have here, I am going to dance—for me, for my soul.

It ended. We curtsied, and I was the very first through the door, running away frantically from the past hour.

Dripping-wet, and suddenly dead-tired, I stretched out on the bench in the classroom, face up and motionless. I remained that way for some time before I could bring myself to change into my street clothes. Meanwhile, a prim lady came in and told us there was no need to wait for the results. According to the rules, they would be sent to our parents later in the week. So we left, carrying with us the uncertainty of the outcome.

At home, I tried to dodge questions. When I was cornered, I answered in generalities, saying that the exam was identical with the Bolshoi and that I could not tell whether it went well or badly. All of this made the family suspect that something was drastically wrong. I wouldn't mention Semenov either. If I had to fail again, I would fail without excuses.

It is hard to describe the change in my state of being. Was it apathy? Inertia? Probably both wrapped up in mental and physical fatigue. I felt drained. I lay on my bed for hours, staring at the ceiling, not wanting anything or wishing for anything, mind dormant, body gathering energy, responding with only routine reflexes.

Before the week was over, Father came into my room and handed me the verdict.

For a second, I saw the printed word steadily, and then it wavered in front of my swimming eyes:

Accepted!

I looked up at Father. He grinned happily and nodded.

I jumped up, fled into the bathroom and vomited.

54

That one word "accepted" changed the course of my life. Everything that followed was a direct consequence of it.

The tempo of living gained momentum; events came fast and furious on each other's heels. Of course, as life will have it, there were some reverses, but the tide was surging forward.

Ten days later I bade an affectionate farewell to Madame Sokolova and Mr. Chekreguin and entered the building of Theatre School as a legitimate student. The "evening" courses began at six and ended at nine. That gave me a chance to continue my studies at the Gymnasia for Young Girls, which was all to the good. Father was right in his appraisal of Theatre School's curriculum; the regular pupils were taught some academic subjects—not too strenuously—but we, the evening intruders, were given lessons in the history of art only. Naturally, the emphasis was on dancing, and we had classes in ballet, character dancing, adagio—that is, learning to be partnered by a boy—and in ballroom dancing. This last consisted of social and court dances of the past such as the polonaise, minuet, gavotte and quadrille.

To differentiate us from the regular pupils, we were denied the blue uniforms, and had to wear our own dresses when not in practice clothes. To remind us further of our inferiority, the regular students were forbidden to fraternize with us, and when we came in, most of them were holed up in the dormitory. All in all, we were second-class citizens.

Still, none of these irritants could erase the fact that we

were there to stay, and that nothing but our own inadequacy could push us out.

From time to time, the directress would come into the studio to observe our progress, and the director frequently made the rounds, chilling us with his contemptuous manner. Grigory Grigorevich (whom, for the sake of brevity, we shall call Mr. G.G.) was a tall, rotund man, who lived in an apartment on the first floor. Having been in charge of the school since the good old days of the Czars, he strenuously objected to this innovation. Caustic by nature, his waspish wit was further sharpened by his dislike of us, and he never missed a chance for a barbed comment that would be both upsetting and humiliating. In no time at all, he christened me "bulldozer," hardly an uplifting nickname.

The crop of boys in the evening course was very small, and when the time came for our first ballroom dance lesson, some of the regular students had to be recruited to partner the girls.

According to the etiquette, we girls lined up along one wall of the studio waiting for the boys to be ushered in. They walked in shyly, looking around them in embarrassment, and lined up against the opposite wall. They were an attractive group, clean-cut, well built and carrying themselves with dignity, very different from the clumsy, pimply youngsters we so hated in the Gymnasia for Young Girls. There was an instant rapport between us.

The teacher gave a sign. The boys crossed the room and bowed to their assigned partners. We responded with curtsies, and then, in pairs, we moved easily into a waltz, like ladies and gentlemen at a formal ball.

We circled the studio a couple of times, and then the door opened and Mr. G.G. walked in with a young man. They stood whispering and chuckling. No doubt the director had gotten a few scornful witticisms off his chest.

The teacher called the quadrille, and the young man deserted Mr. G.G. and joined the ranks of the boys. They greeted him warmly.

"George has a dancing itch," Mr. G.G. called pleasantly to the teacher, and the latter extended his arm in a sweeping gesture as though to offer the young man the floor.

The young man bowed his acceptance, and soon it was he and not the teacher who was conducting the quadrille, inventing combinations, correcting, shifting partners.

He was about five feet ten, slight of build, yet possessing a quiet force. His hair was long and a lock of it fell over one eye, like Father's. His movements were smooth and graceful, and although his voice was soft and his manner polite, his whole presence projected the confidence of a leader. With his aquiline features and Byronic hair, he seemed a combination of poet and general.

The boys obviously liked him. They followed his lead; the girls caught the spirit, and the lesson became a lark. We glided and hopped and whirled in the endless combinations he invented.

He, too, seemed to enjoy himself. In the change of partners, he came to me, took my hand, and we went through a few steps together pleasantly, but without any indication of interest on his part.

But I thought of him for many days afterward, and made it my business to find out all about him. His name was George Balanchivadze, and he was a young dancer and choreographer whose avant-garde tendencies somewhat alarmed the guardians of the old tradition, and with good reason, because even his critics could not deny his talent.

Cut off from his family in the Caucasus, he lived in the apartment belonging to Mr. G.G., who recognized his potential and promoted him vigorously, caring for him as if he were his son.

55

The benefits of the reopened ports which had already affected Moscow were trickling into Petrograd. Shops were springing up all over the city—at least one to every block—and the merchandise was diversified; some shops even handled such luxury items as hats and shoes. Consumer goods were of the poorest quality, but at least you could buy stockings to replace the pair consisting of runs which you had worn for months. That is, of course, if you had money, and a goodly amount. Still, for the first time in years the possibility existed.

The number of little theatres increased, some of them giving special Sunday performances. A few restaurants and even a nightclub or two that had been boarded up since the advent of the Revolution opened their doors. To crown it all, an old mansion was converted into a gambling house.

The government not only closed its eyes to these developments, but actually ran the gambling house. The purpose was to accumulate foreign currency and to bring hoarded gold out of hiding by baiting the trap with gold. I hadn't seen that precious metal since the day Fräulein Rosalia deposited the little pouch on the receptionist's desk at Mr. Chekreguin's school. Now, the "chervonetz" circulated openly. But the upswing toward prosperity and the easing of many rules produced a staggering decline in morality. People who had suffered and hungered for so long now dove into any promise of pleasure. Wild parties flourished all over the city, in private homes, halls and lofts. I think it was then that "love-ins" were invented. Speculators—the glamour boys of the era—had no trouble getting ladies for their festivities because, in addition to the inducements of diversion, decent food and whatever came with it, one might be given a pair of gloves or a bottle of scent.

I stayed away from these goings-on not because of my age (in convulsive times age is irrelevant) but because my days and evenings were eaten up by schoolwork. Classes at the Gymnasia ended at four in the afternoon and classes at Theatre School began at six, which gave me just enough time to grab a bite to eat, straighten my dancing clothes and sew a few protective stitches on my ballet slippers. At night, I was too tired to do anything but sleep. Sometimes, if Konstantin was home, I would sit with him for a while and spin my dreams. His encouragement was unwavering, and the love play underlying our relationship gave me the security I needed as I grew into womanhood.

Irra didn't like our closeness. Once she accused him of trying to rape me, and threatened to expose this foul intent, but her charge sent us into such gales of merriment that she cried and apologized. She had lost her head over him, and was consumed by jealousy. He still kept her on tenterhooks, but I felt he was weakening.

Mother was seldom home in the evenings—between Karpenko and the wild parties, she was having a marvelous time—and this gave Tatiana an opportunity to indulge in her own pleasures freely. There were more men going in and out of her room than one could count.

"Weird family, is it not?" Konstantin commented dryly.

A few days later, his observation proved to be an understatement. In the middle of the night, we were awakened by stamping feet and Mother's wild screams.

"He stole it! He stole it!" she wailed, throwing herself against the entrance door. "The son of a bitch stole my coat!"

It appeared that the son of a bitch was one of Tatiana's shady lovers, who had crept out of her room and made his getaway with Mother's seal coat, the last remnant of her once elegant wardrobe. In the dark corridor, he tripped over the umbrella stand, and Mother, awakened by the noise, ran out just in time to see his tail end vanish through the entrance door. She pursued him down the stairs, but he slid down the banister with the coat wrapped around his neck, and she could not match his speed.

We thought she would surely have an epileptic fit, or at least a heart attack. Belatedly, and half-asleep, Tatiana came sauntering out of her room unaware of what had happened. At the sight of her, Mother turned savage. She let out a piercing shriek, grabbed the first available object—a wooden tray—and cracked it over Tatiana's head. Tatiana fell down in a faint.

"I told you it was a weird family," Konstantin said to me, and calmly retired to his room, leaving the ladies to their own devices.

"Water! Water!" Mother screamed. "I killed her."

Irra ran to the kitchen, and I followed Konstantin's example and went to my room.

But when Father was home, all was quiet and the household was veiled with respectability.

At Theatre School even the evening course was disciplined according to tradition; we were made to speak softly, address our elders with respect, curtsy, and speak to the boys only when it was absolutely necessary. One evening, a boy approached me after class and whispered, "I have something interesting to tell you. Talk to you outside."

We were down the block before he went on.

"Some people are producing an operetta called *Helen of Troy*," he said. "And they're looking for young dancers who can speak a few lines for a scene showing the Judgment of Paris. They need a girl to play Venus, and I thought perhaps you might do. I play Paris."

I, too, hoped I would do. The operetta was to be performed on four consecutive Sundays, and would therefore not interfere with the evening course. And the pay was marvelous—two "chervontzi" for the run, that is, ten gold rubles, a king's ransom.

The boy took me to a dusty office to meet the director, and I was hired. I was ecstatic. My first professional engagement! My first exposure to musical comedy, and the first job I had landed on my own, without Semenov, Karpenko or anyone else!

It was a real theatre, with footlights, a curtain, an orchestra, dressing rooms and hordes of people running around looking important. The theatre was dirty, the performance and presentation cheesy, but what a thrill!

Dressed in a white tunic, my head topped with a coronet, I was discovered together with two other goddesses standing in front of a papier-mâché arrangement vaguely reminiscent of Botticelli's shell. The lines I had to speak conveyed the idea that I was the best of the three, that I was the goddess of love and that Paris had better give me that apple if he knew what was good for him. Having won the contest, I stepped down and danced a few steps à la Isadora Duncan, ending in Paris's arms. I was enthralled and could hardly wait from Sunday to Sunday.

In the meantime, on the periphery of my life, small tempests were brewing.

The bigwigs in the Maryinsky Theatre were beginning to be seriously concerned with the choreographic liberties George Balanchivadze was taking. He had been assigned the staging of the procession in *Coq d'Or,* and what he devised, though beautiful, shattered the traditional approach. It was not what the old guard was accustomed to, and they began a campaign to restrain him and bring him into the established orbit.

True creativity doesn't back down easily, and George began to do choreographic work outside the Maryinsky, creating new numbers which he and other dancers would perform in private halturas.

But again the old guard was determined to block his path. It was made known, unofficially, that appearing with George Balanchivadze, in his choreography, would not be looked on with favor, and although, legally, no penalty could be imposed, it was implied that such appearances could bring "certain consequences." To his surprise, the young man discovered that other dancers were suddenly reluctant to perform with him.

Somewhere, somehow, somebody told him about me. He had no definite recollection of meeting me in that ballroom dancing class. But it was still worth investigating. Students in the evening course were not as rigidly subject as the regular pupils to the jurisdiction of the powers, and so George came to watch me work in class.

I was surprised to see him sitting on the bench by the mirror, and I was excited when he waited after class for me and stopped me on my way out. He introduced himself, and asked if he could talk with me. What amazed me was the shyness, the hesitancy almost, with which he spoke. I had no clue as to what he had in mind, but I was already enough of a female not to let a short conversation on the stairs exhaust this opportunity of getting to know him. I instantly conjured up an excuse for being in a hurry, and asked if he would care to come to our house for tea the following Sunday so that we could talk at leisure. He agreed, and, having given him the address, I ran out in the street winged and breathless.

My announcement that a young choreographer, George Balanchivadze, was coming for tea made Mother look at me strangely. But I had long since learned to read her face. Was it possible that she had underestimated her daughter? How did I manage to contrive all these strange occurrences? First Semenov, then Theatre School and now George Balanchivadze. And all in less than a year.

"What is he coming for?" she asked.

"I don't know, Mama. He said he wanted to talk to me."

"Just make sure there is no hanky-panky," she said edgily.

On Sunday, I counted every minute, besieged by the fear that George might have forgotten, or changed his mind. At the ring of the doorbell, I positively skidded into the vestibule and threw the door open. George stood there, his head bent slightly forward and his dark hair falling over one eye. I brought him in, introduced him to everyone, and we sat and sipped tea in an atmosphere of altogether nauseating gentility. Then George asked if he could speak to me alone. Faces puckered up with curiosity and bodies leaned forward to watch as we left the table.

It was getting cold, but the other side of the apartment had not yet been sealed off, and I took him into the living room to prevent eavesdropping. Here his shyness vanished. He asked if I would mind going through a few movements and attitudes—which he then gave me—and he seemed pleased with my ability to bend low and fluidly. He also asked me to do a few acrobatic tricks. Then he came out with his proposal. Would I like to work with him on a number he would chore-ograph for us, and try it out at his next appearance in a small theatre?

Would I? Straining to keep down a war whoop, I acquiesced grandly.

I remember that first dance well, perhaps not with all its details but with many. The music was Anton Rubinstein's— a piece appropriately called "Romance"—and the choreography included many departures from classical form. It was also laced with erotic overtones that were very effective and, to the old guard, "frightfully shocking."

I was a bit wobbly at the performance, primarily because of Mr. G.G.'s presence in the audience. Conscious of his dislike for me, and fully aware of his influence on George, I trembled at the thought of his reaction. Fortunately, he didn't come backstage, and the performance evidently went well enough for George to start creating a new number soon.

And so I became the first Galatea to his Pygmalion. George and I worked almost every evening after class, except for those days when he appeared in the ballet at the Maryinsky. We often worked on Sunday afternoons. George experi-mented, creating combinations that freed the body from the strict bondage of classical form without destroying that form, but, in fact, extending and expanding it. Because he was an excellent musician (he had studied piano at the Conserva-tory), he was able to play movement against sound in a wholly new way. We also used music by composers until then con-sidered unsuitable for dancing—Scriabin, Prokofiev, Delius and many others. We had many engagements, and no sooner had we tried out a dance in public than George would start choreographing a new one.

The family didn't know what to make of it. Father and Konstantin both seemed pleased but graciously regarded it as my just due after all my struggles. The three ladies, who had only seen me dance the disastrous *Dying Swan,* now could hardly wait for my next performance with George. Mother became my press agent, advertising my achievements to her friends and to anyone willing to listen. Tatiana showed her high regard for me by trying to crawl into my bed and was repulsed. And Irra could only gape at me and repeat breathlessly, "Now, now, who would have thought!"

No sooner had they gotten used to George and our partnership than a new development stunned them. The star of the operetta *Helen of Troy,* in which I had appeared in the role of Venus, was a singing-dancing comedian named Ootesov. He was a considerable matinee idol, successfully combining wit, sex appeal and comedic skill, and his name guaranteed a full house. The operetta had already been closed for several weeks when a note from him was delivered to me by hand. It was a friendly message, asking me to come and see him in the office of the theatre where we had appeared.

I arrived to find him relaxed in an armchair, but when he saw me enter, he got up and met me halfway across the room. He offered me a chair and throughout the interview treated me not as a girl but as a woman.

"Can you sing?" he asked, his eyes appraising me. He had never seen me dressed in anything but the white tunic. "I don't mean really sing—just a little—sort of like a diseuse—carry a tune nicely . . ."

Boldly I said I thought I could, and promptly broke into a Russian equivalent of a torch song. He stopped me after the first phrase.

"Good enough," he said. "How would you like to do a duet

with me? I've just gotten hold of a new song smuggled in from Europe, and I need a sailor boy to do it with me. I think you'll look nice in pants."

Flabbergasted, I naturally accepted, and he gave me the song to learn at home.

Ootesov and I appeared together for the first time in a small theatre right in the heart of the city, on Nevsky Prospekt. It was called Freedom Theatre, and its standing was higher than that of many others. Dressed in sailor suits, we stood in front of a backdrop painted with a profusion of bananas and banana leaves, and harmonized a ditty about the glory of a place called Colombo where life consisted of drinking rum and sleeping in the shade of a banana tree. It ended in a dance that was part soft-shoe, part eccentric gliding. We were a sensation. We had to give two encores, and Ootesov was jubilant.

The whole family came to see us, and they were ecstatic. The ladies came backstage and put on quite a show of their own, gushing over Ootesov, who took it all with polite restraint. He thanked them, told me he would get in touch with me later and locked himself in his dressing room.

On the way home, they couldn't stop talking. In their eyes this was a far greater achievement than my silly notion of pursuing serious dancing.

"You must, you positively must, ask Ootesov to come and see us," Mother insisted, and the other two joined in. Konstantin gave an amused chuckle and winked at me. Then Father expressed his opinion.

"It's all right in its place," he said soberly, "but stick to George."

I never asked Ootesov to visit us.

56

Father was very fond of George. He had so many qualities that Father admired—talent, nonconformity, the determination to follow his own course and convictions despite any opposition. In the old days, Father lived surrounded by such young rebels, to whom he gave his whole support. Now, of course, he was not in a position to help anyone, but his respect for George was unbounded. They might have become close friends had it not been for certain similarities of character that stood in the way. Father was reticent in expressing his feelings, and so was George. Neither could bring himself to abandon his reserve for that spontaneity which is essential in the reach for friendship. A faint distance like a cooling wind forever existed between them, stopping them on the cusp of true closeness.

There was also a definite physical resemblance between them; but with all this similarity, it was not a father image that drew me to George. Other reasons, fundamental and personal on both sides, fostered the relationship.

I was alone, and so was he. A visible family functioned around me, but I lived in solitude with my thoughts, hopes and dreams. My rare moments of communion with Father could not close the gap between the rest of the family—Mother in particular—and me. The umbilical cord had rotted away.

George, too, had no one. He had been cut off from his family for years, and though lately they had begun to exchange letters, there was no real bond. Mr. G.G. had taken him in when, in the toughest years of the Revolution, Theatre School had closed, throwing its pupils out in the street, and George had literally no place to go. George was duly grateful, but I doubt that his life under Mr. G.G.'s wing pleased him. The old man's affection bore unmistakable marks of latent homosexuality and a possessiveness that were at odds with George's masculinity. These were, of course, not the only factors that brought us together. Mutual attraction sparked spontaneously, but those other elements helped to solidify it, and drew us closer to falling in love.

The women of the family took to George nicely, each in her own way. Mother, as usual, displayed all her allure, which was sadly wasted on him; Irra, consumed by her passion for Konstantin, regarded the newcomer with interest and no comprehension of what made him tick; and Tatiana was rather dismayed, for under the circumstances she was afraid to make a pass at him. Konstantin observed our growing unity with amusement. He and George got along very well, yet their rapport remained on a superficial level.

I was fifteen, and much older than my age. George was spending more and more time at our house. He always walked me home after our rehearsals, and came in on Sundays to spend the rest of the day with me. If Father was home, he would sometimes join us and would invariably ask George to play the piano. George was only too pleased to comply. In those days, he not only played well, but he showed a definite gift for composition. I remember one waltz especially that was my favorite, a beautiful piece with interesting harmonies and unexpected turns of melody. Nice interludes! George playing and Father and I listening, brought together by the music. I wished the feeling would carry over after the music had finished, but that never happened. A few pleasant words would be exchanged, and then Father would withdraw to the museum, the invisible barrier still between us. George and I, left alone, would touch hands and cling together.

Mr. G.G., who had at first considered our partnership a business arrangement, was not at all happy with the direction it was taking. He never missed an opportunity to intimidate me at Theatre School, and the nickname of bulldozer was bandied about freely and loudly. If he came to watch class, he would sit stony-faced, and when his eyes fell on me—always as though by accident—his face would twist into a grimace of distaste.

I mentioned it at home, and Mother, confident of her ability to settle anything, said that she would ask Mr. G.G. to tea and straighten him out. I doubted that Mr. G.G. would accept, but he did, probably because an invitation to partake of food and drink was still tempting, especially to someone whose big frame must have craved nourishment.

He arrived and was promptly led to the table. George was not there that day. Mother was dripping with Old World charm and small talk, and Mr. G.G. responded jovially while putting away boiled potatoes and cheese and washing them down with innumerable glasses of tea. The old bird knew what it was all about, and he sat and chatted, and scrutinized everything with interest until he had consumed what food there was, and then got up to go. He shook Mother's hand amiably, and said with a most disarming smile, "It was very tasty, and I thank you very much." Then he paused briefly and guffawed.

"Just the same, she is still a bulldozer," he said.

Pride prevented me from describing this incident to George. We never discussed Mr. G.G. or his attitude toward me, because George chose to avoid the subject, even when Mr. G.G.

belittled me in his presence. For instance, when Mr. G.G. came backstage after a performance, he would say, "It's very good, George, very interesting," and look through me as if I were empty air. "Of course, it could have been performed better. But what can you do! Someday you will dance with another partner."

And George would continue with the conversation as if nothing hurtful had been said. To this day I wonder why he never stood up for me.

Ootesov's behavior, on the other hand, was just the opposite. We had many offers to repeat the "Colombo" song and dance, and Ootesov never stopped praising my looks and generally building up my ego.

Through performing in the halturas, I came to know two young ballerinas, Alexandra Danilova and Leda Ivanova, who often appeared on the same bill. Both were already prominent soloists at the Maryinsky, and both were very talented in different ways. Danilova of the Biblical face and green eyes was the more precise and technical, while Ivanova leaned toward lyricism. She was famous for an extraordinary elevation usually seen only in men. She could rise in a leap and literally hang in the air for a second, leaving the audience breathless. Her looks corresponded to her ethereal qualities—an oval face with an angelic expression, a long Taglioni neck, a tiny waist —but they concealed a wild nature, reckless and sensual. Both young ladies were cordial to me, though noticeably condescending.

They never exerted themselves in the halturas; they would dance something easy to familiar music—Schubert's "Moment Musical," for instance, which they danced, garbed as nymphs, in appalling choreography à la Dalcroze. Our numbers were a far cry from "Moment Musical" and, noticing the audience's reaction, the two ballerinas began to show a definite interest in George's choreography.

With all these activities, schoolwork was bound to suffer. As a result, I flunked more than one subject in the spring exams at the Gymnasia, and was kicked out irrevocably.

I had no qualms about it, my only concern being the effect on Father. To my great relief, he took it comparatively calmly.

"It is of no consequence any more," he said. "Dancing may prove to be a better tool for your survival. Besides, I don't think you ever had the makings of a scientist or a literary figure."

His voice was quiet, but I could detect the undertone of disappointment and resignation.

Get angry, Father! I let you down. Curse me. Show me that you really care. At least your anger might bring us together!

That was what I wanted to cry out, and didn't.

Mother accepted the news of my school debacle with less emotion than if I had been late for dinner. She was immersed in her own woes because of Karpenko. He had dealt her ego a severe blow by announcing that he had transferred his affection to another, younger woman, and by suggesting that Mother get an older man, "more her own age." Mother was only thirty-nine, but Russian women are considered old after forty, and this rejection tormented her as a portent of approaching age. My growing up and the success I was beginning to gather only deepened the wound.

George and I were drawing closer. We had no moon, no romantic surroundings, no chance or time for anything poetic and young, only our work, our loneliness, our bodies always touching, and a natural attraction. Our budding love was amazingly mature.

We continued to dance together, and one day we received

an offer to participate in a recital in Moscow. I remember that they requested a specific number—the pas de trois from the ballet *Harlequinade*—and since it required another male dancer, George asked Nicholas Efimov, another young dancer from the Maryinsky, to make up the trio.

The trip was a replica of my first trip to Moscow: the same crowded car, slow-moving and smelly, the same long night. All three of us cuddled up on a bunk like kittens and slept more or less peacefully in each other's warmth.

The people who engaged us were to arrange our accommodations, but we learned when we arrived that only one room had been provided for us in an apartment occupied by two families. Baffled, we looked at each other. One room with only one bed and one small sofa for two young men and a girl? We took our grievance to the landlady, who laughed in our faces. Moscow was overcrowded, she said. We should be grateful to have an entire room to ourselves.

We returned to our room, and I took it upon myself to lay down the law. Small as it was, I would sleep on the sofa, and the boys would share the bed. With that decided, we spent the rest of the day picking out and crushing tiny vermin entrenched in the creases of the mattress and the sofa cushions.

The performance went well. George had smuggled out beautiful costumes from the Maryinsky wardrobe, and I felt radiant in a pink tutu speckled with little diamonds. It reminded me of the ballet costume Fräulein Rosalia had made for me on that long-ago Christmas. We took several bows, which was more than adequate applause for an antiquated excerpt from the ballet presented out of context. When we had been paid, we packed our costumes and headed for the stage door.

A tall shadow blocked our way.

"A quick recovery for one who failed so recently. Congratulations and salaams!" A powerful voice rang out like a bell in the night. It was unmistakable—there was no other voice like it. "I watched your footwork tonight. Pretty legs! Why didn't your father let me know you were coming? I would have prepared a chariot for you. Fortunately, my roving eye caught sight of the announcement in the morning paper advertising this colossal event."

Beaming at me from his towering height, he took my arm, and we all walked out into the light.

George and Efimov stared at this pillar of power. He bowed to them gallantly.

"Gentlemen, my name is Mayakovsky. May I express my high regard for the light fantastic you have performed."

I was glad to see him and flattered that he had taken the time to come to the performance.

"And now, my dear," he said to me, "you must tear yourself away from your two cavaliers because I am taking you to supper. We shared a moment of despair, so it would be only fair for us to share a moment of triumph."

It was not an invitation to be accepted or rejected—it was a statement of fact and it threw me into a quandary. I wanted to go home with George, yet I owed Mayakovsky so much because of his earlier kindness. He was at once aware of my divided feelings.

"Are you, by any chance, contemplating a refusal?" he asked playfully, knowing perfectly well that I could not decline. I excused myself to George and Efimov, explaining that Mayakovsky was an old friend of Father's and telling them not to wait up for me.

Mayakovsky took me to the same restaurant, and again people recognized him and made a fuss over him, and the gypsies sang, and he was as fascinating as ever, only the excitement was missing. My mind was haunted by the coldness of George's face when Mayakovsky led me away.

Poets have special antennae. Before supper was over, he leaned forward on his elbows and looking right into me said, "I think I am correct in saying that one of your cavaliers has won access to your heart, and that you are longing to return to him?" Again it was a statement, and no denial could persuade him to the contrary.

"Come, I'll take you home," he said. "There's nothing wrong in feeling the way you do. Romantic attachments help us live."

I ran up the stairs of the apartment house, two steps at a time. A sleepy woman answered the doorbell and let me in, and I tiptoed to our room. Carefully, I pushed the door open, inch by inch.

Curled under a blanket, Efimov was sleeping on the sofa, his feet sticking out and resting on a chair.

George was sitting at the foot of the bed, waiting, his eyes on the door. He didn't say anything. He got up and stretched his arms out to me, and that was enough.

That night, George and I slept in the same bed.

57

Perhaps we didn't look the same when we came back from Moscow—maybe we carried what I call the "love-smooth look"—or, possibly, Father had been harboring the idea for some time, but, soon after our return, during one of the piano sessions, he startled us with a suggestion. I'd noticed that his concentration was straying from the music, his face reflecting his preoccupation.

The last chord fell.

"Why don't you two get married?" Father said.

George swiveled around on the piano stool, and I sprang to my feet.

"I mean it," Father continued. "It is obvious that you are crazy about each other. Whether it is puppy love or a real one doesn't matter. Time will settle that. If you find out it was a mistake, you can always get a divorce. Meanwhile, I would feel easier if you were married."

We were too dumfounded to speak.

"What I'm saying isn't so extraordinary," Father went on. "Think about the times we are living in. There is no guarantee of what will happen from one moment to the next, and marriage may give you some protection. Also—" and he turned to me—"you are your mother's daughter, and I know your mother's temperament. It's safer if you are married."

George and I exchanged looks, reading each other's answer. Then George's nose twitched and we both suppressed a giggle.

"Why not!" George said. I think he was in a state of shock.

"Why not!" I echoed.

Father stood up. "Good! That's a load off my mind. And don't let's postpone it with announcements, engagement periods and other trivia. Let's do it now. Afterward, you two can live here with us. I'll tell your mother."

And that is how it came about, the prologue to the sacred vows, and I challenge anyone to match this romantic proposal.

George and I were to be married in the chapel of Theatre School by the resident priest, who was still in circulation. The government had not yet clamped down on the clergy completely.

Preparations for the wedding began at once, and immediately problems connected with it came to the fore.

Being a romantic, I had dreamed of entering the church draped in white, demure and virginal, a facsimile of the brides I had seen in old family photographs. That was not to be. All fabrics were hard to come by, and white was extinct because nobody wanted it. What fool would think of wearing white next to a dirty skin, not to mention the difficulty of laundering it? After an extensive search, we found a piece of pale blue crepe . . . so pale that from a distance a nearsighted person could mistake it for white. The only nearsighted person at the wedding would be Aunt Eugenia, but I had no doubt that some evil-minded person would open her eyes to the compromise. Then we faced another dilemma. There was not enough fabric for a dress with a high neck and long sleeves. The demure look had to be sacrificed. I ended up in a rather tight tunic with short sleeves and a plunging décolletage that was anything but virginal. The veil, also, was too short and narrow to be used traditionally, so I wrapped it around my head like a Hindu turban and let a piece of it stick out like a plume. It is customary for a Russian bride to adorn her veil with wax orange blossoms, but since the veil had become a turban, and there were only two sprigs of the blossoms, I twisted them into loops and attached them to the tiny circles in my pierced ears, thus acquiring a pair of extremely exotic earrings.

On the afternoon of my wedding day, I sat in Mother's bedroom, in front of her dressing table, putting the finishing touches to my unorthodox attire and listening to the chatter around me. We had to wait another half-hour before starting for church, and I was getting restless and a little apprehensive. It was not doubt, but the normal trepidation in the face of an event that was bound to change my whole life.

The chatter got more and more excited. The ladies of the

family, plus Aunt Pauline and Aunt Eugenia, were discussing the guest list for the supper after the wedding ceremony. Mother had refused to invite the priest.

"After all, why should I invite him?" she was saying. "He gets paid and there is no reason to feed him on top of it."

Food was still limited, and though many guests, instead of sending wedding presents, contributed to our own stock of food and wine, there was some doubt as to whether there would be enough for everybody. George's father and brother had arrived from the Caucasus—the wedding provided them with a legitimate reason for a travel permit—and that brought the guest list up to twenty.

"You're crazy," Irra said. "The priest is always invited for supper."

"Always be hanged." Mother was adamant. "He is not my priest. He is from 'that' world. He doesn't know us."

"But he knows George," Aunt Eugenia intervened shyly.

"Then let George send him a bushel of potatoes. It is not my problem," Mother said.

"But he is marrying your daughter," Irra argued, "and he is part of the establishment to which she now belongs."

"I don't care what part of what establishment he is," Mother fumed. "I will not invite him. Priests eat too much."

Barely listening to the bickering, I got up and walked barefoot to the long armoire mirror, where I stood contemplating my image—the turban with the feathery veil sticking out, the large loops of the wax-flower earrings, the pale blue tunic-dress coming just below my knees—and though it wasn't unattractive, it was definitely reminiscent of a young rajah who had forgotten to put on his pants.

"Time to go," Mother said. "Put on your shoes."

From her matter-of-fact behavior since the announcement of my impending marriage, I gathered that she didn't particularly cherish the idea of my becoming a married woman.

I had postponed putting on my shoes because the only pair we could find was a half-size too small for me, and I foresaw an evening of discomfort. Sprinkling the inside of the shoes with flour, I slowly eased my feet into them.

The chapel was crowded. I walked down the aisle on my father's arm through a throng of faces I had never seen, most of them belonging to the members of the ballet troupe. My appearance evoked sounds that were difficult to interpret; they could have been expressions of shock as well as admiration. We came to the altar, and there stood George in a suit of tails borrowed from the Maryinsky wardrobe, his face properly serious but wearing a brand-new look of poetic decadence. The priest took our hands and brought us together, and at that close range I realized what had caused this Byronic transfiguration. He had applied eye shadow under his eyes. I was about to ask him why, but the priest silenced me by piously pressing his fingers to his lips.

"Sorry," I said in all sincerity, which made him roll his eyes in total dismay.

Overlooking the fact that a Russian wedding is intolerably long, and that it requires a certain amount of walking around the altar, which was death on my feet, and that one of the ushers carrying the wedding crown tripped and fell, everything went smoothly until the last few moments.

At the end of the religious service, the bride and groom remain at the foot of the altar to receive a blessing and a few words of advice from the priest or "Batushka," meaning "Little Father."

This Batushka clasped his hands most reverently, took a deep breath, released it and plunged into his tirade.

"My dear children," he said, "it gives me great happiness to unite you in holy matrimony. You, my dear bride, are a newcomer to our midst, but I've known George since he was in knee pants. May you lead a happy and righteous life." He took a slight pause, weighing the next line, and then continued. "My, my, how many famous couples I have married in this chapel. For instance—" and he mentioned a ballerina and her director husband. "What a lovely wedding we had. They asked me to the reception afterward and we celebrated it with a good supper—beef Stroganoff, fish aspic and all that. Of course, those were better times. Still, when I married—" another prominent couple was named—"they also asked me to their house and we . . ."

On and on he droned in an inexhaustible recall of past weddings and receptions, complete with detailed menus and praises for the hosts.

The chapel was getting stuffy from body heat, the candles in our hands were melting and the hot wax was dripping on my fingers, my feet were killing me, and Batushka's gold vestments swam before me in a psychedelic dream.

"Must have been made in Father's factory," I thought, my mind swerving from the spiritual.

"And then, the wedding . . ." the words dripped endlessly like a Chinese water torture.

Behind me there was a shuffling of feet, rustle of skirts, clearing of throats, and then I saw Mother walking up to the altar—which was a sacrilege, because women are not allowed beyond the steps leading to it. She came straight to the saintly orator, whispered something in his ear and retreated to her place in the front row, her head held high. The effect was magical. Batushka smiled benignly, his tone changed, and his rhetoric came abruptly to an end.

"And now, my dear children, I bestow upon you my blessing and may you live in harmony."

We were dismissed.

Batushka came for supper and enjoyed himself thoroughly. It was a gay wedding. The guests ate and drank, and kissed each other in a bliss of brotherhood, and Batushka picked up the fold of his robe (the gold vestments remained in church) and performed a sedate dance to the clapping of hands. In the privacy of her boudoir, Mother ranted. "The stinker! The blackmailer! He would have kept us there until tomorrow morning."

My tight shoes were driving me to tears, and I kicked them off and walked around in my stocking feet for the rest of the evening.

George's father sang us a Georgian toast, and Father and Mother presented us with a wedding gift—the famous gold and crystal set.

The evening was turning into night, but the guests showed no intention of going home. At 3 A.M., when George and I went to bed, the party was still in full swing.

58

George had an impregnable face. His eyes, alert, vaguely suspicious and full of wonder, guarded his emotions and the endless images in his mind like two little animals protecting their hideaway. Even excitement could not alter that façade; it exhilarated his speech and widened the pupils of his eyes, but his countenance kept its enigmatic mold.

Therefore, I was astounded to see him visibly annoyed when he returned home from a rehearsal at the Maryinsky a few days after the wedding.

"That Semenov is really a bastard," he said.

"Why?" I asked, though it was no revelation to me.

"He came up to me at rehearsal today and in front of all the other people he said, 'Why did you marry that trollop?' "

I gasped. "And you? What did you do?"

"Nothing," he said. "What could I do? I turned my back on him and walked away."

The hurt of Mr. G.G.'s past insults returned in full force and inflated this new incident beyond endurance.

"You didn't say anything or do anything?" I wailed. "You didn't defend me—your wife?"

I felt crushed. The tears that flowed from my eyes could have flooded the whole Maryinsky Theatre and its occupants. George looked on helplessly. It was quite clear he had never anticipated this reaction.

The next afternoon brought even more startling news. George was sickly pale when he came home, accompanied by a tall, nice-looking young man whom he introduced as a fellow dancer named Michalov.

"What is the matter?" I inquired.

"I've been suspended for two weeks," George said without any emotion.

"Why?"

"I hit him," he said laconically, and that was all he would say.

"You hit who?" I kept on probing.

Since George remained silent, Michalov answered.

"He hit Semenov," he said. "Right in the face. In front of everyone in the rehearsal hall. He asked him to apologize for yesterday's remark, and when Semenov refused, he hit him so hard that he almost fell backward."

I screamed with the thrill of vindication and threw my arms around George's neck. He stood completely passive.

Two weeks later, he was back in the theatre with no apparent change in his status, but for me this episode had an unexpected outcome. Two men, one solidly established, the other of great promise, had collided openly over a girl—a former "private." The incident was unprecedented in the memory of anyone in the troupe. The "Lady's Champion" again rode his white charger.

And I became notorious.

Notoriety breeds curiosity, and curiosity invites exploration, and in a complete turnabout those who had formerly ignored me now sought me out. The two young ballerinas promoted me to the rank of a near-friend, and many other members of the Maryinsky maneuvered to be invited to our house.

But there was another consequence of the battle royal: Mother took one look at Michalov and he promptly filled the place vacated by Karpenko. Nor did the young man consider it necessary to hide this relationship from his friends. Also, Tatiana's affairs increased with the influx of new people. Gossip flew.

"Your house has a bad reputation," Nina said to me one day. "Not you," she hastened to add, "but the others." She was too charitable to identify them by name.

It was a slap in the face, but I couldn't find any rebuff or reply.

Since the nightclubs and cabarets which had opened around town all wanted floor shows, we could count on more work. One such place was especially popular. It was called Donon, and it had kept all the luxurious fittings of the past—red velvet curtains and upholstery, marble columns, gilt and crystal, and even private alcoves on an upper landing which offered a view of the entertainment below. The prices were out of reach for the general public, but every era manufactures its own elite, and the upper crust of government officials and speculators could afford to get whatever they wanted. Both elements vied for the favors of young dancers, seducing them with food and gifts, and many a young girl succumbed to the lure. Leda Ivanova was often seen at Donon's, supping in the company of questionable characters, and one night, when taking a bow, I spotted her at a ringside table with the dreaded one-eyed sailor.

The madness of the times even extended to the upper echelon of the arts, and it was announced that a masked ball would be held at the Maryinsky Theatre. This desecrating of the sacred precincts was met with horror by some purists, but they had no voice in the matter.

A medley of different dances was to be presented on the stage, and since, under the circumstances, the authorities didn't care how avant-garde it would be, George was given the chance to display his choreography and I would achieve my goal of appearing on the famous stage. The dance George created was called *Enigma,* and it lived up to its name: it combined classical technique with acrobatics, and we danced barefoot, in chiffon tunics barely covering our torsos.

That night stands out in my memory as a Roman orgy. Orchestra seats were removed to let the audience mill around; the boxes were transformed into restaurant booths; and bars selling wine, sweets and sandwiches were installed in halls and lobbies. The symphony orchestra was charged with the determination to live it up to the full. In no time at all half the crowd was reeling.

Standing in the wings as we awaited our turn, I felt a painful letdown. I was about to step out on the stage I had only dared to dream of, but it was far from what I had imagined. The lights in the auditorium were only partly dimmed, the audience was standing, none of the important dancers were taking part, and one could hear distant voices and laughter.

Never mind, I lashed out at myself mentally. Be grateful that you are allowed to stand here. Two years—only two more years—and you'll appear on these boards in different circumstances. I glanced out at the vast stage, and it filled me with a renewed thrill.

Our time came and I ran out, George a few feet behind me.

In the hullaballoo, it was impossible to determine the degree of our success or failure, but we took three bows. I think the audience was a bit stunned.

When we had changed into our street clothes, we went down into the audience, having first arranged a meeting place in case we should get separated. That happened almost immediately.

The crowd of well over a thousand, bizarre in its conglomeration of fancy costumes, ordinary clothes and a few leftover evening dresses and dinner jackets, was getting unruly. People ate and drank gluttonously, spending their last rubles on what had been denied them for years. Unaccustomed to drink, they were thrown off balance, and though in Soviet Russia any public display of affection was suppressed, eroticism was rampant. One had only to open a door to the antechamber of a box to come upon entwined bodies. It was madness—a ball during a plague. The theatre, the beautiful, blue and gold, dignified theatre, was the scene of a drunken carnival.

It was close to dawn when George and I found each other and walked home, leaving the insanity on the other side of sunrise.

On another artistic level, a very different event took place soon after. In those days George contended that dancing, like sculpture, should be complete and interesting to view from all four sides. To give him a chance to prove his theory, he was granted permission to stage a spectacle in the arena where the short-lived Duma, or parliament, had formerly convened. Having complete freedom of choice, he decided to choreograph Chopin's "Funeral March" and to create another dance to a rhythmic reading-aloud of Russian limericks, called chastushki.

The idea of choreographing a dirge of death was startling. In the second act of *Giselle,* there are indeed dead souls, but they are pretty ethereal, flitting about in white tutus to lilting music in a romantic setting. And here we were, twelve youngsters in stark linen tunics, our heads encased in tight hoods, building a design of uncompromising grief to the dark downbeat, changing from the mourners into the dead, into whirling spirits, our bodies twisting into arches and crosses.

The chastushka, danced in national costume to fifty voices speaking in unison, was also a departure from the norm. It was George's variation on a Russian square dance done to a boldly changing rhythm that at times approached syncopation.

It was all too much for the traditionalists, and George was never again offered a similar opportunity.

59

The opera singer signed a contract with some provincial opera company and departed, forsaking her abode. This caused Mother great inconvenience because the government immediately filled the vacancy with new tenants. A new pied-à-terre had to be found for her amorous adventures, and that was easier said than done, for Petrograd, like Moscow, was beginning to feel a housing shortage, and anyone with extra living space was likely to be forcibly invaded by nonpaying tenants. Because of Father's position and his museum no one had yet been foisted upon us, despite the size of the apartment, and we were still enjoying the luxury of ample quarters.

Meanwhile, family life acquired new variations. At long last, Irra had weakened Konstantin to the point of going to bed with her, and she was now openly sleeping with him. Tatiana, on the other hand, underwent a temporary moral renaissance: instead of diversified sleeping, she switched to a steady boyfriend. Granted, it didn't last more than two months, but it was a step in the right direction.

Konstantin took his new alliance lightly, assigning it no significance, but accepting it as one would accept a cup of coffee in the morning; it was offered, it was hot, and it was good for one.

"She is useful," he said to me, taking a long draw on his cigarette.

What with the evening courses, rehearsals with George, and occasional halturas, I had little time at home and even less inclination to have more. I saw Father only two or three times a week, for he, too, kept busy and away from home. George had a busy schedule; he and Michalov had to rehearse almost every day and appear on the Maryinsky stage twice a week. On those nights I would grab a tram as soon as I was through at Theatre School, and dash to the Maryinsky to catch part of the performance and then return home with George. One evening, however, I twisted my ankle during class, and although the injury was not serious, I was ordered to go home and rest my foot.

I arrived to find a party at high pitch.

Animated talk and laughter were coming from the dining room, and a man's drunken voice was bellowing a song to the accompaniment of a guitar. No one noticed me come in.

The singer, glass in hand, was steadying himself on his wobbly legs, and the guitar player's eyelids were drooping in the ecstasy of his art, which consisted of three chords changed ad libitum and without any relation to the song. On the banquette, Tatiana was necking with a bearded man.

And Mother? Dressed in a lacy peignoir, she was locked in an embrace with a man I had never seen before.

The picture of Mother and Stepan on the stairs surfaced for a second.

On the table there were several bottles, overflowing ashtrays, scraps of food and broken pieces of bread.

I stood there, my eyes registering everything with icy accuracy, until Mother saw me. She recoiled from the man, her hands still on his shoulders, and stared at me with the eyes of a cornered animal that is about to be killed. Before she could say anything, I walked out.

In my room, I closed the door and sank into a chair by my desk. I felt strangely cold but not a bit unnerved or upset. The proverbial straw had fallen and broken the camel's back, and the camel refused to move or feel any more. I remember leaning my elbows on the desk, with my head down, relieved by my reaction, my mind's eye watching particles of thoughts find each other and jell into a decision.

The noise in the dining room was diminishing. I could hear a few exclamations, and it quieted down completely. They must have left through the "black walk" since no one walked past my room.

The doorknob turned slowly, and Mother stood on the threshold, partly hidden by the door.

"They've left," she said apologetically, like a child admitting his mistake.

I didn't answer, watching her silently.

She eased into the room and looked at me apprehensively, waiting for me to speak. I kept silent.

"You won't tell Father?" she asked pathetically.

"No," I said, "I won't tell Father. I didn't tell him when I saw you with Stepan on the window sill, and I won't tell him now."

Her eyes opened wide and she clutched her stomach as if someone had pierced it.

"You saw me and Stepan?"

"Yes, Mama, I did. And would you like to know who stopped me from telling Father? The woman you hated—Fräulein Rosalia! Remember her? She did!" I was driving my point in cruelly. "No, I won't tell him . . . and I won't tell George or Michalov either . . . and do you know why? Because I'm ashamed. I'm ashamed, Mama!"

She threw her hands up dramatically, swung around the room and then dropped to her knees by my side, clutching my arm.

"You don't understand," she sobbed. "You are so very young. . . . Life is short and living is not what I expected it to be. . . . I want to get everything out of life. . . ." She was breathing hard, but I didn't believe any of it. I had seen her throw fits before, and this resembled too closely some of her faked hysterics.

"Stop it, Mama," I said through clenched teeth. "Don't grovel. You mustn't grovel before me." My anger was honest: I hated to see her lose all dignity, and I stood up, trying to pull her up with me.

"No . . . no . . ." She resisted, her hands clenched in supplication. "You must try to understand . . . you must not judge. . . ."

"I will not judge you, Mama," I said. "But I cannot stay here any longer. I'm leaving. George and I will move out as soon as we find a place to live."

She jumped up.

"But you can't do that!" she wailed. "How will I explain it to Father!"

"I don't know, Mama. It's up to you. I'll take care of George and you take care of Father. Let's do it quietly."

"You can't walk out on me," she cried, trying to grab me. "You are mean and horrible. . . . You can't leave me. . . . I'm your Mother. . . . I love you."

I backed away, slipping out of her grip, and she stopped, confused, realizing that on my part it was not a scene, but stark honest truth.

"Please, Mama." I was forcing myself to say what I felt was necessary. "Believe me. There is nothing we can do about it any more. Nothing."

"No, no!" she cried. "You can't do that!"

"It's done, Mama," I said.

Her dramatics vanished. Her hands dropped to her sides, and she looked forlorn.

I felt sorry for her—and for myself. For the love that could have been and had got lost somewhere, and now would never be.

60

The transition came about smoothly. I don't know how she explained it to Father, but he took it graciously.

"I hear that you have decided to move, to be on your own," he said to me. "Perhaps it's wise. One must learn to stand on one's own feet."

George also accepted it without any questions. Like most potential geniuses, he was self-centered and too absorbed in his own interests to be bothered by anything so trivial as a change of location. We'd be living somewhere, we'd have a roof over our heads, and where was immaterial. He took everything the way it came—that is, in the present tense, never delving into reasons and causes. Even with me—he took me as he found me, and though I'm sure he loved me, he never showed any curiosity about my life before we met, and consequently never knew much about it.

We found an unfurnished apartment on the Moika Canal, with a view of a church and the National Arts Building, where, before the Revolution, Father had built a chapel. Our apartment was on the first floor, but it was several feet above street level, so that our windows looked out over the heads of passing people. It had two very large rooms on the canal and a big kitchen facing the backyard, where the previous tenant had left an enormous heap of old books in the corner by the stove. The books were useless, their bindings dry and cracked and the type faded, but we didn't throw them out; should we stay till winter, we would use them for firewood.

Mother's pathos turned to anger, and she was anything but helpful in furnishing our new dwelling. She consented to my taking some of the pieces from my own room, such as the bed, the bedside table, one armchair and a chest of drawers, but she vetoed the draperies and the desk. Aside from that, she provided us with the bare essentials—a simple wooden table, six chairs and a set of shelves, though the storage room above the factory was packed with furniture from her previous apartment. Added to this bounty were two sets of bed linen, four towels, a few dishes and kitchen utensils and a student lamp. But, irrationally, she insisted that we take our wedding present, the gold and crystal set, which was of no possible use or value to us.

Of course, I could have gone to Father for arbitration, but it was not my plan to cause any more friction; I felt he already had more than his share of unhappiness.

And so our new home looked more like an empty barracks than the cozy nest of two newlyweds. Bit by bit, I scrounged a few more things vital to basic housekeeping, but the over-all look remained bare and cold. In this setting, the gold set sparkled on the shelves with the malevolence of a vicious joke. We tried desperately to get rid of it, offering it at a fraction of its value to anyone who ever admired it. There were no buyers. We even lured indoors one of the Tatar peddlers who roamed the streets looking for bargains, and showed it to him. Dazzled, he stared at it and then dismissed it with a hoarse laugh and a wave of his hand. However, on his way out through the kitchen, he noticed the pile of books, and his face lit up. He was back next morning at the crack of dawn with a scale and a cart, and, having weighed the whole heap, he bought it at a certain price per pound. He loaded his acquisitions into the cart and trotted away as happy as a mouse in a cheese shop.

George had his regular salary from the Maryinsky. Still, with the added expense of rent and food, we could barely make ends meet. We had neither the knack nor the means to deal in the black market. To make matters worse, shortly after we moved there was another purge of the speculators, which curtailed activity in every field. Halturas became less frequent, many shops went out of business, and the gambling house, the meeting place of the elite, closed because the government didn't need it any more. Some nightclubs still held their own, and one entrepreneur of a cellar café, remembering my success in "Colombo," had the bright idea of trying me out as a diseuse. George accompanied me on the piano, and it worked. Thinking back, I'm sure I presented a ludicrous sight—a girl in a rented, long dress warbling German songs about monkeys in the trees or ladies pinning flowers to their muffs. But the mere sound of a European tune was intoxicating to the audience, and I was engaged several times to repeat the same feat.

Ivanova came to hear me, escorted by a stranger, and was very amused. It was rumored that she was on intimate terms with some shady government official.

Having broken away from the family, we seldom went back to visit them and, to my best recollection, only Konstantin ever came to see us. If we had a haltura, he trailed along to see us dance. Michalov, too, seemed to prefer our company to Mother's, and he and other chums of George's would drop in for the evening. We would sit drinking tea, and talk or play dominoes. I hoped secretly that one day the doorbell would ring and Father would be standing there.

It was becoming more and more apparent that the authorities at the Maryinsky had no intention of advancing George's choreographic ambitions. No assignment came his way, nor were there any promises or hints of such a possibility. They used him only as a dancer, and George hated to dance, although he was very good—agile and wiry. Everything seemed to have been stymied. We were caught in the dreary monotony of our days. We had no piano for George and very few books, and I refused to go home to borrow any.

And so we sat in the empty apartment, with nothing much to look forward to, and dreamed. George's dreams were big—immense, in fact, completely out of scale with what our lives could offer. We dreamed and waited for something neither of us could define—some brilliant promise, some bridge over the river to the land of Oz, unaware that the pilings for that bridge were already in the water.

That mysterious force which had changed the course of my life before was at work again. It had started months before, while the gambling house was still in operation. A very clever, calculating man named Dimitriev had manipulated himself into the profitable job of croupier at the gold table. It is the rule for croupiers to get a percentage of the winnings, and at that table the stakes were high—and in gold. By the time the gambling house was shut down, Dimitriev had accumulated a small fortune, which could not be confiscated, at least for the time being, because it had been earned legitimately in the government's employ.

The question was, what was he going to do with it? Spending it inside the country would be stupid—there was nothing worth buying—and keeping it would be dangerous because one never knew when government policy might change.

To escape from the country was too risky—many people had perished in that attempt. The Iron Curtain was down tight.

Dimitriev must have worked on his scheme for a long time, probably while he was still at the casino, because there he became friendly with many important government officials. At any rate, he never disclosed how he achieved the incredible result, but somehow he got to the very top people in the government and presented his idea. As a loyal Soviet citizen, he said, he didn't want to spend the money on himself. Instead, he proposed to spend it on some talented young people in the arts, whom he would take on a two-month educational tour of Germany at his expense. He would bring the group back in time for the fall season, with information and photographs of what was happening in the outside world. He suggested, also, that it was high time for Europe to get a glimpse of Soviet culture, and, with that in mind, he would arrange for the young artists to give one or two recitals in Berlin. He confessed modestly that he wanted nothing for himself but a chance to serve the Soviet Union and its great art. But he wanted the assurance of a good job when we returned.

Incredible as it seems, he got permission. It was one of the first cracks in the Iron Curtain.

He must have been watching us very closely because his first choice was George, which automatically included me. Next came Danilova, Ivanova and Efimov, who often partnered the two ladies.

When Dimitriev came to see us and explained his plan, which had already been approved, we thought he was some maniac escaped from an asylum. Yet he didn't look like one. Tall, distinguished, conservative in speech and manner, he invited confidence and respect.

"Of course," he said, "you could reject my proposition, in which case I'd have to choose some other dancers. But you've already been cleared by the government."

Who would reject an impossible dream come true? For days, we behaved as if we'd been hit by lightning.

61

White nights fall upon the city in the late spring and linger for about three weeks. They erase time; if it were not for the moving hands of the clock, one would not know that the day was following its normal circle. Darkness never falls and night never comes; everything is bathed in the milky luminosity of a foggy day when the sun is fighting to break through the clouds. Midnight differs from morning or afternoon only in the faint tinge of violet that glazes the sky. People sleep in spurts, manufacturing darkness by curtaining their windows heavily, but it doesn't help—white nights penetrate the stifling air and disturb the spirit.

Those nights are brothers to the mistral, or sirocco, or other mischief-makers, and though, unlike their windy relatives, they are calm, the very absence of any stir produces the same effect: people are sleepless, edgy and restless.

It was about ten in the evening. George, Efimov and I sat on a bench some distance away from a mall where an open-air stage stood, backed by a shell. A performance was going on in the miniature park; it would be our last haltura before our journey.

It was intermission time. We had already appeared in the first part of the program, and were waiting for Danilova and Leda Ivanova to perform their inevitable "Moment Musical" so that we could all go back to our house together. We had sat around our table until dawn the night before, planning our repertoire for the promised recitals, discussing details, wondering what it would be like and talking, talking, talking. Ever since we had the luck to be chosen for Dimitriev's tour, all differences of age and standing had disappeared. We had become close friends, united by the adventure we were about to share.

The park was crowded. The benches in front of the stage were packed and other people were milling around, pausing to glance at the stage over the heads of the seated audience. It was warm and balmy and a little oppressive, and the new green of the grass and trees looked frosted in the milky light. Lovers strolled hand in hand, and, leaning against a tree next to us, a young man inspired by the white fantasy of nature was audibly composing a poem and scribbling it into his notebook for posterity.

The performance began. Our bench was on a knoll and we could clearly see the stage, where a juggler was tossing plates in the air.

My mind was wandering. I was thinking of my pitiable wardrobe and wishing I could get something new and fresh to wear when I stepped on a foreign shore. I had one pretty dress which had been given me, but since it was cerise jersey it was not exactly suitable for traveling. If only I could find some extra money, I could afford a blouse or a skirt on the black market.

"I wish we could sell that damn gold set," I said, my thoughts coming out aloud.

Efimov, who sat between me and George, pondered my wish for a while, and then, being a practical young man, came up with a suggestion.

"Why don't you ask Ivanova to help you sell it?" he said.

"She's close to all the Communist biggies. They might be interested in getting something like that. Make them feel like Czars."

"Oh, no," I said. "I'm afraid they'll take one look and confiscate it."

"Not if Ivanova is in on the deal. She's in the know about everything. I sometimes think she knows too much. It isn't healthy. Anyway, it's worth the gamble. The set is no good to you sitting on the shelf."

"You're right," I said. "I'll talk to her tonight."

George was not listening to our conversation.

"Funny," he muttered, looking ahead.

"What's funny?" Efimov asked. We both turned to George, whose eyes were fixed on the stage.

"They were supposed to be second, and look . . . someone else is coming out."

It was a woman singer, who took the right stance and began an aria.

"I wonder what happened," Efimov mused.

"Oh, probably a broken hook or a torn ribbon," I said, accustomed to such minor tragedies. "So they took time out for repairs."

It seemed logical, and we listened to the lovely voice, trilling gently in the stillness of the evening.

When, however, the singer was followed by three balalaika players, and they, in turn, were succeeded by a comedian, we skidded down the slope and ran backstage.

Danilova stood in the stage door, wide-eyed with anxiety. She was made up and dressed in her nymph's tunic.

"I'm so glad you came," she stammered, her voice shaking with worry. "Leda isn't here yet . . . she hasn't come in . . . she said she would be back by seven. . . ."

Behind her, the figure of the stage manager appeared out of the dark.

"Look here," he said, obviously annoyed. "If Ivanova doesn't show up in the next five minutes, we might as well forget it. It will be too late." And he disappeared into the shadows.

"Oh, Lord," Danilova moaned. "I wonder what it means. I can't imagine why she isn't here. She promised to be back by seven."

"Back from where?" The question popped out from all of us almost simultaneously.

"Back from boating. She went boating with those three men she goes out with. She asked me to join them, but they said the boat was too small to take more than four people. Anyway, I didn't feel like going. They called for her at three this afternoon and promised to bring her back by seven. Oh, God, what could it be?"

Her explanation brought a chill of apprehension, but none of us would voice our alarm, resisting the possibility of an accident.

"Go out and see if she is coming," Danilova pleaded.

We ran out and sprinted down the alley that connected the stage door with the park gate.

The crowd was thinning. Groups of people were strolling toward the gate and out into the street. We wove in and out among them, straining our eyes, peering, searching, and desperately clinging to the belief that at any moment she would come running toward us.

But there was no sign of her.

The last number on the program was on the stage, and now people were leaving in droves, pushing their way out. Defeated, we stopped in the alley and watched the departing crowd hopelessly.

And then we saw a man elbowing his way into the park against the human tide. Everything about him attracted our attention. He wore a heavy coat, conspicuously too heavy for this time of year, his body thrust forward like that of a man fighting a storm. He walked with urgency, but his step was jerky and unsteady; his upturned collar was pulled higher by his hunched-up shoulders and hid most of his face. As he passed us, he threw us a glance that was a flick of burning coal. In that look there was recognition instantly withdrawn.

We stared after him, blind intuition connecting him with Ivanova. He was heading toward the stage door, and we followed him, apprehension growing into foreboding.

We caught up with him inside the stage door, where he was already speaking to Danilova. His back was to us, but we could see her face.

"No need to wait," the man was saying in a dry voice. "She will not come. There's been an accident—and that's that. Pack up and go home."

He spoke rapidly, like a man who hated what he was doing but was driven to do it by some compulsion.

Blood had drained from Danilova's face and she could only stare at him.

"What accident?" George asked, stepping forward, and the man turned to us, showing his full face for the first time. It was a face rutted with hatred and torment and self-doubt, the lips trembling and the eyes glistening with fever—the face of Judas.

"Don't ask questions," he snapped. "Stay out of this. I just came here to tell you so you wouldn't wait all night. She won't be back."

He swung around and was gone.

What accident? Where? Was she dead or alive? Was she in the hospital?

The manager of the park had stood by listening, and he was the first to regain his senses and connect the words "boating" and "accident." He offered to drive us across the river to Vasily Island, where we could check the different harbors on foot—a mileage restriction on his government car prevented his driving us to each one. We waited for him to lock up the park, and then climbed into a small four-seater, badly painted and creaky. He let us off on the other side of the bridge and we split into two groups, George and I heading for one side of the island and Danilova and Efimov for the other.

We agreed to meet at the largest harbor, the outlet to the fortress of Kronstadt and the Baltic Sea, where the bigger ships came in.

George and I walked the river route. We walked like somnambulists, hardly talking, knowing in our hearts that we had one chance in a hundred of finding out anything. The man's warning to stay out of it and not ask questions meant only one thing—foul play, and if the foul play involved anyone in the official world, there would be no trace left. Still, we kept walking and stopping at every dock and small harbor and anywhere a small boat could have anchored. The answer to our questions was in each case the same: no, they didn't know anything, had not seen any boat, and no accident had been reported. The streets were emptying and the harbor people were going home, and it was becoming harder to find anyone to question. It was hours later when we reached the big harbor. Despite the pale lustrous light around us, we knew that we were deep into the night.

The harbor was deserted. A gray destroyer stood solidly rooted in the water across from a building that looked like a warehouse, and, farther down the pier, a big two-decker ferry that took people to the fortress of Kronstadt was moored to the heavy pilings. There was no one around.

315

Waiting for the other two to arrive, we walked idly along the edge of the pier, our hearts empty and our eyes aimlessly skimming the waters below. We passed the destroyer and came to the double-decker and were going by it when we suddenly caught sight of an object too close to the pier to have been visible from a distance.

Tied to the stern of the double-decker, a motorboat was wobbling in the ripples. One side of it was so badly smashed that it was almost broken in half; the motor was dangling from the one remaining strip of metal still attached to the craft.

This was it—we knew it instantly.

We stood numb, looking down.

Danilova and Efimov came up from behind us.

"What are you looking at?" she asked. And then they, too, were staring silently at the wreckage of the boat.

Slowly, we came out of our trance. If this was the boat, then we had to make sure of it. Someone around this harbor must know what had happened, must be able to give us the details, and, heaven be kind, maybe some hope. But there was not a living soul to be seen.

The gangplank to the two-decker was still down, although the entry to the ship itself was closed off with lashings of heavy rope. We raced up the gangplank to the rope and began calling, with no real expectation of being heard.

Anyone there? Anyone there? Our cries rose to a hysterical pitch.

To our astonishment, an old man appeared on deck, rubbing his eyes and grumbling his displeasure at being awakened.

No, he didn't know anything about that broken boat. He was only a night watchman, he said, and what was all the hurry about anyway? If we wanted to know anything, we'd better ask the captain. He lived in that small cottage behind the big building, but we had better be prepared to catch all hell if we dared wake him up at this hour. Cursed be the young, he growled. They have no consideration.

His curses were lost behind us as we made for the cottage. It was a square, wooden shack with windows on three sides. All the curtains were drawn, and we circled it cautiously, appraising our situation. If the watchman was correct about the captain's temper, then, surely, by waking him we would gain nothing but more trouble. Perhaps it would be wiser to wait till morning, which was not far off.

That was when we noticed a light through a slit in one of the curtains. One by one, we put an eye to the slit.

All we could see was the captain's forearm lying on the table, his hand clutching a mug, a pot of coffee standing next to it. That was all we needed. The captain was awake.

The response to our knocking was slow, and when he opened the door, we were faced with a thin, balding man stooping with weariness. His no-color eyes were rimmed with red, his mouth drooped, but he didn't seem to be drunk.

Nor was he angry. He was nervous and suspicious. His bloodshot eyes studied our faces.

Who were we and why did we want to know about the broken boat? We explained ourselves and began firing questions at him.

He was evasive; he contradicted himself repeatedly, retracted what had slipped out, gabbled double-talk. He claimed not to know a thing. But slowly our relentless interrogation and our obvious despair made him give in, and the truth began to leak out.

Yes, he said, there had been an accident. He was bringing his ship back from Kronstadt and it collided with the small boat.

"But it was not my fault," he added wildly, a man caught in a whirlpool of someone else's stirring. "It was their fault. They were aiming straight at the bow of my ship. I kept tooting my horn, but they wouldn't stop. I couldn't stop either, because I was going full speed ahead. To stop would have endangered the lives of the two hundred people on board." He paused and then explained, "You see, we have no lifeboats."

"What then?"

He replied with reluctance. "I hit the small boat and it turned over."

"What happened to the people in it?"

"Well, the men—there were three—they held on to the side of my ship. Someone had let some ropes down from the bow, and they grabbed them, and it was easy to pull them up on deck. But the girl . . ." He hesitated. He looked into our anguished faces and tried to soften the blow.

"No . . . no . . ." he muttered. "I think there were two girls . . . and one was saved by the fisherman from the other shore. . . ."

We knew there was one girl only, but we didn't contradict his well-intentioned lie.

"And the other?"

"The other?" His eyes were downcast and his hand was rubbing the back of his neck as if to relieve an ache. "The other . . . she fell into the water and was sucked under the boat into the propellers."

Suddenly, his eyes glimpsed something beyond us and deadened into a stare. His tone changed.

"That's all I can tell you. Maybe your friend was the other girl."

"What other girl?" Efimov almost shrieked.

"Well . . . the other . . ." The captain hurriedly repeated his lie. "I told you I think there were two. . . . I mean the one saved by the fisherman."

He pushed us away and slammed his door.

We turned from the door, and then we saw what had prompted the change in the captain's attitude.

About a hundred feet away from the shack stood the man in the heavy coat. He stood like a figure of stone, watching us. Had he followed us, or had he known that eventually we would end up at this harbor? Or was it a compulsion to return to the scene of the crime?

We had to pass him, his face gnarled, the features twisted, and his eyes even more feverish than before. As we walked by him, he said, "Who is going to tell her mother?"

None of us answered, walking in a nightmare.

"All right, I will do it," he shouted after us, but we didn't look back.

We walked all the rest of the night.

62

A bleak, gray morning—very early, not yet eight o'clock. The white nights have gone, taking with them the lustrous sheen, and the sky is matte, shedding a thin drizzle like sieved dew.

We are standing on the same pier where not so long ago we stared down at the smashed boat, and the memory of that night is vivid. It is ironic that fate should bring us here at this moment Ivanova should have shared with us. Her death has erased all the joy from this adventure, and we stand cold and quiet, chilled not only by the morning dampness but by the thought of her.

The navy destroyer is still here, and next to it a barge is heaving under its cargo, but in place of the double-decker, there rises an immaculate, freshly painted ship, on her prow the name *"Der Preusse."* She will take us away.

As had been the case in Stepan's hanging, the mystery of Ivanova's death was never unraveled. Every attempt to investigate it was promptly squelched, with a warning to lay off the subject. Although it was officially ruled an accident, remembering the ropes ready for the three men, reason insisted that it was a premeditated crime. It was whispered that she had been in possession of some secret that represented a threat to the three men. Yet why was it necessary to simulate an accident in such a dangerous manner? One was forced to assume that the three were afraid of being caught at it—afraid of someone higher up.

Whatever the truth, she is gone, our marvelously gifted friend, and we are not yet ready to accept it.

We stand in silence surrounded by family and friends. Nothing to say.

The hidden hand of fate is charting our course, and we are keenly aware of it and uncertain of ourselves, our potential, our plans and even the very next minute. Are we really leaving? Leda Ivanova was sure of it, but it turned out quite differently.

Father is standing with his hands behind his back and his head down, looking at me from under his brows. A serious, penetrating look. I wonder what he is thinking. My own mind is a blank, and I move like an automaton, according to what I am told to do.

Mother shows signs of impatience, and Anatol, whom she

holds by the hand, is squirming and brushing raindrops off his nose. Irra and Tatiana are ogling the people around us. There is another group waiting. They are Germans who have been granted permission to return to their Fatherland.

Konstantin hasn't come. He had to work, and felt it wrong to take time off. He said he'd rather meet us on our return—there would be much more to say then.

Our baggage has been taken away, into the building we had taken for a warehouse but which in reality houses the offices of immigration and customs. After our bags are searched, they will be deposited directly on the ship.

We are waiting to be called in for the passport examination. I am shivering. We have been standing here a long time, and Dimitriev, our impresario, is beginning to worry. He walks to the building, pokes his face inside and returns to tell us it will be soon. George alone is calm. He is deeply religious and has the unshakable conviction that God is always at his side to help him, whatever his need may be.

On the deck of the destroyer, sailors lean over the railing and gape at us, commenting on us loudly and rudely. We are an oddity, a breakthrough—Russians leaving the Soviet Union —and they are speculating about the reason.

Another hour goes by, and then a man in a shabby leather jacket comes out of the building and motions us to follow him inside.

We enter a long room divided by a partition and are steered to the corner where a man is sitting at a table littered with documents. Without glancing up at us, he carefully examines our papers. Meanwhile Dimitriev, genteelly solicitous, is supplying him with details he obviously considers irrelevant, since he pays no attention to what is being said.

The man is a stone mountain, hard and hostile.

"Next," he says, handing Dimitriev the passports.

Like a flock of buzzards, the militiamen surround us, separate the men from the girls, and we are led to two different alcoves behind the partition. A plump woman is waiting for us in a cubbyhole, and she orders Danilova and me to undress. Painstakingly, she goes through pockets, hems, shoes and shoe linings, any bulge or hollow that could hold what we might be trying to smuggle out of the country. She does it with detached precision, never looking at our faces.

When we are dressed again, and she dismisses us, we go back into the long room, where we are joined by the men, who have undergone the same search. Here we are informed that we will be escorted directly to the ship, and that we are forbidden any physical contact with the people outside. No embracing, no handshaking, no accepting of gifts or packages, not a touch.

In accordance with this ruling, we are marched across the pier under guard—two militiamen on either side.

Those who surge toward us are pushed back with a warning to keep away. Bewilderment comes to their faces, hands flutter weakly in farewell, words of good-bye fly back and forth.

At the top of the gangplank, we are handed over to the German captain, and the militiamen go back to Russian soil.

I stand on the stern deck as the ship disengages from the pier and begins to move. On the receding shoreline Father's lone figure is looking up at me.

All the well-wishers are gone, tired of waiting for us to leave, and the pier is empty of people except for a few officials huddling in the background, and the sailors still watching us from the destroyer.

Mother blew me a kiss a long time ago and left, talking vivaciously to Irra and Tatiana and dragging Anatol along.

We are withdrawing fast, and Father's figure is diminishing in the distance, the sea pushing us apart.

His figure loses shape, shrinks to a pinpoint and disappears, and the shore itself becomes a pencil line, and then that, too, vanishes in the meeting of sea and sky.

The drizzle has stopped and the fresh and salty air is beginning to revive my brain. I shake my head to help it. My companions are below deck, probably looking over the vessel, but I have no inclination to join them yet, and so I stroll to the bow and stop at the tip. Now, water all around me, the sea flat and glossy as a mirror top, the ship slicing through it like scissors through a piece of fabric. Ahead, the elusive, ever-retreating horizon, the guardian of the future, releasing it a minute at a time.

I gaze at the horizon and wonder what is waiting for me beyond it, wishing I could get a glimpse of things to come.

Remembering how in childhood I was able to bring the impossible to life by squinting, I try it now. I throw my head back slightly as I used to do and tighten my eyelids.

Nothing happens. The power of the little girl has dissipated with the years, and reason has devoured magic.

But had I been granted that glimpse ahead, I would have learned that I had just cut myself off from my native land forever, and that I would never again see Father, who was destined to be killed by a bomb in World War II, and that Anatol, too, would fall victim to the great tragedy and die a prisoner in a German camp.

We were coming out into the open sea. A sudden gust of wind blew savagely, lashing the still waters, and drops of rain began to fall again, big and heavy this time.

I waited by the railing, and when it became too menacing, I descended the stairs to our cabin.

It was empty. I sat down on one of the bunks and pressed

my hands to my temples, trying to make myself realize where I was and what was happening.

There was a knock on the door and a stewardess walked in, carrying a silver tray with a silver tea set on it and a plate of cookies. Her uniform was spotless, her apron, cuffs and cap snow-white and starched into paper stiffness, the cap sitting on top of her perfect coiffure like a crown.

"Willen sie ein bisschen tee haben?" she asked, probably mistaking me for one of the German passengers.

I stared at her idiotically.

My, my, I thought. Right out of Pola Negri's movie. Maybe people do live like this somewhere.

"Danke sehr," I said recovering. "Vielleicht später."

"Gut," she smiled. "Ich will zurück kommen." And she walked out.

I wonder what made me refuse the tea. Was it because I sensed there was no longer any need to grab at food, or because a pleasant calm was spreading throughout my body and I wanted to enjoy it quietly. I stretched out on the bunk and relaxed completely.

The boat rolled and pitched, carrying me into a new tomorrow.

POSTSCRIPT

Tomorrow came. We arrived at Stettin, a German port on an outlet to the Baltic Sea—our steppingstone to Berlin.

Bright weather, blue sky, cheerful little town. Houses shining with fresh paint, flower boxes outside windows, greenery carefully clipped, surreys with fringe on top—a picture out of a children's book we once saw and then forgot.

We climbed into a surrey and asked where we could find inexpensive lodgings—that is, I asked, since I was the only one in our quintet who spoke German. Dimitriev was able to put a few sentences together, but he got lost in conversation.

Obligingly, the driver took us to a pension, the surrey gliding smoothly on its good tires. How different from the bare rims squeaking along our city streets! We stopped at a two-story house. Here, too, everything was neat and orderly—a garland of shrubbery surrounding the house; the stairs to the front door flanked by rows of plants; inside, spotless walls; chintzy furniture; comforters beaten into fluffy heaps on top of beds; brass gleaming. Fortunately, we had washed and scrubbed ourselves on the boat; otherwise, I wonder if we would have had the nerve to enter this spotless haven.

But the most glorious experience was the meal. On board we had had a nice supper, better than any we had had in years, but here we found real German home cooking: hot bread, and butter, and cookies and a plethora of rich sauces and vegetables and other culinary marvels, all temptingly fragrant. What's more, no limit was put on the intake, although I must admit that when we all dove for a third helping, lost in the ecstasy of eating, the proprietress showed some concern. She was obviously relieved to learn that we would leave the following day.

Early in the morning, we were on the train to Berlin. Order and efficiency everywhere, glossed with harsh, Prussian politeness; everything moving like clockwork. Half-dazed, we gaped around us and out the windows, trying to digest the new world drawing us into its midst.

Finally, Berlin—blazing with lights in the indigo of the

325

early evening, brilliant store windows, girls with bobbed hair, electric signs, horns tooting, traffic—it was enough to take one's breath away.

We drove to an address on Potsdammer Platz given us by a porter at the Bahnhoff, and settled down in a boardinghouse suitable to our budget. It was not as quaint and cheery as the place in Stettin, but it offered comfort enough in a heavy German style.

Although we were among the first to enter the country legally from the Soviet Union, our arrival went unheralded except for a paragraph in one Russian newspaper. That brought a few curious Russian refugees to our door. We were grateful for their assistance and friendship, and to them we were not unlike visitors from Mars.

It soon became evident that Dimitriev had greatly overstated his financial position and that he had made no plans or preparations for the recitals. Thwarted by the new metropolis, he was totally inadequate, and that was when our new Russian friends proved to be invaluable. Tirelessly investigating all the possibilities, they guided him to the people who could help him organize a performance.

While waiting, Danilova and I strolled about the city, continually staggered by the sights. Berlin, in that pre-Hitler era, was a city of decadence, and though in my naïveté I could not diagnose it as such, the climate of the cafés disturbed me and I was shocked by the suggestive posters and the young men and women flagrantly soliciting in the streets even in daytime. I was told that an apricot-colored shirt on a man meant a silent "for sale." I cannot vouch for the authenticity of this information, but there certainly were a great many apricot shirts.

In no position to buy anything, we gloated over the window displays. Finally, we could not restrain ourselves from making one purchase—not from a shop, but off a cart on one of the side streets. Each of us acquired a hat with a wide brim and a long veil and immediately slapped it on. God only knows what we looked like in our pommeled sweaters and scuffed shoes, our veils drooping to our shoulders. I probably looked especially ludicrous because of the long braid hanging down my back. But we thought ourselves irresistible.

A month passed before our performance became a reality, and the delay took a substantial bite out of our finances. The recital was a disaster. It took place in a gloomy hall, no better than some in which our halturas had been staged at home, and since we knew nothing about advertising and couldn't have afforded any, the attendance was poor. By European standards, our costumes were niggardly, the tempo of the performance slow, and the whole presentation, to the tinkling of one piano, amateurish. The tainted Berliners didn't respond to the classical excerpts danced by Danilova and Efimov, and George and I didn't fare much better. We were most definitely behind the times. Besides, we couldn't help feeling an underlying hostility to anything connected with Soviet Russia.

The option for the second recital was canceled by the owner of the hall, and we had to look elsewhere for work. Days went by and the situation was getting to be precarious.

At long last, Dimitriev got hold of some impresario in Wiesbaden who offered us a contract for a series of recitals along the Rhine. We were given a definite guarantee, but he refused to specify any details or give us an advance until the group, or at least part of it, arrived in Wiesbaden—with the costumes. I presume he didn't trust any Soviet citizens.

We were not in a position to bargain, and so Dimitriev and the boys, carrying the suitcases that held our costumes, started out for Wiesbaden, leaving Danilova and me behind as hostages for the unpaid hotel bill. Should everything go well, we were to be sent the tickets and the money.

Alone in the big city, we waited, our allowance shrinking no matter how stingy we were. Furthermore, our limbs were getting stiff. Dancers need practice.

I am slumped in a barber's chair. The man standing at my side snaps his scissors closed and puts them down.

At my feet, snips of hair are scattered on the floor like the torn wings of insects. In front of me a rich harvest of thick, long strands carefully tied with ribbon is laid out on the table. The barber picks up one of the strands, runs his hand over it caressingly and says, "Solche schöne haare."

He is a wigmaker and he has just made a profitable deal. There are many wigs on the dummy heads standing around, but none of this color.

I felt tearful. I can't take my eyes off my shorn plumage. So much of my life is tangled in those ash-blond strands, and now it's all in the barber's hands.

He goes to the cash register, comes back and hands me the money.

A sigh rises in my throat, but I squelch it. Don't sigh. There was nothing else to sell. After all, many girls have bobbed hair.

The tickets and the money arrived. We paid the bill and immediately set out to join our fellows in Weisbaden.

We lived in another pension, this one very middle-class and overburdened with wicker furniture. We found a pitiful imitation of a studio, where we rehearsed, trying to improve our repertoire, and when we weren't working we ate. We ate three meals a day and we ate between meals, plus a lot of extra goodies we bought daily and consumed before retiring.

The recitals began. We danced every week, sometimes more often. We danced in Wiesbaden, Ems, Mosel and other, smaller towns of the Rhine provinces. We danced in dingy halls, in summer theatres, on open stages, in ballrooms for private parties, in beer gardens and for the inmates of an insane asylum. The last was a terrifying experience—performing before rows of expressionless faces, eyes focused on some intangible, private planet, no reaction, no applause, not even at the end, only a shuffling of feet as they moved out of the hall, herded by male attendants. I wonder if they saw us at all, leaping and whirling in front of them. One of those shuffling inmates was Ernst Toller, the famous Socialist poet and playwright whose *Hinkemann* was much admired in Russian. In 1933, Hitler would exile him from his native land.

The series ended. Our last appearance was in a vaudeville show in a Mainz beer garden. Birds flew overhead, the stage was slippery, and the hale and hearty audience was drinking beer and occasionally bursting into song. We followed a dog act.

The date for our return home was approaching rapidly. The split second of decision was at hand.

Up to then, not one of us dared broach the subject. We brooded over it secretly, battling doubts and fears, measuring pros and cons. Granted, we had made no impression so far, gained no recognition, but maybe somewhere ahead there was a silver lining. On the other hand, we trembled to think of the steps our government might take if we defected. Ivanova's death was still fresh in our memory.

It was not logic, however, that swayed us to a decision, but a sudden blast of realization that we could not—never, never—go back to the dreariness, the privation and restrictions of our past existence. We had had a taste of the world and we wanted more. Come what may, we were going to stay. We would take our chances.

A few days later we received an offer to appear for two weeks, with an option for two more, at the Empire Theatre in London—the Palladium of the day.

What a thrill! We were going to the great city of London.

"What's up? Hurry!" The stage manager was banging on the dressing room door.

"Be there in a minute!" I called back panting, my fingers struggling with the hooks and eyes of my costume and getting entwined with the fingers of the wardrobe lady who was trying to help me.

I had finished my first number and was getting ready for my second, but this Egyptian sheath was a nuisance and the pas de deux danced by Danilova and Efimov in the interim didn't give me time enough to complete my change of costume.

The stage manager pushed the door open and nearly jumped into the room, his hands clutching his bald pate in a gesture of despair.

"You're late! The orchestra is repeating the introduction for the third time!" he yelled in an outburst not befitting an Englishman. All this in French, since I didn't understand English.

I was not alone in this predicament. Our whole group was equally guilty of the same offense. We knew nothing of the precision required in a music-hall presentation, our costumes were not constructed for quick changes, our timing not correctly gauged. We were all often late for our entrances.

The great city of London didn't last very long. We were given our full salary and fired at the end of the second week.

The London fiasco restricted our travels to one place—Paris. Return to Germany was out of the question—we had no contract that would entitle us to a visa; the same provision was required by other governments; and our Red passports were not looked on with favor by the British authorities. Within a week, we were politely ushered out of England. France was the only country that gave anchorage to the homeless.

So Paris it was. Dejected, with no expectations to cheer us, we crossed the Channel, took a train to Paris, and found ourselves at the end of our journey in a cheap hotel on the Place de la République—not a first-class locale. The quality of our residences was diminishing with our every move.

The glories of Paris were not on our agenda; we seldom ventured out for more than a breath of air. Cloistered in our rooms, our heads together, we desperately searched for some way out of the deadlock. There was absolutely nothing in the offing, nobody knew us, and our dismal record was no help. Doubt and fear were surfacing. Had we made a mistake? Should we have gone home? But our return date had come and gone, and there was no turning back.

We sat around the table, nibbling cheese and crackers and playing dominoes to distract us from our morbid thoughts. It was our fifth or sixth day in Paris and we had estimated that our fortune would last two more weeks.

Dimitriev lifted his head, his face set with some idea.

331

"Why don't we risk our money on a trip to Monte Carlo, to see Diaghilev?" he said. "The company is there, getting ready for the season. Maybe he'll give you kids a job."

The legendary Ballets Russes of Diaghilev! The home of Pavlova, Nijinsky, Karsavina—the pictures and photographs in Father's museum, the dream of childhood! My heart was pounding.

"Ah, he won't give a damn about us," said Efimov, who was the most pessimistically inclined. "Everybody's been trying to get into that company for years."

"How do you know?" I said. "You haven't been here for years."

He didn't deign to answer me.

"Perhaps we should risk it," Danilova said. "But if it doesn't work out, will there be enough money left to get back to Paris?"

"No," Dimitriev said laconically, and that put a damper on the subject.

"But you could save us," George said to him teasingly. "You could become a croupier at the Casino—you've done it before —and maybe you will break the bank of Monte Carlo."

George was the only one who took the situation philosophically. He seemed much less perturbed than the rest of us, and when I would ask him, "What do we do now?" he would reply calmly, "Nothing. We wait." I often wondered if that state of being was a product of his superconfidence in himself, or of his firm belief that God would not let him down.

Gloomily, we continued our domino game until it was interrupted by a knock on the door and the concierge walked in before we could say "Come in." Paris concierges are notoriously rude.

"Téléphone pour Monsieur George," she said, George's last name being unpronounceable. "C'est en bas."

A look of astonishment passed between us. We didn't know a soul in Paris and had certainly not been seen anywhere.

Puzzled, we waited for George to come back. When he walked in, he was pale and spoke slowly.

"It was Diaghilev," he said. "His agents traced us from London, and it took them five days to find us in Paris." He took a deep breath. "He wants to see us all tomorrow."

We auditioned for Diaghilev and were signed under individual contracts to join the company in Monte Carlo. Danilova and George were to be the most highly paid because of their rank at the Maryinsky (Diaghilev kept track of everything in the theatre world); Efimov came next; and I, with nothing but Theatre School to back me up, was at the bottom of the ladder.

The casino, the theatre and the rehearsal hall were all in the same palace-like building, the front opening on the plaza of the Hôtel-de-Paris and the rear facing the Mediterranean, aquamarine under the cliff of the promenade. A lane weaving between lemon trees descended to the entrance of the rehearsal hall at basement level.

The routine of the company was strenuous, beginning with a class at nine in the morning, conducted by Maestro Cecchetti, followed by a rehearsal till five, with only an hour-and-a-half break for lunch. During the actual season, the afternoon rehearsal was shortened by an hour to give us a chance to rest before reporting to the theatre at seven.

Serge Diaghilev was an extraordinary man and a despot. He had all the characteristics of Dr. Jekyll and Mr. Hyde, his personality changing from overwhelming charm to the roughness of a truck driver at any sign of opposition. He had perfect taste and an unfailing sense of discovery, and there was no other man in France who commanded equal respect in the world of the arts. Surrounded by great painters, composers and authors, he ruled his domain and manipulated his people like puppets. When this hulk of a man with a protruding jaw and a white streak cutting through his dyed black hair entered the rehearsal hall, one could feel everyone's nerves tighten.

In status, as in salary, I was pushed way back. Danilova became a ballerina almost at once, and George's gifts as a choreographer caught Diaghilev's interest. They were constantly in conference preparing projects for him to develop. But I was stuck in the corps de ballet. Quite a comedown after the equal billing throughout our tour.

My first break came when Bronislava Nijinska, sister of the famed dancer, left the company, and Anton Dolin, the premier danseur, intervened on my behalf in the choice of her replacement. I was given the lead opposite Dolin in the ballet *Train Bleu*. It was lovely while it lasted, which was not very long. Dolin soon quit the company also, leaving no one skillful enough to duplicate his role, and the ballet was taken out of the repertoire. I was delivered back into the corps de ballet.

Gradually, solo parts began drifting my way, though I was still kept in the corps, which meant a double job. We gave three ballets a night, and if I soloed in one, I had to dance in the corps de ballet in the other two.

I have something in common with race horses—small feet and thin ankles, great attributes from the aesthetic point of view, but not serviceable under pressure. An overworked race horse, when forced to do its best, is apt to injure itself because of its delicate underpinnings, and the same applied to me. I was forever twisting my ankles or pulling tendons.

Meanwhile, George's career was blossoming. Now rechristened George Balanchine by Diaghilev, he was choreographing one ballet after another, and the world was accepting his work with delighted appreciation. He was totally immersed in the new milieu of talented, creative people who crowded around Diaghilev—a circle that excluded me. I was nothing but George's dancer-wife, left somewhere in the shadows.

And the dancer-wife began developing an appetite for the world, and a strong compulsion to be accepted for herself. Solo parts increased, taking me out of the corps more frequently, yet I was not satisfied. The curiosity Father had implanted in me was growing, and Mother's genes were spreading through my body a lust for life.

George's emotional pattern was to be in love with his Galatea, and he now had several. I no longer had exclusive claim to that pedestal. Nevertheless, whenever he choreographed a new ballet, he would create a part for me if it was at all possible, but I was never sure if he did it because of my ability or my marital status.

A lot was missing in our relationship, and the gap between us was widening. And then one day, having seen him cast an eye toward a new Galatea, I took it as an excuse and, after a heart-to-heart conversation late at night, walked out dramatically and took up residence on my own. In keeping with his character—he was never a demonstrative man—George never discussed the break again, but he did send an emissary who asked me to come back. I declined.

Our professional routine didn't suffer, and the discipline of our training kept us in check. We saw each other every day, worked together, and kept a subtle distance to allow the discord to simmer down into friendship.

It was the end of the season. We were in Paris, and only four days were left before vacation time. Diaghilev and his entourage, including George, had already left for Italy, leaving us in the hands of our general manager, Grigoriev. He was not particularly fond of me, chiefly because he thought I represented a potential threat to his aging wife, ballerina Tchernicheva, and Diaghilev's absence gave him the opportunity to assert his power and put me in my place, which he considered to be the corps de ballet. He ordered me to join the corps in the second scene of *Boutique Fantasque*, although I had to dance a solo in the first scene and the change of costume was virtually impossible. Naturally, I failed to accomplish this metamorphosis, and that gave him his chance. He accused me of having missed out on purpose, and unleashed a storm of such wounding and violent abuse that I could not help answering back. If he was not satisfied with me, I said haughtily, I could always leave the company. He latched onto my words.

"Good riddance!" he shouted. "Go! Leave! We don't need you!"

He didn't renew my option for the next season, and there was no one left at the helm with whom I could register a complaint.

Paris is not the right place for a young girl alone and without a job. I found that out soon enough.

At first, I didn't worry. Surely, when the ballet season started again, Diaghilev and George would find out about the injustice done me, and they would call me. And I had enough money saved to last me through the two months of vacation.

I rented a room in one of those cheesy hotels that Paris is full of, ate at a bistro across the street, and enjoyed this respite. It was summer and it was beautiful, and I wandered around the city, learning a lot about it. My knowledge of French helped me make a few friends, but still it was then, for the first time, that I came to know the forlorn feeling of being all alone in the world.

And then leaves began to fall and the date for the new ballet season splashed on the calendar. By corresponding with one of the girls in the company, I made sure that my address was easily available, and I waited nervously for someone to get in touch with me. But every evening ended in disappointment.

I still had a little money left, but to insure myself, I began making the rounds of what were described to me as managerial offices. Outside of a wink, a pinch on the behind and the nebulous possibility of a job, contingent on a drink and a late visit, I got nowhere. Weeks went by. I locked a small sum of my remaining capital into my trunk, rationed myself to a minimum, and stubbornly hung on in the wishful expectation of a call or letter.

The silence persisted. Reluctantly, I had to admit to myself that there would be no call and that I was alone in Paris with a few francs and no prospects.

Mama Mottie, the owner of the bistro where I ate, seemed to me a kind woman, and I decided to confess my dire state to her. Pretending that I was waiting for a contract to materialize at any moment, I asked her if she would let me have my meals on credit. Shaking her head in sympathy, she consented. All went well until the pinches, slaps and passes of her husband became so vigorous that I objected. It was a mistake. Over Mama Mottie's protestations, my credit was canceled.

For a while, she managed to smuggle me through the back entrance up to the attic and feed me oysters and white wine (two items not easily checked), but ultimately her illicit generosity was discovered and stopped.

Winter came and added to my woes; having lived in the south of France the previous year, I had no warm clothes, and I was forced to wear two dresses under my coat to keep from freezing. Then a short reprieve came with an invitation from a Russian dancer-acrobat to assist him in two performances at the Théâtre Édouard VII sponsored by his rich patron. Grateful as I was for the money, I was glad when it was over and I was still alive after being tossed through the air like a handball between my partner and another muscular young man. Acrobatics of that sort were not my métier.

The salary for those performances gave me a breathing spell, and then my situation became desperate again. Soon there would be nothing but the money locked in the trunk between me and destitution. Anticipation of that moment was tearing me apart, and, finally, I decided to meet it head-on—if it had to be, let it be tomorrow.

That evening, I took the money out of the trunk, invited two equally poor friends to join me, and bought us the most elaborate dinner my finances could afford.

When I returned to the hotel, I had three francs left to my name. Surprisingly, I fell asleep with a sense of relief.

Next morning, when I awakened from a black, dreamless sleep, the folly of my actions hit me with full force. The money spent the night before would have kept me going for a few more days, and who knows what changes might have occurred in that span of time?

Emptyheaded, I lay in bed all day, foolishly observing the molding around the edge of the ceiling. By six o'clock my stomach as well as my head was so empty that I felt faint. I endured the pangs in billowing despair, and then, as at other

times in my life, despair churned into anger and blind defiance.

I would not be hungry again! I would eat. If I had to con-
nive until my fortunes changed, I would do so. I would go
to a restaurant, order dinner, eat it and then pretend that I
had lost my purse. Or maybe I'd tell them the truth—or maybe
. . . I was not sure what I would tell them. Looking back, I
think I was out on my feet.

I chose a restaurant in Passy, mainly because I had heard
it employed a few Russians, who, I hoped, would commiserate
with me. I entered with aplomb. The drama of the moment
appealed to me, boosting my courage and pushing away the
questionable outcome.

I sat down, ordered a complete dinner and gulped down
the soup with comparative ease. The second course didn't go
down so smoothly; spasms constricted my throat, and though
I chewed my food into mush and washed it down with vin
ordinaire, it still clogged my gullet; meanwhile, bite by bite,
my false courage was taking leave of me.

A few tables away, a big stodgy man with a hooked nose
was eying me steadily. Accustomed to attempted pick-ups, I
paid him no heed.

I left the dessert untouched. Then coffee was placed before
me and the bill was gently slipped next to the cup. I went
cold and stiff, my mouth suddenly dry. Never before had I
been in a position where I had to plead for leniency, and I
cringed under this humiliation. Delaying the dreaded moment, I sipped my coffee slowly, the cup unsteady in my hand
and my mind going dead blank.

The pudgy man got up.

"Oh, no!" I prayed. "Don't let him come here. I'll have to
get rid of him, and that will make everything worse." French

restaurateurs were not fond of girls who chased away customers, especially if those girls could not pay for dinner.

The man walked straight to me and leaned over the table. "Excuse me, please," he said, "but I think I know you."

A new approach, I thought.

"Permit me to introduce myself," the man continued. "My name is Rode. In the old days, in St. Petersburg, I owned a famous restaurant called Villa Rode. One of my clients and friends was a rich man who had a lamé factory, and was well known also for his art collection. He had a daughter whom I last saw when she was about seven years old. Forgive me for studying you all evening—and it might be my imagination— but you bear a striking resemblance to that little girl. By some quirk of fate, you wouldn't be . . ." And he spoke my name.

I nodded, gone mute. It seemed impossible. Rode . . . Rode . . . yes, I had heard that name, and now it was quivering in my memory.

"Good," he said and sat down, his face breaking into a cherubic grin. "You know, I'm deeply indebted to your father; at one time he saved me from bankruptcy and, with the Revolution on our heels and my subsequent escape, I was never able to repay him. And now I meet you. How nice. Count me as a friend."

Tension left me. My jaw dropped and I felt beads of perspiration building on my forehead. The man looked worried.

"What is it?" he asked. "Is there anything I can do for you?"

"Yes," I said, "pay this." And I pushed the bill toward him.

He paid my outstanding bills, fussed over me like a big uncle, made me promise not to worry and, of course, that was when the call came.

I was sitting opposite Diaghilev in his suite.

"Why did you leave?"

"I didn't leave," I said. "I was fired."

"Who fired you?"

"Grigoriev."

"I was told you had left saying you didn't ever want to see the company again."

"He is a liar!"

"Never mind that." The edge in Diaghilev's voice instantly quelled my agitation. "Come back. Sokolova is about to retire, and you'll inherit her repertoire." (Sokolova was one of the incumbent ballerinas—no relation to my teacher.)

"But Grigoriev hates me."

"He'll have no jurisdiction over you."

I returned to the company triumphant. The company met me warmly. George, too, seemed pleased by my return. Time had brushed down the bristles of separation, and he was friendly, and easy, and more like his old self. I reciprocated, though in my heart I could never reconcile myself to his lack of concern during my absence. I thought he knew me better than to believe I would leave the company of my own accord. Grigoriev had the audacity to act as if he had had nothing to do with my dismissal.

My star was in the ascendant. I was given new solos, several variations, and assigned one of the two leads in George's new ballet, *Pastorale*, which was soon going into rehearsal. In the interim, and quite unexpectedly, I was given the lead in *Prince Igor*. It was almost supernatural to find myself putting on the very same costume I had so often admired as a child in Father's museum. The audience's response to my performance was gratifying, and the next morning I was summoned into Diaghilev's presence. Expecting praise, I was taken aback by what he had to say.

"You were quite good—" he was known to be stingy with any expression of approval—"but curb your personality. You were about to set the stage on fire. A dancer is an instrument in the choreographer's hands, and nothing more. The dance pattern speaks for itself—don't add anything to it."

What he said left an indelible impression on me. For the duration of my stay with the company, I could never recapture the same freedom.

Meanwhile, another surprising situation was developing. Diaghilev's extravagance in staging his productions often left him on the brink of bankruptcy and forced him to seek backing from private sources. That particular year, it was Lord Rothermere, a burly, gross man, and the co-owner of the London *Daily Mail*, who undertook the subsidizing of the company. Unfortunately, he also chose a mistress from the company, and, wielding the threat of withdrawing his money, he insisted that his lady-love be given more important roles. Consequently, we all watched this young woman of boyish build and mediocre gifts being pushed to the top, to the disadvantage of more talented dancers. I was beginning to lose my illusions about the integrity of the famous company.

It was only a matter of time before the rise of Rothermere's mistress was to affect me directly. I had been told that she and I would alternate in the lead of a ballet called *Les Biches*. Suddenly, and with no explanation, the decision was reversed and the role handed to her exclusively. It was quite a pill to swallow. Even Danilova, secure in her position as a ballerina, suffered indignities because of that woman.

My disappointment deepened. My few professional gains

could not compensate for the weariness and the general sense of futility, and the whole environment was beginning to dishearten me. The world of the ballet is narrow and self-indulgent; its interests are limited and mental stimulation is not one of its virtues.

Then came spring, and in the spring a young man's—and a young girl's—fancy turns to thoughts of love. Emotionally I was barren and very lonely, assailed by spurts of melancholy. Although I had no dearth of beaux, none of them caught my fancy, not even a composer named Dukelsky, later to become famous as Vernon Duke, who relentlessly tried to persuade me to elope with him, his choice of place for this adventure getting wilder with each attempt.

My most rewarding relationship by far was my new friendship with Ivor Novello, the British playwright and composer, a man of beautiful countenance and soul to match. Being a balletomane, he was spending his vacation in Monte Carlo, and between rehearsals or at the end of a day, I would rush out looking for him, and would usually find him in the Café de Paris at the other end of the plaza. We would sit under an umbrella and talk and talk, and he would tell me about his work and life in England, and then the scope of the conversation would broaden, and through him I lived in the big world outside our circle.

He was a man of great sensitivity, and could easily read my discontent.

"You're dissatisfied, my girl," he said, "and these lemon trees in blossom make you lonely."

"Yes," I said. "Dancing is fine, but something is missing."

"Of course," he said gently, "you need a lover, someone who, if only for a moment, will put you on a cloud."

"Maybe you're right," I laughed, not too gaily. "There must be a prince somewhere."

There was—only he was a marquis.

I have found that when the subconscious sets the stage, some inexplicable force in the universe will supply the actor. In this instance, he came to life in Spain, during our season in Barcelona, immediately following Monte Carlo.

One night, a party was given for Diaghilev and his entourage, and I was included with two other dancers in that select group.

Our host, the wealthy heir to some dukedom, spared no effort to make the evening elegant. Supper was served under the stars in a flowering courtyard; music played in a hidden gazebo; liveried lackeys ran around carrying candelabra; and the male guests, outnumbering the ladies at least three to one, were most gallant and solicitous.

After supper we were led into a large studio, where we sat on cushions, Moorish fashion, while three flamenco dancers entertained us with their electrifying art.

In the midst of this, a new guest walked in. He was dark, not too tall, and handsome, and he wore a black mourning band around his left sleeve. He didn't join any group, but greeted people with a nod as he passed them, walked quietly to a sofa at one side and sat down alone and remote, taking no part in the gaiety.

A Frenchman next to me was very impressed.

"That is Antonio, a brother of our host," he told me. "His nickname is 'Le Beau Marquis,' and he is a very unusual man. I am surprised to see him here. Since his wife's death two years ago, he seems to have lost all interest in living, and he hardly ever goes out."

He waved to the man on the sofa, who acknowledged his greeting with a slight bow.

The gitanas finished their dancing and sat down at a side table, drinking champagne and strumming guitars for their own pleasure. It was getting late. Someone suggested that before calling it a night the whole party should drive up the famous Tibidabo Mountain, and the suggestion was seconded at once. With the scarcity of ladies, the men began rushing from one of us to another, inviting us to go in their respective cars.

Guided by instinct, I kept staving off the invitations. The man on the sofa remained impassive, watching me.

When the first rush after the ladies subsided and some of the people were already outside, he got up, walked to me unhurriedly and, as if it had been prearranged, offered me his hand as one invites a child for a walk.

"Will you come with me?" he said in flawless French, and that's how it began.

Antonio, Marquis de Mizar, was the perfect answer to a girl's impossible dream. He was in his early thirties, handsome, rich, titled, intelligent, selective—and he was crazy about me. His largess was of another century, and he showered on me flowers and presents and an attention such as I had not known before, easily sweeping me up to that cloud Ivor Novello wished for me.

On the debit side he was—a Catholic, a widower with a six-year-old son, and a member of that impenetrable society, the Spanish aristocracy.

The drawbacks didn't bother me. I accepted what we had for what it was—a dazzling fling, a passing love affair made of hearts and flowers, and, literally, castles in Spain.

For the rest of the season, I was spinning in a romantic whirl, cured of my spleen, desired, alive. I was pleasantly surprised by the effect our liaison created among his friends. And when it was over and the hour came for us to part, I had no regrets and no heartache, but rather a bittersweet pang at leaving something beautiful behind.

He drove me to the train that was to take us to Paris for the remainder of the spring season and, ignoring the inquisitive stares of the company, stood under the compartment window looking at me with a whimsical smile until the train left.

I sat down, closed my eyes and, to the rumble of the train, swam in the recollection of the past weeks.

Three days later, he was in Paris. Walking out the stage door after a rehearsal, I felt someone's arm coil around my waist and there he was, cool and smiling and amused at my amazed reaction. He wore a light suit, and I noticed that the mourning band was gone.

Except for one short trip to see his son at their home in Madrid, he remained in Paris, and this time, quietly and with complete assurance, he took possession of my life. Overriding my objections, he moved me from my modest hotel to a better one—"not too conspicuously exclusive"—and I realized that, discreet and careful though he was about my reputation, with a little encouragement on my part I could be well on my way to becoming a kept woman. It was inevitable that the situation would remind me of my mother's life.

Paris with Antonio was different from the Paris of my miserable days. Now it was all glamour and glitter and excitement, as Paris usually is pictured and seldom is. We visited all the best restaurants and boîtes, took drives through the Bois, and spent a lot of time in photographers' studios—he had a mania for having me photographed, the results never satisfying him. His collection of my portraits was prodigious, and when I suggested that he wanted to include them in the gallery of his conquests, I received a searing Spanish look.

I had to dance six times a week, but on one of my free nights we went to see a black revue imported from America. At the first strain of the blues with the horns wailing, my hair stood up in a thrill, and I felt my pores soaking in every sound as if I had finally found the music I had been looking for. Next day I bought sheet music of "Mandy" and "St. Louis Blues." When no one was around, I played them in the orchestra pit, always getting the same dreamy lift.

That season our ballet company was a huge success, thanks mostly to a riot on opening night deliberately provoked by Diaghilev. The Surrealists had recently signed a manifesto refusing to work for any commercial enterprise. Nothing more was needed for Diaghilev to decide that Miró should design the sets for a new *Romeo and Juliet*. Miró agreed, and the Surrealists broke up the first performance with a fracas that required police intervention. But the season was sold out.

My position in the company had not improved an iota. I danced the same solos and a couple of leads, but an effective duet created for Danilova and me in the Miró ballet was cut to the bone because, I presume, it showed up the inadequacies of Rothermere's girl friend, who still reigned.

And there was no further mention of Sokolova's retirement. Clearly, I had no chance for advancement under the current setup. My disillusionment with the company and its intrigues was increasing, and I saw nothing to look forward to unless some drastic changes took place. Vacation would soon begin, and then back again to the same grind and fatigue, the same ballets and the same cities, the same limitations and boredom.

Fused with my professional woes, I felt a growing concern about Antonio. I was getting in too deep in a relationship that had no future, and I had begun to cling to it involuntarily. A young Spanish grandee and a ballet dancer—it was a combination that would never do—and we both knew it. I had broken the deadlock of his isolation, but there was no real place for me in his life. His private world was closed to me; he never mentioned his family, his son or his activities when he was away from me. I didn't resent it; I, too, had a life of my own to follow; I was fully eighteen, and I believed I had a career ahead of me. What disturbed me was that the lightheartedness of Barcelona had disappeared, and I was beginning to feel trickles of real anguish at the thought of our inevitable parting.

Something had to come along to pull me out of this double dilemma and fill the gap, and in my unfailing belief in miracles, I waited for one.

In the course of a casual conversation with a friend, I learned that Nikita Balieff, the producer of a company called Chauve Souris, was looking for someone young to revive his tarnishing company.

"What about me?" I said lightly.

She looked at me queerly. "Would you go? You would leave Diaghilev? You know, the Chauve Souris is not of the same caliber."

"I don't care," I said, still taking it as a joke. "They are going to America, aren't they?" The blues were singing in my ears.

"Yes, they are," she said, "and soon. They've been to America several times before."

Undoubtedly, the conversation was reported to Balieff, for his offer came within a week. I vacillated. It was a big step to take—to tear myself away across the ocean—and I left the decision to fate by putting up very stiff terms. Refusing to participate in any of the Chauve Souris repertoire, I insisted on being presented as a guest star with three separate spots of my own in which to dance whatever I wanted. There was no argument.

The contract was sent to me at once, and I signed it quickly so as not to give myself a chance to change my mind.

Only when the contract was returned with Balieff's signature, and thus irrevocable, did I go to Diaghilev to inform him of my departure.

He threw up his hands.

"You're crazy! The craziest girl I've ever had around," he shouted, a piece of paper fluttering in his hand. "Here! Here is Sokolova's resignation. She won't be with us next year. It's all yours!"

"Too late," I said. "You should have told me before."

"You will regret this!" he went on ranting. "America is a barbaric country. They know nothing about art! It is all Indians, and bankers, and gangsters in checked suits. They are cave people!"

He was still shouting when I left.

I kept putting off saying anything to Antonio about the turn my life was taking, afraid to damage our last days together, and I might well have waited until the last moment had not a certain incident prompted me to break the news.

One day his wife's picture slipped out of his wallet. I had only a brief glimpse of it, but there was no missing the likeness between us.

The discovery disturbed me and sent me into a maze of doubt.

That night as we were sitting at a late supper, and I was looking at him across the table, his eyes jet-black in the candlelight, questions were flying through my mind.

What am I to him? Does he really see me as I am, or am I

only a vague replica of the dead woman? Was that the reason for all the photographs—to keep her alive in my face?

He remarked that I was unusually quiet, and then told me his plans.

"I have decided to take a house for you in Biarritz for your vacation," he said. "Then I can come and visit you often."

His hand covered mine, and I was glad that I had already signed the contract.

"I am going away, Antonio," I said weakly. "Far away. To America."

There was a long pause and then a slow question.

"When will you be back?"

"I don't know." I felt my voice fading out. "I really don't."

He let go of my hand, and not much was said after that.

On the eve of my departure, he told me he would not wait until I left the next day. He was returning to Spain on the early-morning train.

The New York skyline was at its most spectacular when, at eight in the evening, our ship was tugged into the harbor. The sight of the steel-laced metropolis transparent with lights and reaching toward the sky mesmerized me, and I stood transfixed at the railing.

By ten all the Americans had disembarked, but we, the aliens, had to remain on board until next morning to be checked out by the immigration officials.

At daybreak, we lined up on the deck in front of the immigration officers' table. Our manager stood by, acting as interpreter, and I hated myself for not understanding what they were saying. At ease in three languages, this was a new experience for me, and I felt nervous and uncomfortable.

Everything went smoothly; the company was checked out

one by one; but when it came to me, the official's eyebrows tightened. With his head down and his finger tapping my papers, he started a discussion with our manager who stood by, perplexed and worried. The discussion tensed into an argument, the official shaking his head and the manager getting meeker and more distraught, and then out of the incomprehensible verbiage two words fell clear and deadly:

Ellis Island!

The manager turned to me helplessly. "I don't know what to do," he said in Russian. "He is just picking. The discrepancy in your papers is not worth mentioning."

Ellis Island was a frightening name to a foreigner. Anyone who ever contemplated migrating to America knew what that name implied, and I begged him to plead my case again.

Some note in my voice made the official lift his head. His look was stern, and then his cheeks began to quiver and his face split into an uncontrollable smile. I must have looked the picture of terror, like a young rabbit ambushed by hounds, because he put his hand over his eyes and laughed. His other hand picked up my papers and handed them to the manager.

"Okay," he said, "go on."

Those were the first three words I learned in English.

I flew down the gangplank weightless. My first American had smiled at me and let me through. What a country!

Much as I wanted to see New York, I didn't allow myself that luxury until after the opening night, restricting myself to the half-block between the Great Northern Hotel, where we stayed, and Carnegie Hall, where I rented a studio. I had only sketched out my dances in Paris, and now I had two weeks to work them into my body and perfect them.

I worked hard, in unusual peace of mind and a surprising

absence of nerves. I was doing my best—and that was all I could do. Freedom was back. I would repeat each dance twice without any rest in between until it became a breeze. The dances were carefully thought out to sneak up on the audience gradually, not to scare them with this new kind of dancing. The first was a romantic madrigal, fluid and danced on point between two white wooden borzois; the second was a take-off of a bullfight, and the third a virtuoso abstraction to the music of "Sarcasm" by Prokofiev. They were all technically difficult, and they all departed from the expected form.

Balieff presented me well. Before each number, he came out to the footlights and spelled out my name in his broken English, vowing to the audience that they would hear that name again.

I was an overnight success. Reviews were raves, and John Martin, the dean of ballet critics, wrote editorials about me. Magazines picked up the same song of praise, and I became the draw of the Chauve Souris.

But the season was too short to do me any real good. Two weeks later we went on tour, and when we returned to New York, interest in me had simmered down.

Before returning to Europe, Balieff had tried to extend my contract, but I would not agree. It was never my intention to affiliate myself with the Chauve Souris for any length of time, and basically I used them as a means of crossing the ocean. Moreover, I had decided that America was the place for me even before the success of opening night. Balieff warned me that because I had no legal papers warranting my stay in the United States, I would be liable to deportation, but I replied that I had taken chances before and saw no reason to change now.

And so I stayed. I felt a peculiar affinity with this country, with its pace, which I found invigorating, its way of life, its rhythm, and the English language was coming fast and easy.

To stretch out my savings, I moved from the hotel to a room on Ninety-sixth Street, and began charting my course of action.

It never occurred to me that after my success it would be difficult for me to find a job, but all the agents I turned to shied away from me. Oh, they remembered me all right, some even saw me perform, but compared with the pussy-footing of Marilyn Miller, and the backbends of Harriet Hoctor, I was not unlike a shot of heroin, and they were afraid I would not fit on the American stage.

Time was flying and my money was running out. Was life playing the game of cat and mouse with me again?

This doleful period was broken by Morris Gest, the impresario and friend of Balieff's, who tracked me down. Gest told me he was taking me to someone he called Flo, and, on our way, revealed to me that Flo was, of course, Florenz Ziegfeld.

I was impressed with the opulence of Mr. Ziegfeld's office, and with the gentleman himself. Tailored to perfection, with a tiny rose in his lapel, he got up from behind his desk to greet us, took one look at me and, although he had never seen me dance, signed me on the spot.

The musical was *Whoopee*, starring Eddie Cantor, Ethel Shutta and Ruby Keeler, and shortly after our first meeting, Ziegfeld called me in to tell me what he had in mind for me. His intentions were generous but his notion of what I was or could do entirely wrong, running somewhat along biographical lines.

Because I came from Russia, I was to perform a gypsy

number, and because I was now in America, my second number was to be an Indian dance.

Both ideas threw me into a mild state of dementia. My memory of gypsies didn't inflame me with inspiration—and as to the Indians, I had never seen a live one and all I knew about them was that when they danced, they hooted, pressing hand to mouth.

"In the Indian number, you'll come down a hill on a white horse followed by showgirls on brown steeds," Ziegfeld said proudly. "We'll have a sunset behind you."

The mention of the horse rendered me completely frenetic. I had never sat on one even while it was standing still, and here I was to ride downhill—and bareback. And all that before dancing.

I tried to dispel my distress by concentrating on the pursuit of some interesting choreographic form for these banalities, and, of course, ended with something quite different from what was expected, and rather confusing for the audience.

We were to open in Pittsburgh.

At the dress rehearsal, I discovered that in the gypsy number I was surrounded by tents, each tent adorned by a half-naked six-foot showgirl, leaning against it in a provocative pose. That certainly took the edge off the audience's interest in my dancing. And in the Indian scene the ladies following me on "brown steeds" wore only beads on their bodies, which gleamed in the artificial sunset.

I am five foot four, and I doubt if I was even visible. There was hardly any applause, and at the end of the week the Indian number was out. The gypsy number, too, underwent a considerable transformation; it was cut down to half its length and became a kind of introduction for the showgirls, who, while I danced, slunk slowly down toward the footlights displaying their pulchritude from all sides.

We were less than three weeks from the Broadway opening. A showgirl came up to me and addressed me in poisonously dulcet tones. "Did you get your notice yet?" she said.

"What is a notice?" I asked.

"That's when they fire you, hon." She smiled deliciously. "I hear that gypsy bit of yours will be out too. You didn't expect them to carry you with nothing to do."

I shall always be grateful to that showgirl. Had she not spoken, my theatrical life might have taken a sad turn.

I ran to Ziegfeld.

"Please don't fire me," I implored. "Please, let me try another number."

He looked at me kindly and with the softness of regret.

"Sorry," he said, "the show is set, there is no place for you any more. The only spot would be the finale, but that's eleven-thirty at night—the audience is tired and ready to go home."

"I don't care what time it will be," I pleaded. "Just let me try once more—and my own way, please."

He was adamant. "The score is all used up."

"Any refrain will do!" I was on the verge of tears, and he succumbed, though without conviction.

The number had to be invented and staged quickly—there was no time to lose. Frantically, I racked my brain for some intriguing idea, something that would attract attention, and could find nothing.

Out of despair and to clear my mind, I went out that night with one of the boys from the show. To amuse me, he took me to a local dive that featured a floor show. I looked on listlessly until a young Negro came out. He wore an alpaca suit, a white sequin vest and spats, and with his head tilted to one side, he did a magnificent strut—all elegance and disdain.

I almost screamed. Here it was—what I'd been looking for.

Next morning I went to work, integrating six chorines (short) into the background of the dance.

On Thursday of our last week on tour, at eleven-thirty at night, I stepped out on the stage of the National Theatre in Washington. It was the finale, the set was a gold and orange ballroom and the whole company was on, grouped in a semi-circle against the background.

I wore a tight, hip-length jacket of sapphire-blue velvet, white gloves and the traditional pink tights and ballet slippers. A large clump of violets was pinned to my left shoulder, and my hair was cut short in Roman ringlets. To the tune of "Come West, Little Girl," played in a languid blues tempo, I did a take-off on the strut—on point—embellished by technique and with a deliberate air of arrogance.

The applause started way before the dance ended and persisted long after I disappeared in the wings, so when the principals came downstage to sing their final song, they had to retreat twice to let me take my bows. That shot of heroin the agents were afraid of worked.

At the fall of the curtain, Ziegfeld was in my dressing room, bubbling with excitement. He had two ideas that would, he said, give the number more importance. Having been exposed to tents, showgirls and horses, I became apprehensive, but this time he was right. And when we opened in New York, in place of the velvet jacket, I wore top hat and tails, black tights coming up to my waist, and black ballet shoes. The other innovation was Paul Whiteman, who came with his orchestra a few minutes before eleven-thirty to play the finale.

The reviews were splendid, and I became a high point.

Several months after the opening, I read in the paper that Diaghilev had died and that the ballet company had been disbanded.

From then on, it was easy. In my second musical, *Three's a Crowd,* I danced, played comedy and even crooned a song that Vernon Duke had written. Then the reviews came in and rocketed me to stardom. My face was in the papers and magazines, my name in the columns, and I was welcomed to its bosom by the crème de la crème of the theatre and its fringe society. I will not go through those famous names because they have been listed so many times in theatrical biographies that I see no reason to give them an encore.

But two more events are worth speaking of.

I was in *Flying Colors,* my third show, when my doorbell rang and I was surprised to see George on the threshold, looking very pale and tired. It was a nice reunion. He plunked down on the sofa and told me he had been brought to America by Lincoln Kirstein to organize a school of American ballet and create a ballet company, an undertaking that had no precedent in this part of the world. The project was interrupted when George fell seriously, frighteningly ill. Many a day I sat by his bedside at the Barbizon Plaza. But he slowly got well and, on his recovery, the enterprise was resumed.

The first performance drew near. The company was young and very good, but there was no one experienced enough to carry a certain ballet George wanted to present that night, and he asked me to appear with them as a guest star. And on that first night, the birth of the American Ballet (now the New York City Ballet), I danced George's choreographic marvel called *Errante* to the music of Schubert's "Wanderer Fantasy." It was a revelation to the American dance audience, and we took seventeen curtain calls.

It was a year or two later when Richard Rodgers and Dwight Wiman recalled me from Hollywood to co-star with Ray Bolger in their new musical, *On Your Toes*. They also signed George to do the choreography. I doubt that anyone will dispute that *On Your Toes* was a milestone in the history of musical comedy, changing the format, eliminating the chorus line and incorporating dancing into the story. Once more George and I were destined to be reunited in the creation of something new.

On Your Toes was a huge success. My role was that of a glamour dame, and each act ended in a long dance sequence. The first was a satire on classical ballet done so subtly that, until the fun began filtering through, the audience was convinced that I was performing a serious pas de deux with all the technical tricks.

And the final segment was "Slaughter on Tenth Avenue," a dance drama and Richard Rodgers's masterpiece.

The opening night was a night to remember. When the final curtain fell on "Slaughter," leaving me shot dead, and, after a momentary silence, the audience erupted into roars, I said to myself, "This is it, girl!"

Behind my closed eyelids I saw a tiny girl sitting beside the dressing table in a mauve boudoir, watching her mother bedeck herself with jewels.

72 73 10 9 8 7 6 5 4 3 2 1